THE CRUCIB

"It is *impossible* to th...
to do in intense com...
did was start to ram th... ...German airplane with my left
propeller. When the German saw me coming, he
immediately turned to the left. As he did, his tail
hit my left wingtip. The collision demolished the
Me-109's tail assembly, the pilot lost control, and
the Me-109 dived into the ground. I looked around,
but there were no more Me-109s in the air. . . ."

—Captain Newell Roberts, U.S. Army Air Corps,
in *Aces Against Germany*

"Hammel is one of our best military historians when
it comes to presenting that often complex subject to
the general public. He has demonstrated this facility
in a number of fine books and now he does so
again. . . . A nitty-gritty insider's view packed with
information and human drama. Along with the words
of the pilots involved, Hammel has woven a narrative
that gives the reader a clear overview of the progress
of the war from its early dark, uncertain days right
through to the final victory. Not to be missed."

—James H. Flanagan, *BookPage*

"Astounding. These remarkable septuagenarians have
almost total recall of events they experienced half-a-
century ago. . . . These old warriors fly again, activating a Mustang's flaps to make it turn inside an
Me-109, nursing the throttle of a Thunderbolt to keep
it in a Lufbery without stalling and making the most
of the K-14 computing gunsight. . . . Simply a great
book."

—Richard Marchant, *Air Pictorial*

Books by Eric Hammel

CHOSIN: Heroic Ordeal of the Korean War
THE ROOT: The Marines in Beirut, August, 1982
GUADALCANAL: Starvation Island
GUADALCANAL: The Carrier Battles
GUADALCANAL: Decision at Sea
KHE SANH: Siege in the Clouds, An Oral History
AMBUSH VALLEY: I Corps, Vietnam 1967
ACES AGAINST JAPAN
ACES AGAINST GERMANY

ACES AGAINST GERMANY

ERIC HAMMEL

POCKET BOOKS
New York London Toronto Sydney Tokyo Singapore

POCKET BOOKS, a division of Simon & Schuster Inc.
1230 Avenue of the Americas, New York, NY 10020

Published by arrangement with Presidio Press

ISBN: 0-671-52907-2

First Pocket Books printing June 1995

10 9 8 7 6 5 4 3 2 1

POCKET and colophon are registered trademarks of
Simon & Schuster Inc.

Front cover photo of P-51D Mustang "Tika IV," 374th Fighter
Squadron, 361st Fighter Group, over England, mid-1944; photo
courtesy of Jeffrey Ethell

Maps by Moody Graphics, Kansas City

Printed in the U.S.A.

*This book is dedicated to
all the American airmen
who helped bring about the
great victory against
the Nazi empire
in World War II*

CONTENTS

CONTENTS

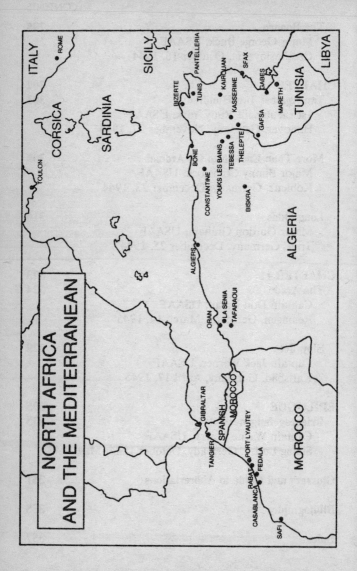

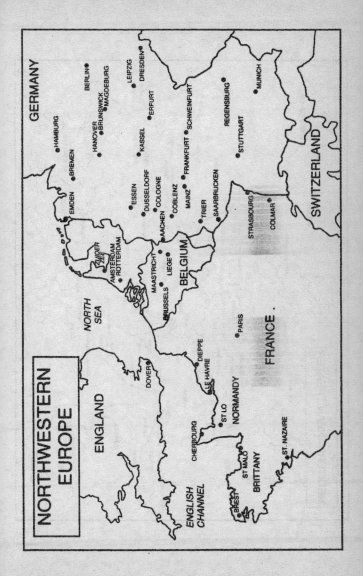

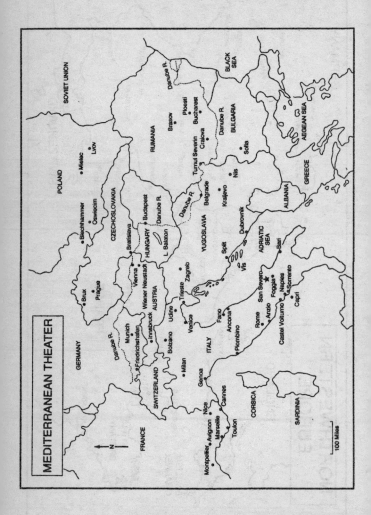

MEDITERRANEAN THEATER

PROLOGUE

The popular conception of the struggle in the air over Europe during World War II is of pairs and quartets of sleek fighters racing over the German heartland to protect contrailed streams of lumbering bombers, stretching beyond sight. This is as it was late in America's air war against Germany, but it was far from the truth at the start of that great aerial crusade. In the beginning, the fighter was a short-legged creature whose role of protecting the bombers was quite far down the list behind its role of guarding friendly territory and installations. The difference, which is crucial, was the product of technology—range and the power of aircraft engines—and intellect. Until surprisingly late in the war, the use of the fighter as an offensive weapon was stunted by the defensive mindset of even the leading "pursuit" acolytes of the inter-war decades.

The pursuit airplane had evolved over the fixed battlefields of Western Europe during World War I. The pursuit's essential duties at the start of the war—the reason the type was developed—was to prevent enemy reconnaissance airplanes from overflying friendly lines and to protect friendly observation airplanes from enemy pursuits while the observers overflew enemy lines. The pursuit was conceived as a tactical and a defensive weapon, and it was limited to these roles both by conception and by the technologies of the day.

Between the world wars, the development of the American pursuit aircraft was hobbled by budgetary restrictions that for many years slowed or obviated altogether the creation of new technologies or even methodical experimentation with new tactics. The U.S. Navy and, especially, the U.S. Marine Corps did advance the use of the single-engine pursuit as a close-support weapon to bolster the infantry, but the interests of various intra-Army constituencies prevented similar advances in what had come to be called the Army Air Corps. To the degree that it developed at all, the Air Corps saw increasingly heavy and longer-ranged bombers in its future. And, as the limited available research-and-development dollars were expended on speedier bombers, the pursuits of the day were increasingly outranged and outrun. Inevitably, an ex post facto argument gave a voice to reality, and the American bombers of the late 1930s were designed to be "self-defending" because they could fly much farther and at least somewhat faster than could the pursuits of the day. The pursuits, which were being developed at a much slower pace, were relegated to a point-defense role—guarding cities, industrial targets, and air bases. When World War II began, the Air Corps, shortly to be renamed the Army Air Forces, was divided into two distinct combat arms, fighters and bombers; and by virtue of the fighter's stunted development, there appeared little chance that the two would spend much time working together. (The combat radius of the B-17 heavy bomber was approximately 400 miles in late 1941, and the combat radius of the Army Air Corps' best fighter was around 200 miles. Put another way, the B-17 could stay aloft for more than seven hours, whereas the *best* American fighter could stay aloft for seventy to ninety minutes at most.)

As soon as the Army Air Corps was pulled into World War II on December 7, 1941—right away, at Pearl Harbor and around Manila—it became focused on the defense of the United States' East, West, and Gulf coasts; several Caribbean islands; bases in Greenland and Iceland, and on the strategically indispensable Panama Canal. There were few airplanes of any type to devote to these defensive missions, and those that were deployed defensively also had to serve as on-the-job trainers for hundreds of the raw young pilots who were beginning to emerge from the Air Corps's burgeoning flight schools. The early attrition in training accidents—inexperienced pilots strapped into bad or simply unforgiving high-performance airplanes—would have been scandalous had there not been a war to be won.

Through the first half of 1942, all of the very few pilots and airplanes that could be spared from the defense of the United States coasts and sea lanes were rushed to defend Australia and the South Pacific. Dozens of these precious airplanes and pilots were lost in the pathetic defense of the Dutch East Indies, and many more were lost in the early battles around Port Moresby, New Guinea. But, combined with other stop-gap measures, and with a valiant effort by the U.S. Navy, the thin line managed to hold. The pressures exerted by the war against Japan continued to mount, however, and the Pacific and even China drew off the entirety of the Army Air Forces's slowly rising spare strength. Meanwhile, at home, the flight schools and several new operational training units were beginning to catch up with combat and training losses as well as with the heavy burden imposed by the formation of new fighter, bomber, and other-type groups. And fighter aircraft with a higher probability of survival were beginning to reach the Pacific and Asian war zones and coastal-defense air groups.

Fortunately, the United States could afford to be a bit late off the mark in her war against Germany. German efforts in 1940 to bring Great Britain to her knees had failed miserably and, by the end of 1941, the bulk of Germany's air and land forces were mired in a frightful war of attrition deep inside Russia. For many months, the only point at which the United States and Germany met was at sea, where German submarines were beating the pants off American maritime power. The Army Air Forces helped marginally in the war against German submarines, but the main effort naturally fell to the U.S. Navy. In Great Britain, the British had the situation reasonably well in hand, though they would have collapsed had it not been for vast infusions of weapons and supplies from the United States. The land war in Egypt and Libya was teetering on the edge of collapse, but there was little the United States would be able to do for many months to affect the outcome, assuming the British held on that long.

So, while the Army Air Forces devoted the bulk of its limited expendable resources to aiding China and Australia, and to bolstering the U.S. Navy's early efforts in the Pacific—defensive programs, all—new air groups were being built up in the United States, and new and better bombers and fighters were rolling off scores of newly created assembly lines. Finally, in the spring of 1942, it was decided in high Army Air Forces circles to begin the actual commitment of American air power in the United Kingdom. At first, commitment would be more symbolic than real—little more than a meager show of force masking an advanced combat-training program to be overseen by the Royal Air Force (RAF). Only later, when training bases and factories in the United States had caught up with the planning, would the United States Army Air Forces take on what its leaders had already billed as the decisive strategic campaign projected to be waged against the German industrial heartland.

As early as February 20, 1942, Brigadier General Ira Eaker arrived in England to establish the headquarters of the new VIII Bomber Command. To the accompaniment of much public fanfare, Eaker formally opened his headquarters at High Wycombe, England, on February 23, 1942. However, VIII Bomber Command had no combat airplanes to its name; they would not be available for several months.

It fell to General Eaker to argue with his British hosts in favor of an independent role for the forthcoming Army Air Forces in Europe. Eaker knew going in that the RAF and the British government both wanted America's commitment to the air war in Europe to be subordinate to or an adjunct of the British theater air war. The Americans, however, wanted and felt they deserved an independent role, and it was Eaker's job to win the British to this viewpoint.

The American notion was strongly bolstered—in argument, at least—by the fact that the Army Air Forces had developed over many years a theoretical strategic air doctrine that was quite different from the RAF's experience-based strategic doctrine. The Americans favored and had equipped their bomber force to wage a precision daylight bombing campaign against industrial targets hundreds of miles inside enemy territory. The RAF, on the other hand, was the only other air force in the world to have developed long-range four-engine heavy bombers, but its doctrine—the result of bloody experiences early in the war—

opted for "area" bombing at night. Doctrinal arguments aside, the British victims of the Nazi Blitz of 1940–1941 were less squeamish than their American allies about bombing German civilians. Besides, the RAF had few long-range heavy bombers to its name and thus felt it needed to co-opt the promised infusion of American heavies. In any case, for whatever reason, the RAF commanders argued forcefully for the VIII Bomber Command heavy bombers, once they arrived, to join in the night-bombing curriculum.

For the time being, Eaker's arguments with the RAF hierarchy were moot. There would be no American air combat units in the United Kingdom for several months, and then there would not be enough of them to make a dent in Hitler's Fortress Europa for many more months.

The first VIII Bomber Command unit to reach the European Theater of Operations (ETO) was the 97th Heavy Bombardment Group, which arrived on May 10, 1942 equipped with Boeing B-17 Flying Fortress four-engine heavy bombers. This was a symbolic commitment, for the 97th had been activated in February 1942 and thus had not had time to be adequately trained to fly combat missions over heavily defended European targets. It would be several months, at minimum, before the 97th saw any live action.

Around the time the 97th Heavy Bombardment Group became the first combat unit to join Eaker's VIII Bomber Command, Brigadier General Frank "Monk" Hunter arrived in England to establish the headquarters of his VIII Fighter Command, also at High Wycombe. Unlike Eaker, Hunter, a rather flamboyant World War I ace, quickly came to terms with British beliefs and aspirations regarding the employment of forthcoming American fighter groups. The RAF had opted for powerful short-range fighters that could defend friendly air bases and attack nearby enemy air bases, and their doctrine had more than proven itself during the Battle of Britain and the Blitz. Monk Hunter, who had spent most of his career arguing the point-defense case for the U.S. Army's fighters, was more than satisfied to augment the British fighter plan, at least until it came time for the Allies to prepare for the invasion of France in mid-1943 or mid-1944.

On June 10, 1942—a few days after the U.S. Navy won the great aerial victory in the Pacific, near Midway—the personnel of the United States Army Air Forces 31st Fighter Group arrived in England by ship. After being outfitted with British Spitfire fighters, the green American fighter group began a rigorous advanced combat-training program overseen by a number of the RAF's leading Battle of Britain aces. As with the 97th Bombardment Group, the 31st Fighter Group was not expected to begin combat operations for several months.

On June 18, 1942, Major General Carl "Tooey" Spaatz arrived in England to establish the headquarters of the Eighth Air Force at High Wycombe. A World War I combat commander with several German airplanes to his credit and decades of being at the leading edge of the growth of the Army Air Corps, Spaatz was one of the handful of leading Army Air Forces officers with the moral authority to win an independent role for American air units over the forceful arguments of Britain's top military and political leaders. Leaving the training of pilots and aircrews to Eaker and Hunter, Spaatz set out to accomplish this. It was Spaatz's brief from his superiors to integrate and modulate the projected American daylight air offensive with, but not subordinate it to, Britain's night-bombing effort.

The Army Air Corps's first combat mission against a German-held target took place on July 4, 1942. Intended as a symbolic attack—note the date—it was a poor symbol, for the six American-manned RAF Douglas A-20 Havoc light attack bombers that accompanied six British-manned A-20s were emblazoned with RAF roundels, not U.S. markings. In their attack on German airfields in Holland, two of the American-crewed A-20s were shot down by flak (seven crewmen were killed and one was captured), two failed to reach the target, and a fifth was severely damaged. The U.S. Army Air Forces could not have asked for a less auspicious or more humiliating inauguration of what would become the greatest aerial offensive in the history of the world.

While half the world away the air battles for Port Moresby, New Guinea, continued, the very first U.S. Army Air Forces fighter mission over Occupied Europe took place on July 26, 1942. As part of their training syllabus, six 31st Fighter Group senior pilots took part in an RAF fighter sweep to Gravelines, a town on the English Channel coast fifteen miles southwest of Dunkirk. German fighters challenged the American and RAF Spitfires, and the 31st Fighter Group's deputy commander was shot down and captured.

The 97th Heavy Bombardment Group had to wait a bit longer. Finally, on August 17, a dozen of the 97th's B-17s, with General Eaker along as an observer, conducted an afternoon raid against railroad marshaling yards near Rouen, France, thirty-five miles from the Channel. Escort for the bombers was provided, not by American fighter groups, but by four RAF Spitfire squadrons. The results of the bombing were negligible—the target was hit, at least—and the RAF Spitfires held off all but two of the German fighters that came up to attack the American B-17s. One B-17 returned to base with a burning, smoking engine, but there were no losses and no injuries. Six other 97th Bomb Group B-17s that conducted a diversionary flight over the French coast that afternoon were not molested.

Two days later, on August 19, the entire 31st Fighter Group joined with the RAF for a "big show" across the Channel.

FIRST TO FIGHT

Captain FRANK HILL, USAAF
308th Fighter Squadron, 31st Fighter Group
Dieppe, France, August 19, 1942

Frank Ackerman Hill's boyhood visions of flight took tangible form when he and a dozen other students at Hillsdale, New Jersey's Westwood High School formed a club and purchased an old Cessna Primary glider for fifty dollars. The glider, which had been in storage since the early Depression, was a forgiving platform on which the youths could learn to fly. After Hill graduated from Westwood High in 1937, he worked as a plumber's helper by day, attended an aircraft mechanics course at night, and took an aeronautical engineering course by mail.

In September 1939, six months after his twentieth birthday and after nine months of waiting in vain for a response to his application to join the U.S. Army Air Corps to attend aerial photography school, Hill traveled to Chanute Field, Illinois, and enlisted. He passed the two-year college-equivalency test at Chanute and, in January 1940, joined Class 40-G as a flying cadet. Hill earned his silver aviator's wings and received his commission as a second lieutenant in the Air Corps on November 15, 1940, at Kelly Field, Texas.

Lieutenant Hill joined the 31st Pursuit Group at Selfridge Field, Michigan, immediately after graduation from Kelly Field, and he was assigned to the 40th Pursuit Squadron, which at the time was flying the new Curtiss P-40 Warhawk. Shortly after Hill checked out in the P-40 and passed through an aerial gunnery course, the group transitioned to Bell P-39 Airacobra fighters and then took part in Army-wide maneuvers near Savannah, Georgia, and, later, near Jackson, Mississippi. In mid-September 1941, during the Jackson maneuvers, the P-39 Lieutenant Hill was piloting lost power on takeoff, hit a tall tree, and fell to the ground. Hill was in a body cast until shortly before he rejoined the 31st Pursuit Group in February 1942.

Early in 1942, all three of the 31st Pursuit Group's original squadrons and half of the group's experienced fighter pilots were detached and rushed to Australia, which was being threatened by Japanese advances across the South Pacific. Three newly commissioned squadrons—the 307th, 308th, and 309th Pursuit squadrons—replaced the departed units, and 1st Lieutenant Frank Hill was assigned as the commander of a flight of eight airplanes and pilots in the 308th.

On May 19, 1942, the newly redesignated 31st Fighter Group was ordered from New Orleans Air Base to Grenier

Field, New Hampshire. There the airplanes were equipped with 500-gallon belly tanks and we prepared to fly the P-39s over the Atlantic to England. At the last minute, the chief of the Army Air Forces, General Henry Arnold, apparently worked a deal with the Royal Air Force (RAF) to equip us with Supermarine Spitfire fighters. The P-39s were turned in, and the 31st Fighter Group, including all its mechanics and other service personnel, sailed from New York on June 11, 1942, aboard an old British ship. We were the first U.S. Army Air Corps fighter group to reach the European Theater.

When we arrived in England in early July, we were based at Atcham, near Shrewsbury, northwest of London. We were provided with Spitfire Vb fighters, and we began working with them right away.

The Spitfire was really a welcomed airplane. After only a few flights, we were unanimous in our praise for it and thankful not to have the P-39. The Spit was an easy plane to fly and to get used to—something like an AT-6 advanced trainer, only more powerful and maneuverable. The only thing that was hard to get used to was the air-brake system used for taxiing. You pressed the rudder pedal as usual, then squeezed the handle on the control column, which was similar to the brake on a ten-speed bicycle. We had a few taxiing mishaps, a forced landing due to fuel starvation (there were only 110 Imperial gallons aboard), and one fatality due to an approach on final that was too slow. On the whole, however, the Spit proved to be an easy plane to fly and maneuver, and our mechanics were quick to adapt to the engine and armament. In less than thirty days, we were ready to go.

Beginning August 5, 1942, the group flew indoctrination —sightseeing—missions along the coast of France. The 308th operated from the RAF station at Kenley, which was about fifteen miles south of London. Wing Commander Brian Kingcombe, a hero of the Battle of Britain, was assigned as our liaison, and he led these early missions. On several missions, we escorted Army Air Forces B-26 medium bombers and A-20 light attack bombers against targets along the French coast, usually Le Havre. Most of the missions were flown on the deck until we got to within about ten miles of the French coast. We would then climb rapidly to 10,000 to 12,000 feet, stay with the bombers during the bomb run, dodge flak, and dive to the deck to escort the bombers back to England. The 308th Fighter Squadron saw no enemy aircraft at all during this period, but on August 8, Major Harrison Thyng, the commander of the 309th, damaged a Focke-Wulf FW-190 radial-engine fighter a few miles off the English coast. This was the first credit of any kind given to an Army Air Forces pilot for air-to-air combat in Europe.

On the evening of August 18, 1942, we were briefed for a "big show" that was to take place the following day— Operation JUBILEE, a raid-in-force against the French Channel port of Dieppe by several battalions of Canadian infantry and tanks. The 31st's job was to be part of the top-cover force.

The 308th took off from Kenley at 0717. There were twelve Spitfires in the squadron formation, arranged in three flights of four airplanes each. My "B" Flight was stepped down a little to the right and behind the squadron commander's flight, and the third flight was stepped down to the left and behind mine. Each flight was arranged in the finger-four formation. My wingman was to my left and a little behind me, the leader of my second element was to my right and also a little behind me, and my element leader's wingman was to his right and a little behind him. By flying in this manner, we could all see behind the other airplanes in the flight, and we were able to maneuver smoothly as a unit and react to any sort of attack.

As we approached the French coast, we could see a number of ships near Dieppe harbor, and a large number of aircraft were flying in the general area. At our altitude, it was hard to tell if the ships or planes were friend or foe. We arrived over Dieppe on schedule at about 0740 and split into separate four-ship flights in order to patrol the area inbound to Dieppe at altitudes between 8,000 and 10,000 feet. We orbited more or less over the port.

We had been over Dieppe for only a few minutes when the RAF operations center that was controlling all the fighters —Mickey Control—reported that a dozen or so enemy aircraft were approaching Dieppe from the direction of the big German airdrome at Abbeville, which was to our east. A few minutes later, a flight of aircraft arrived above us, at about 12,000 feet, and immediately rolled over and commenced an attack on my flight. I could see that the attacking airplanes were FW-190s.

I wanted to keep my flight together and avoid giving away the advantage. As the Germans attacked, their formation broke up into pairs. I turned up toward them and flew at them head-on as they came down. This made it hard for the German pilots to keep their sights on us, and it forced them to attack us head-on.

One pair of FWs came in real close, and that gave us an opportunity to fire our guns directly into them. On this pass, my number four airplane, piloted by Lieutenant D. K. Smith, received a burst of cannon fire through its left wing, about two inches from the aileron. It left an eight-inch hole on top and took out about two feet on the underside of the wing.

After about three minutes of trying to keep my flight from being hit—by constantly breaking and turning into the Germans—I found myself in position to get a good shot at one of the Focke-Wulfs, so I fired all four .303-caliber Browning machine guns and both Hispano 20mm cannon at it. The German swung out to my left, and I got in another good three-second burst of cannon and machine-gun fire. I fired into his left side at a 45-degree angle from about 300 yards down to about 200 feet. The Focke-Wulf started pouring black smoke. He rolled over and went straight down.

I followed the smoking FW down to about 3,000 feet, but at that point I had to pull out because the ack-ack coming from the ground was really intense and I didn't want to lose any of my planes to ground fire. The last I saw of the Focke-Wulf, it was about 1,000 feet over the Channel, north of Dieppe. It was still smoking and still in a steep dive.

We climbed back to 8,000 feet. It was quiet for a few minutes, and then more Focke-Wulfs came down. We headed up and kept breaking into them. As my wingman and I turned into them, making it harder for them to track us in their sights and forcing them to come at us head-on, my second element was given an opportunity to fire on them. This was our first combat and we didn't know much else to do except turn into them and fire as best we could. We were fighting defensively, but we had a chance to hit them as they came down to hit us.

It was constant look-see-turn for about thirty-five minutes. Then we started to get low on fuel. I had run out of cannon ammunition by then—there were only sixty 20mm rounds in each magazine—but I don't think I did much damage after I hit the first Focke-Wulf. I made one last attack on another Focke-Wulf from above and behind with only .303 bullets. I was quite a distance away when I fired, and I don't think I hit him. If I did, I didn't damage him very much.

I was getting ready to turn for home when, all of a sudden, my element leader, Lieutenant Robert "Buck" Ingraham, called, "Snackbar Blue-Three going down." I thought he was going down after something, but then I saw him bail out at about 7,000 feet. We were over the water, off the coast. I watched him going down for quite a while. His parachute strung out and opened only halfway. It didn't look like it was going to open the rest of the way, but it finally did. As Buck approached the water, I saw two boats heading toward him. I figured he was going to be picked up okay. I later found out that the boats were German E-boats, and they got him. He was a prisoner for the rest of the war.

After we left Buck Ingraham, we hit the deck and headed back toward England. As we went, D. K. Smith pulled up alongside of me and showed me the hole in his wing. It was the first I knew of it; he hadn't said anything when it happened at the beginning of the action. I was really surprised.

When we got back to Kenley, we refueled and had the

airplanes ready to go in about ten minutes. We picked up another pilot to fill in for Buck Ingraham, and D. K. Smith got another airplane. I was wearing a leather jacket and, when I landed after the first mission, I discovered that it was soaking wet from sweat.

"B" Flight flew four missions that day, and we had quite a time. I fired my machine guns and cannon on each mission. We learned a lot. Flying and firing on each mission was quite an indoctrination to fighting.

Captain Frank Hill's smoking FW-190 was initially treated by victory-hungry American reporters as the first full air-to-air kill scored by a U.S. Army Air Forces pilot over Europe in World War II, but the rules and conventions for awarding victories were, at the time, borrowed from the British. Thus, since no one had actually seen the German fighter crash into the English Channel, Hill received credit for a "probable" victory. Hill himself never claimed more than a probable. The Army Air Forces's first official full air-to-air victory credit— scored over Dieppe at 0900 on August 19—went to the 309th Fighter Squadron's 2d Lieutenant Samuel Junkin, who was severely wounded and shot down in the same action.

Captain Frank Hill's first official victory was a Junkers Ju-87 Stuka dive-bomber that he downed over Tunisia on February 22, 1943. He next downed an FW-190 on March 25, 1943. Then, after he was reassigned to serve as the commander of the 309th Fighter Squadron, Hill shared in the downing of a pair of Messerschmitt Me-109 fighters on April 22. Newly promoted Major Frank Hill achieved ace status on May 6, 1943, by downing two Me-109s over Tunisia. His sixth aerial victory was an Italian Air Force Macchi Mc.202 fighter that he downed near Pantelleria Island, in the Mediterranean south of Sicily, on June 10, 1943, and his seventh and last victory credit was for a Junkers Ju-88 twin-engine bomber that he shot down over Sicily on July 10, 1943.

Lieutenant Colonel Frank Hill, then only twenty-four years old, commanded the 31st Fighter Group through the summer of 1943. He was ordered home in September and, after leave,

13

spent the remainder of the war in command of an operational training unit charged with preparing P-47 pilots for the rigors of combat.

Frank Hill remained on active duty after the war, earned a Bachelor of Science degree in industrial engineering, and held a succession of important command and staff assignments, including command of the 33d Air Division, until his retirement from the Air Force with rank of colonel in August 1969.

Following its four missions over Dieppe on August 19, 1942— for which it was officially awarded two confirmed and two probable victories—the 31st Fighter Group continued to fly fighter-sweep missions over coastal France, but it was awarded only one probable and no confirmed victories before it was withdrawn from combat operations in October to prepare for its upcoming role in Operation TORCH, the invasion of French Northwest Africa. Meantime, on September 12, 1942, the RAF's three independent Eagle squadrons—fighter units composed entirely of American citizens who had enlisted in the Royal Air Force or Royal Canadian Air Force—were absorbed into VIII Fighter Command as the newly commissioned 4th Fighter Group.

Thanks to the withdrawal and diversion of other VIII Fighter Command groups for the North African Campaign, the 4th Fighter Group, which was outfitted with Spitfires, was the only operational American fighter unit in northern Europe until March 1943. Already endowed with experienced combat pilots, including a number of aces, from its RAF days, the 4th did about as well during its first six months of combat service as did RAF Spitfire units that were taking part in similar fighter-sweep missions over France. Between September 1942 and mid-April 1943, the 4th Fighter Group was awarded credit for fifteen confirmed victories over France, Belgium, and the Netherlands.

While the 4th Fighter Group alone was upholding the honor of American fighter units in England, nearly the full weight of the American air effort against Germany and her allies shifted southward, to French Northwest Africa.

CHAPTER 1

At 2140 hours on the evening of Saturday, October 23, 1942—following nearly two years of costly, indeterminate warfare in the Western Desert—General Bernard Law Montgomery's British Eighth Army opened the great El Alamein offensive against General Erwin Rommel's *Panzerarmee Afrika* with a ground attack supported by the fire of 1,000 artillery pieces. In the vast array of tanks, troops, big guns, and airplanes Montgomery brought to bear in his all-or-nothing bid to deny Rommel access to the Suez Canal, one group of P-40 fighters was all the United States had on the table.

The Curtiss P-40 Warhawk fighters were in the hands of the 57th Fighter Group, which had arrived in the Middle East in late July 1942 and had trained with the RAF in Palestine until September. Though the 57th Fighter Group was credited with two probable victories in action over Egypt in September 1942, it was not until October 9 that the group received its first confirmed victory credit, for a Messerschmitt Me-109 fighter downed over a temporary Luftwaffe landing field behind the El Alamein front. Thereafter, the aggressively led, attack-oriented 57th Fighter Group pilots settled in and did as well as or better than Army Air Forces defensive fighter units had been doing over comparable periods in the Pacific War. Two German fighters were shot down by 57th Fighter Group P-40 pilots on October 13; four Germans were downed on October 25; four Italian fighters fell to three 57th pilots on October 27; four Italian and three German fighters were shot down on October 28; and five

Me-109s were downed on October 29. By then, the 57th Fighter Group had several pilots well within range of the coveted "ace" status, and all the group's pilots were determined to press their apparent advantage to the hilt.

Even though the airplanes and a number of the pilots were showing signs of wear and tear, a raid on a temporary German landing ground behind the El Alamein front was scheduled for dawn on October 30, 1942.

DESERT RAID

2d Lieutenant ROCKY BYRNE, USAAF
64th Fighter Squadron, 57th Fighter Group
El Daba, Egypt, October 30, 1942

Robert Joseph Byrne was born in St. Louis on January 24, 1917. He enlisted in the U.S. Navy in 1935 and served aboard a destroyer until he took his discharge in early 1939 so that he could accept an offer to play professional baseball. Byrne kicked around the minor leagues for two seasons, but when he was about to be drafted in late 1940, he applied for flight training in the Army Air Corps. He passed the entrance exams in early 1941 and was called to active duty in July of that year.

Cadet Byrne began his Primary flight training at Ryan Field in Hemet, California, in August 1941, and he went on to Basic flight training at Gardner Field in Taft, California. After earning his wings and a commission with Class 42-C at Luke Field, Arizona, on March 6, 1942, Byrne was ordered to a group equipped with North American B-25 Mitchell medium bombers. After only a short time in B-25s, however,

Lieutenant Byrne requested a transfer to a fighter unit, and he was sent to a Curtiss P-40 group at Baton Rouge. While Byrne was on leave in June 1941, his group was precipitously transferred to California, and Byrne was left behind. He was put to work training P-40 pilots at Eglin Field, Florida, but when the training unit switched to the inferior Bell P-39 Airacobra, Byrne asked to be transferred to any fighter unit that was in combat anywhere in the world. There was no shortage of openings in the late summer of 1942—attrition in Pacific-based fighter units was on the rise—so Lieutenant Byrne's request was approved in very short order. Though Byrne reasonably expected to end up in New Guinea, he soon found himself aboard a Pan American Airways Clipper bound from Miami to Egypt.

Lieutenant Rocky Byrne reported in to the local American military authorities as soon as he reached Cairo, and he was immediately assigned to replace a pilot who had been lost from the 57th Fighter Group's 64th Fighter Squadron. The flat spot in the desert where Byrne joined the 64th Fighter Squadron in the closing days of October 1942 was merely one in a forgettable series of temporary landing fields from which the P-40 group had operated since its combat tour had begun. Conditions were unbelievably crude. The pilots and ground crewmen lived in tents, maintenance was conducted under the open sky, and the entire operation was required to be ready to move to a new site at a moment's notice.

My first mission against the German forces was a 64th Fighter Squadron strafing sweep against a Luftwaffe landing ground at El Daba, Egypt, which was some fifty miles behind the neutral bombing line that marked the El Alamein front.

Twelve P-40s from the 64th Squadron took off under the leadership of the squadron commander, Major Clermont "Pudge" Wheeler. It was dark when we took off and formed up over our landing field. I was flying the fourth P-40 in Major Wheeler's flight. I joined up on the wing of a Lieutenant Lancaster, and, in the pitch dark, I stayed there by sticking close to the blue flame from the other P-40's engine exhaust stacks.

After we formed up, Wheeler led the three four-plane flights out over the Mediterranean at less than 100 feet over the water. This was to evade the German radar. We quickly lost sight of the coast and continued on in a very tight formation.

We flew along over the water like this for about forty minutes, and then, just as it was getting light, I heard Major Wheeler say, "Turn the guns on." Then I sighted the coastline.

I was thinking, "There's no way we could be close to El Daba." Since we had flown out over the Mediterranean from our base, there had been no landmarks and no guides even for direction. But, to my great surprise—and admiration—we hit the El Daba landing ground right on the button. I was immediately aware of what a great effort of navigation Pudge Wheeler had expended.

We caught the Germans by complete surprise. They were in their chow lines, for breakfast. As we came in, I saw that their landing ground was pretty much the same as ours—desert sand and tents. It was temporary and mobile, just like ours.

We were through the base in less than ten seconds. That's all we were supposed to do—one strafing pass at whatever targets we felt like hitting. We spread out and hit them from less than 100 feet. I shot up some planes on the ground and hit some other equipment and, probably, some people, too. There was no antiaircraft fire—no time for them to man any guns—but they must have been throwing their helmets up at us as we passed right over their heads. I was so low that I'd have flown into the ground if I had depressed my gunsight any farther.

It turned out that the Luftwaffe wasn't completely asleep. They had a gaggle of Me-109s in the air, even at that early hour.

Major Wheeler's flight was the last one off the target, and I was the last man in it. By the time we got over the German landing ground, I sensed that the rest of the squadron had already climbed out and was heading east across the desert, toward home.

When we came off the strafing run and started to climb to clear the landing ground and re-form, the 109s were at 1 o'clock high. I saw them first and called them in over the radio. I was just lining up on Lieutenant Lancaster, getting ready to rejoin on his wing, when I saw the 109s. Lancaster tried to pull his plane in to avoid the fire from one of the 109s, but he pulled it in too tight. His P-40 stalled out and, at that low altitude, it crashed and burned. Maybe it was hit by German bullets, too. Lancaster was killed in the crash.

The 109 that had opened fire on Lancaster had me on a platter. He was coming up at an angle, from about my 1 o'clock. I was dodging tracers the size of golf balls—20mm. I flipped over on my back because my airspeed was so low, and the German plane flashed into my sights almost at once. I blasted him to pieces as he soared up past me, only a second or two after he had opened fire on Lancaster.

The kill was confirmed by Captain Glade "Buck" Bilby, the squadron executive officer. Buck must have been flying wing on Pudge Wheeler for some reason because he was still around when Lancaster and I came off the target. I never saw Buck during the encounter.

The 109s were after my ass, and I was a loner. The only thing I had going for me was the six .50-caliber machine guns in my wings. I turned them on whatever 109s I could reach as they made repeated passes at me. As I climbed to get away from them, however, I used up all my ammo, and I still wasn't free of them.

I was at about 2,000 feet when I happened to remember that the Qattara Depression was only a little farther south of El Daba. The depression was a wide, deep valley in the desert, 300 to 400 feet below sea level, much like California's Death Valley. It was my only out. I dove to the deck and, at full throttle, headed south.

Sure enough, I found what I was looking for. I dove right over the edge, straight into one of the ravines, and flew straight down to the floor of the depression. Somehow the Germans lost me.

When I leveled out on the floor of the Qattara Depression, I headed due east at full power, with the throttle bent over the firewall. I was going flat out on the deck when I glanced up one of the ravines to my north—and spotted a column of troops wending its way in single file over an outcropping on the side of a canyon. I wheeled around in a 180-degree turn and came back. The soldiers—about 120 of them—were waving their weapons and jumping up and down. They were Italians. I had no ammunition left, so I just waggled my wings in salute and headed back on course to the east.

When I hit the other side of the Qattara Depression, I flew up to the desert floor and turned on a heading for our own landing ground. It was a long way home, but I got there in one piece without further incident. I reported my sighting of the Italian troops as soon as I landed.

I was amazed to find out that other members of the squadron had tangled with the German fighters. Pudge Wheeler had damaged a 109, the leader of one of the other flights was given credit for a probable, and two lieutenants damaged a total of three other 109s. Unfortunately, one of those lieutenants, Gordon Ryerson, returned to base with a few bullets in him. They got Ryerson to the hospital, but he died on the operating table.

This was a remarkable mission, mainly because of the unbelievable rate, time, and distance navigation accomplished by Pudge Wheeler. It was a truly amazing feat. And it was an important mission because we let the Luftwaffe in North Africa know that the U.S. Army Air Forces was now in the air after them.

Lieutenant Rocky Byrne flew many missions against the Luftwaffe and General Erwin Rommel's Panzerarmee Afrika *through the long, lonely autumn and winter of 1942 and 1943. In all that time, as the British Eighth Army pressed the Germans westward toward Tunisia, and then northward toward Tunis, action was frequent and the pace was wearing, but Rocky Byrne scored no additional victories until April 18,*

1943—Palm Sunday. On that day, the 324th and 57th Fighter groups caught a vast fleet of fighter-escorted German transports and bombers as it was bringing German reinforcements from Italy to Tunisia. In little more than an hour, pilots from the 57th destroyed fifty of the seventy-seven German airplanes downed over the Gulf of Tunis that afternoon, and Rocky Byrne was credited with three Me-109s.

In an action over the Tunisian desert and hill country south of Benghazi on April 26, 1943, Rocky Byrne's flight got into a lopsided battle of survival with a much larger German fighter force. All three of the P-40s flying with Byrne were shot down and Byrne himself was wounded, but he downed two of the Me-109s—his fifth and sixth victories—and managed to land his crippled fighter at his own base. He returned to flying duty following a month-long stay in an RAF hospital in Egypt, but he did not shoot down any more German airplanes before he was shipped home in September 1943 at the conclusion of a year-long combat tour.

Rocky Byrne spent the rest of the war training new pilots, and he mustered out of the service in 1946. Giving in to an itch to fly again, however, Byrne joined the Delaware Air National Guard in 1947. He was activated with his unit for the Korean War, but he saw no combat.

United States forces invaded French Northwest Africa—Algeria and French Morocco—on November 8, 1942. The landings themselves were covered by U.S. Navy Grumman F4F Wildcat fighter squadrons working from the decks of light carrier *Ranger* and several escort carriers. In two days of action against Vichy French aircraft, the Navy pilots downed a confirmed total of twenty-four aircraft, plus five probables.

On November 8, the 33d Fighter Group, a P-40 unit, landed at Port Lyautey, French Morocco, and the 31st Fighter Group's 309th Fighter Squadron flew its Spitfires from Gibraltar to Tafaraoui Airdrome, outside Oran, Algeria. Both came under the control of Major General James Doolittle's Twelfth Air Force, whose advance headquarters went ashore in Algeria on November 9. On its arrival at Tafaraoui during the afternoon of

November 8, the 309th was attacked by Vichy French fighters while in the landing pattern. Several Spitfires were downed in the bounce, but so were three of the French fighters. The next morning, a Vichy mechanized column attacked Tafaraoui as the 31st Fighter Group's second echelon was landing, and the 31st beat back the French Foreign Legion light tanks and motorized infantry in a devastating aerial counterattack.

Shortly thereafter, on November 13 and 15, two fresh, unblooded American fighter units—the 1st and 14th Fighter groups, respectively—flew all the way to Tafaraoui from England in Lockheed P-38 Lightning twin-engine fighters. On November 18, the fresh 79th Fighter Group, a P-40 unit, arrived in Egypt to bolster the blooded, aggressive 57th Fighter Group. The 57th and 79th, plus an assortment of medium and heavy bomber groups, were placed under Major General Lewis Brereton's Ninth Air Force, which had established its headquarters in Egypt on November 12.

Almost upon arriving at Tafaraoui, the fresh 1st and 14th Fighter groups joined the blooded 31st in action, supporting ground troops and escorting freshly committed XII Bomber Command medium bombers against targets as far away as Tunisia's east coast. On the hills along the Algeria-Tunisia frontier, infantry and armored divisions from the British First Army and the U.S. II Corps were waiting to link up with Montgomery's British Eighth Army, which in a matter of weeks had driven Rommel's forces all the way across Egypt and most of the way across Libya.

"YOU SEE THEM, YOU DRIVE UP BEHIND THEM, AND YOU SHOOT THEM DOWN"

Captain JOE OWENS, USAAF
27th Fighter Squadron, 1st Fighter Group
Bizerte, Tunisia, November 30, 1942

Joel Amos Owens, Jr., was born in Bigheart, Oklahoma, on May 8, 1920, and raised in nearby Skiatook. He graduated from the Oklahoma Military Academy before enlisting in the Army Air Corps as an aviation cadet in October 1940. Following his graduation from flight school in May 1941, 2d Lieutenant Owens was assigned to the 1st Pursuit Group's 27th Pursuit Squadron at Selfridge Field, Michigan.

By the time the 1st Fighter Group flew its Lockheed P-38 Lightning twin-engine fighters to England via Iceland— Operation BOLERO, in August 1942—and then to North Africa on November 13, 1942, Captain Joel Owens was the regular leader of the 27th Fighter Squadron's "A" Flight.

The first home of the 1st Fighter Group's headquarters and 27th and 71st Fighter squadrons in North Africa was Nouvion, a converted wheat field a few miles southeast of Oran, Algeria. At the time—two weeks after the group's arrival in North Africa from England—the 27th was commanded by Major John "Willie" Weltman, and the 1st Fighter Group was commanded by Lieutenant Colonel Ralph Garman.

I commanded "A" Flight of the 27th. My deputy flight commander and best friend was 1st Lieutenant Harold "Mendy" Mendenhall, who, like myself, was twenty-two years old. Mendy and I both were graduates of Class 41-D, and we had flown together since June 1941. We had shared a lot of experiences, in the air and elsewhere. He was the best acrobatic pilot in the squadron. I knew that no matter what sort of stunt I pulled, Mendy would be where he was supposed to be. By the end of November 1943, Mendy and I each had around 700 hours total flying time, including over 450 hours in fighter aircraft of various types: P-35s, P-36s, P-43s, and, primarily, P-38 variants.

My wingman on the November 30, 1942, mission was 2d Lieutenant Marcus "Junior" Linn, a nineteen-year-old former Royal Air Force or Royal Canadian Air Force type who had joined the unit in England a short time before our move to North Africa. Junior had a high-pitched voice that was very difficult to understand. He was a good pilot and utterly fearless, but he was never able to fully comprehend or manage all of the systems on the P-38.

Mendy's wingman was 2d Lieutenant Henry "Smitty" Smith, who was twenty-one. Smitty had joined the squadron at Mines Field, in Inglewood, California, in the spring of 1942. He was an experienced pilot and was rock solid in his flying. He was also an avid poker player, perhaps best known for the horrendous bluffs he tried to run on his buddies.

The 1st Fighter Group was equipped with the Lockheed P-38 Lightning twin-engine fighter. We had conducted in-service testing of the P-38 in 1941, and eighty-odd P-38Fs had been delivered to us in April 1942. Each of these airplanes had been modified with RAF-compatible radio gear and low-pressure oxygen systems. They had also been fitted with pylons underneath each wing to accommodate the 165-gallon wing tanks that allowed the group to fly across the North Atlantic to England, via Greenland and Iceland, in Operation BOLERO. The visual difference between the F-model P-38s and earlier models was the mast antenna in front of the nose wheel. This replaced the pitot tube, which had been moved underneath the left wing. Also, if you looked real hard, you might note that there was a slight change in the canopy to accommodate a rear-view mirror.

I usually flew the same P-38F: serial number 42-7546, which had the squadron marking, HV-E. I flew this airplane all the way from Mines Field, California, to Nouvion. The plane had been named *Daisy Mae* by the crew chief, Technical Sergeant John Clark, in honor of a young lady he had been dating. Daisy Mae herself invoked the Lord's blessing on the plane and the crew by burning a candle for each of us, and I suppose it worked because I flew sixty-five missions in her namesake without any serious trouble.

On November 30, 1942, we had been in North Africa for almost two weeks and had as yet had no contact with the enemy. The 94th Fighter Squadron of the 1st Fighter Group and the 14th Fighter Group (which at the time consisted of only the 48th and 49th Fighter squadrons) were somewhere near the front lines, in eastern Algeria, and they were encountering the Luftwaffe on nearly every mission. The 27th and 71st squadrons were the bomber-escort force. We and the heavies had been out on two occasions, but we had been thwarted by bad weather over the target area. On the November 24 mission, we had to turn back after reaching a point about twenty miles south of Sardinia. And on November 29, we got only as far as Cape Serrat, about thirty miles from Bizerte.

On November 30, 1942, sixteen P-38s of the 27th Fighter Squadron were to escort eighteen B-17s of the 97th Heavy Bombardment Group to Bizerte. The target was the North Quay at the naval base. The timing of the mission was much as it had been on the earlier missions: Takeoff when it was light enough and touchdown before it got dark. On this mission, the time over target was 1215. An open-air briefing was conducted by Major Weltman; as the pilots gathered around, he spread his maps out on the hood of his jeep and gave us our headings, callsigns, and assignments.

The bombers were to proceed to an initial point (IP) midway between Tunis and Bizerte at 24,000 feet. At the IP, they were to turn left on the run-up to the target. This was to be followed by another left turn after bomb release. The four flights of P-38s were to rendezvous with the B-17s over our base and follow at the bombers' pace—around 170 miles per hour—above and "up sun" in relation to the bomber group.

The B-17s were in three of their usual "box" formations. Each box consisted of two three-plane vees, one stepped down behind the other. The three boxes also were deployed in a loose vee. The up-sun box was about 200 feet below the lead box, and the down-sun box was about 200 feet above the lead box.

As we approached the IP, the P-38s were to increase their speed and climb to their assigned altitudes. The squadron leader and seven pilots were the close escort. It was their job to make wide, sweeping S-turns back and forth at 500 to 700 feet above and near the bombers. One flight of four was the support force, whose mission was to be ready to protect up sun and prevent the close escort from getting "bounced." The top cover was provided by my "A" Flight. We were to be about 1,200 to 1,500 feet above the support flight and were allowed quite a bit of leeway in positioning ourselves in relation to the bomber force.

The squadron was off on time and the missions proceeded as briefed. Junior was on my wing and Mendy and Smitty were the second element. The weather was clear when we took off, but it gradually deteriorated as we went along. The cloud deck below us was solid after we passed Algiers. It appeared that the weather ahead of us was going to create yet another dry run. But, as we approached the IP, there was a hole in the clouds over the target. The B-17s dropped their bombs through this hole. There was some flak as they made their bomb run, but no fighter opposition.

The 97th Bomb Group was off to my right and about 2,000 feet below me as it turned left and headed for home. The other P-38 flights were close to the bombers as the entire formation passed below us. We were making a wide right turn to clear the area behind the withdrawal. At that moment, I saw a single-engine fighter climb up through the hole in the clouds. I started down after it by making a steep spiral dive. I had the presence of mind to check and make sure the guns were hot and all the switches were on.

We started our dive at about 26,000 feet and had to lose about 9,000 feet. As the speed built up, the plane became nose-heavy and the controls started getting squirrely as it approached the edge of compressibility. As I neared the enemy plane, I identified it as an Me-109E; it had the square wingtips that were unique to the model. I was closing much too fast to make a good attack, and I was pulling a lot of Gs as I started to fire from 150 yards at an angle of around sixty degrees above and behind him. I fired a short burst, and, wonder of wonders, I managed to hit him in the left wing and the aft part of the fuselage. The German pilot did a half-roll to the left and popped down into the clouds. I pulled up into a steep climbing turn to the left and headed west to rejoin the formation.

I looked around to see how "A" Flight was doing. Mendy was the only one in sight. I asked where the rest were. Junior said something, but all I could make out was "Over." Smitty then called to say that he and Junior were together, but Junior had an oil-pressure gauge that was bothering him. They were just above the cloud deck and heading for home.

At that moment, I saw another Me-109 about a quarter of a mile to our left and slightly below us. He was climbing on a southwesterly heading that would put him in position for an attack on our bombers. I put "the balls to the wall," and Mendy and I started after him.

I managed to get directly behind and slightly below the Me-109 as we closed to a range of 100 yards. My pulse rate matched my airspeed as we passed through 25,000 feet at 220 miles per hour indicated. I was getting extremely nervous, apprehensive, and just plain scared as I recalled the words of an RAF pilot who had told us, "The most dangerous time, chaps, is when you've got your pipper on the bloke."

I had closed to about 200 feet when the 109 banked slightly to the right. I thought, Oh, oh. This is it. You had better do what you are going to—and right now! I fired a short burst. When I saw that I had him boresighted, I clamped down on the gun button until there was an explosion in the Me-109's fuselage and the tail blew off. The Me-109 started tumbling, and a great deal of smoke was coming from the midsection. Mendy hollered, "You got him! You got him!" I replied, "Yeah, I got him!" Then I uttered the immortal words used by fighter pilots to this very day: "Let's get the hell out of here!"

We found Smitty and Junior stooging along just above the clouds. Junior had feathered an engine for some reason.

Mendy and I joined up and headed for home. Along the way, Willie Weltman called and wanted to know, "Where in the hell are you and what is going on?" I told him that we were all right, but we would be a little late getting home.

The rest of the squadron returned to base about thirty-five minutes ahead of us. They were not aware of what had happened, since in all of our radio talk there had been no mention of enemy aircraft, *no* talk of "bogies" or "bandits." No one had associated Mendy's "You got him!" with enemy activity. Due to his delicate condition, Junior landed first. Then, after Mendy and Smitty had landed, I proceeded to give the base a "buzz job," followed by a victory roll.

My little air show attracted a good deal of attention from the folks on the ground. There was a good-sized group of crew chiefs, armorers, and others at my hardstand when I taxied in. My crew chief, Technical Sergeant Johnny Clark, was beaming as he waved me in. He pointed to the guns, which of course showed signs of having been fired, and he gave me a sort of quizzical thumbs-up. I gave him the joined thumb and forefinger—"Okay"—as I shut everything down. We had been flying for a mere six hours and forty-five minutes.

I could hardly wait to tell the world of my astounding feat. I was doing my best "There I Was" story when the staff car arrived. A grim-looking Lieutenant Colonel Ralph Garman, accompanied by a downright angry-looking Major Willie Weltman were striding toward my airplane. I thought, Maybe I shouldn't have done the slow roll, as my mind flashed back to Bangor, Maine, where Weltman had placed me under house arrest awaiting a court martial for blowing over a sailboat as I was doing a low-level navigation mission. I had escaped the hangman at Bangor because a senior officer interceded in my behalf, but now I was thinking that I was in *real* trouble.

The 1st Fighter Group policy regarding low flying and other dumb stunts was well known; it had been implemented shortly after the group's arrival in England. Sure enough, Weltman's first words were something like, "You $-!*£%$! What the hell are you trying to do?" Colonel

Garman was a bit more restrained, but he wasn't smiling as he spoke. "Joe," he said, "you know the policy. What's the idea?" I was searching for some way to extricate myself when, luckily, I remembered Garman's closing remarks in the speech that he had made to the group when we first arrived in England. So I said, "Why, Colonel, sir, don't you remember? You told us the rule didn't apply if we shot somebody down." Suddenly the colonel was all smiles. "You mean that you *got* one? Tell me about it!" So I repeated my "There I Was" story. Willie also cooled off and offered his congratulations. I was off the hook.

The only thing left for us to endure was the Intelligence debriefing. The Interrogation, as we pilots called it, was the final act of a mission; it was where the Intelligence specialists attempted to gather factual data about the mission. They had a rather detailed checklist that they followed. I was always rather impatient with them, and I never underwent an interrogation that I liked. They rigidly applied their rules, and no amount of rhetoric was able to sway them. They weren't too impressed with my claim for a damaged aircraft because there was only one supporting witness, Mendy Mendenhall. And since no one had actually seen the second Me-109 crash, they decided to submit the claim to review. Luckily for me, the Review Board allowed the claim. The rules probably had been drawn up in 1917 or 1918. In my view, they were not practical in our place and time because there was little or no likelihood of anyone engaging an enemy aircraft at high altitude and actually seeing it hit the ground. The gun-camera film at the time was of little or no value because the camera on F-model P-38s was mounted about six inches below the muzzles of the four .50-caliber machine guns and the 20mm cannon. The vibration from the guns produced a very blurred image, which was invariably inconclusive. In the end, I was officially credited with the second Me-109 destroyed and the first Me-109 damaged. For the moment, I was the top-scoring pilot in the 1st Fighter Group. That was a distinction I enjoyed until December 2. *Sic transit gloria mundi.* A post-war review of Luftwaffe combat losses in North Africa revealed that on November 30, 1942, Unteroffizier Otto Reuss, of *Jagdgeschweder* (Fighter Wing) 53's IV *Gruppe* was wounded in action by a P-38 while on a routine test flight over Bizerte. Also on November 30, 1942, Leutnant Horst Wunderlich, of *Jagdgeschweder* 51's II *Gruppe* failed to return from a mission near Bizerte.

After a few drinks in celebration of the day, it was time to hit the sack. As I lay in bed, I reflected on what had happened. This air-to-air combat, I determined, is a snap— you see them, you drive up behind them, and you shoot them down. It seemed as simple as that. But it never happened to me like that again. The few additional victories that I was able to gain came as a result of *re*acting rather than acting. In a matter of weeks, our fighters were to cede the initiative to the Luftwaffe because we became committed to the role of close bomber escort. In fact, we never seemed to get close enough to suit the bomber crews.

At times, we put a flight in line-abreast formation directly beneath the lead box of bombers. The idea was to compensate for the lack of firepower that an early-model B-17 could project forward. It became our job to deter the enemy fighters from making sustained head-on attacks against the bombers. We experimented with new formations and tactics almost daily in an effort to increase our effectiveness as escorts. We eventually settled on a loose, finger-four formation for the individual flights, with the entire squadron right down on top of the bomber formation. Within the flight, if it was operating alone, the two elements would fly abreast and space themselves widely enough apart to allow either element to turn inside and protect the other. The key word was "protect"—we were on the defensive.

Even when our squadron fighter strength dwindled to the point where, on December 15, 1942, two of us wound up escorting eighteen B-17s on a mission to Tunis, we *stayed with the bombers!* The two P-38 pilots shot down four Me-109s and two FW-190s on that particular mission, but no claims were made due to lack of corroboration.

In the beginning, we had little or no experience in bomber escort. The RAF had offered little advice during our brief stay in England. They had scads of experience in *intercepting* enemy bomber forces, but their short-ranged fighter units had done very little escort work. The Luftwaffe had the most experience in daylight escort work, but their record in the Battle of Britain had not been at all great. Besides, they were unavailable for consultation.

Our formations and tactics clearly were not designed to attack and destroy enemy fighters. They were designed to prevent the bombers from being shot down by the sustained attacks of the enemy fighters. To this end, I believe that we were successful because the majority of the bomber losses in the Tunisian Campaign were due to antiaircraft fire or mid-air collisions. We didn't know it at the time, but we were facing some of the Luftwaffe's elite pilots. *Jagdgeschweder* 53 had at least a dozen pilots with twenty or more victories each, and three of their pilots each had more than 100 victories. The top gun in *Jagdgeschweder* 51 was Leutnant Anton Hafner, who would score 204 victories before he was shot down.

The tactics we used and the discipline that enabled us to carry out our mission in the face of such formidable opposition are a credit to our early combat leaders—Major Glenn Hubbard, of the 94th Fighter Squadron; Major Ray Rudell, of the 71st; Major Willie Weltman, of the 27th; and Lieutenant Colonel Ralph Garman, our group commander. They started from square one and built from there.

Captain Joe Owens shot down a second confirmed Me-109, also near Bizerte, on December 4, 1942. Within the month, Owens was elevated to the command of the 27th Fighter Squadron, and he received credit for probably downing an Italian Reggiane Re.2001 fighter while leading a long-range reconnaissance mission to Tripoli on January 12, 1943. Owens's next confirmed victory was an Me-109 he downed near Gabès, Tunisia, on January 31, 1943. In April 1943, Owens was promoted to major and reassigned to the 14th Fighter Group as deputy group commander. He achieved ace status when he destroyed two Me-109s on May 10, 1943, while leading a mission over Sicily.

In December 1943, following home leave and a brief tour of duty in the United States, Major Joe Owens was transferred to England to become the operations officer of the 71st Fighter Wing. He served in that capacity until June 1944, when he assumed command of the 370th Fighter Group's 402d Fighter Squadron, a Lightning-equipped ground-attack component of the Ninth Air Force.

By war's end, Lieutenant Colonel Joel Owens had flown 147 combat missions, every one of them at the controls of P-38 fighters. In fact, between his first flight in a P-38, on July 29, 1941, and his last, on August 23, 1945, Joe Owens accumulated over 950 hours in the twin-engine Lockheed fighter.

ARMED RECONNAISSANCE

Captain NEWELL ROBERTS, USAAF
94th Fighter Squadron, 1st Fighter Group
Tunisia, December 2, 1942

Newell Orville Roberts was born in Little Rock, Arkansas, on August 7, 1916. After his mother died in 1920, he and his older brother were cared for by a number of relatives in Arkansas and Kentucky until 1923 when the boys finally went to live with their mother's aunt on a farm near Greenfield, in central Indiana. Roberts graduated from high school in Greenfield in 1934, worked for four years, and attended Ball State College, in Muncie, Indiana, during the 1938–39 school year. He majored in aeronautical engineering at Purdue University during the 1939–40 school year, but he earned his private pilot's license in September 1940 and enlisted in the Army Air Corps instead of returning to school.

Roberts was inducted into the Air Corps as an aviation cadet on November 21, 1940, and he reported to the Spartan School of Aeronautics in Muskogee, Oklahoma, three days later to begin Primary flight training. He earned his wings and a commission at Randolph Field, Texas, on July 11, 1941, with Class 41-E.

Special Order 161, dated July 12, 1941, relieved me from the Air Corps Advanced Flying School at Brooksfield, Texas, and assigned me to duty at Selfridge Field, Michigan, with the 1st Pursuit Group. When I arrived, I was assigned to the famous 94th "Hat-in-Ring" Pursuit Squadron, which had been commanded by Captain Eddie Rickenbacker in World War I.

In the summer of 1941, we were flying the Republic P-43 Lancer, which was a smaller and less-powerful forerunner of the famous P-47 Thunderbolt. However, in September 1941, a group of us was sent to the Lockheed Corporation's Burbank, California, plant to be taught to fly the new YP-38, a pre-production training and in-service test model of the twin-engine Lightning fighter. After a brief transition course, we flew this batch of YP-38s back to Michigan.

During our period of testing the YP-38s, several of the airplanes buried themselves in the earth while doing combat or acrobatic maneuvers from high altitudes. On one occasion, I had a YP-38 up to 20,000 feet and was doing acrobatics. When I did a slow roll, the airplane would not come out of the dive. The Lockheed technical representative who had been assigned to the 1st Pursuit Group had told me earlier that, if I ever got the airplane into a dive and it would not come out, I should quickly roll back the trim tab and, if I was lucky and had enough altitude, it would come out of the dive.

I quickly rolled the trim tab back and the airplane came out of the dive at about 100 feet off the ground. I immediately brought the airplane back to Selfridge Field and landed. The technical staff went over that airplane from stem to stern. They found that the wings were buckled and it wouldn't be able to fly anymore. They then took the airplane apart and discovered the problem. On the counterbalance shaft controlling the back horizontal rudder were two stop bolts that kept the shaft within a certain arc. When the airplane vibrated, the bolts worked loose and turned downward in such a way that it became impossible to get the airplane out of a dive at high speeds without using the trim tabs. This aeronautical engineering monstrosity was corrected at the Lockheed factory and we had no more difficulty bringing the airplane out of a dive.

By the time the correction was made, most of the YP-38s had either buried themselves in the ground or were unable to fly any longer. Of course, when several of the YP-38s had buried themselves in the ground following uncontrolled dives, they had also buried the pilots. Shortly, we were supplied and outfitted with improved production P-38s, which were excellent airplanes.

In the autumn of 1941, we participated in the big Army maneuvers in the Carolinas and then we went back to Michigan. Then, on December 4, 1941, we were ordered to the West Coast. On December 7, I was flying one of twenty P-38s from our home base in Michigan to Southern California. It was during a fuel stop at Biggs Field in El Paso, Texas, that we learned of the attack on Pearl Harbor.

During the following six months, the three squadrons of the 1st Pursuit Group operated from three separate bases in Southern California, performing coastal patrol missions—looking for the Japanese fleet everyone expected to invade the West Coast of the United States. The 94th Pursuit Squadron operated from both North Island, in San Diego, and from Long Beach. In June 1942, however, the group—now called the 1st Fighter Group—moved to Bangor, Maine, to prepare for Operation BOLERO, the first mass flight of fighters and bombers to England via Labrador, Greenland, Iceland, and Scotland.

Ferrying a group of fighter aircraft over the Atlantic to the war zone in England was a real first. All of us were proud to be part of it. On the way, in Iceland on August 14, one member of the 27th Fighter Squadron even took part in downing a German FW-200 Condor long-range reconnaissance bomber, the very first aerial victory of the United States war effort against Germany.

We remained in England for approximately three months and trained in tactics and gunnery. We actually flew about twenty or twenty-five short-range escort missions over enemy territory in France, but we never met the enemy during the whole time.

Allied forces invaded French Northwest Africa on November 8, 1942, and both the 1st and 14th Fighter groups received orders to fly their P-38 fighters non-stop from England to Algeria. This extremely long flight (nine hours and fifteen minutes) was completed when we landed at Tafaraoui Airdrome, near Oran, Algeria, on November 13. Within a few days of our epic flight, after much-needed aircraft maintenance had been performed on our P-38s, our group was considered to be a fully operational unit, and we began combat operations from a rudimentary air base at Nouvion, Algeria.

The airdrome at Nouvion was merely a wheat field that had been turned into a landing field. It was not really what should be called an airdrome. It was just a space where we had our airplanes and where we all lived in tents and foxholes. We officers stayed in holes we dug ourselves and covered over with pup tents.

Normally, we provided close air support for our ground troops, but we also raided enemy bases and defenses deep inside neighboring Tunisia. We also provided high-altitude escort service for the two American heavy-bomber groups that also were operating from bases in Algeria.

Our early losses in pilots and aircraft were unbelievable, both from enemy action and from maintenance problems caused by lack of spare parts and the wearing effects of dust and sand on machinery. In two instances during our first months in North Africa, the total number of aircraft in our three squadrons ran from the usual total strength of eighty aircraft down to approximately only thirty aircraft. And in most instances this involved the loss of the pilots as well.

On November 28, the 94th Fighter Squadron began operating from a crude advance fighter strip at Youks-les-Bains, in eastern Algeria, near the Tunisian frontier. On November 29, I was involved in the 94th Fighter Squadron's first confirmed victory of the war. It was a Messerschmitt Me-110 twin-engine heavy fighter that I encountered along with my wingman, 1st Lieutenant Jack Ilfrey, while we were flying home following a raid on the German airdrome at Gabès, Tunisia. In fact, this was the first full victory credit awarded to the 1st Fighter Group in the war.

On December 1, our group commander, Lieutenant Colonel Ralph Garman, called me back to his headquarters, which was still at Nouvion, and asked me if I would volunteer for a mission. As far as I know, the mission had been dreamed up by Major General Jimmy Doolittle, the commander of the Twelfth Air Force, and it had been sent down to our group headquarters. Lieutenant Colonel Garman was a very fair individual and would oftentimes ask for a volunteer for a hazardous mission. He never at any point in time ordered any of his men to do anything; he always asked them to do it.

The mission, due to be flown on December 2, was to be an armed reconnaissance to the Tunisian coast by four P-38s from our squadron. On the way out, we were to strafe enemy positions at Faid Pass, which was ninety miles from Youks-les-Bains. Faid Pass was a target because, during that period, German tanks, troops, and supplies were all passing through it on their way to fight our troops elsewhere in Tunisia. The Germans had built pillboxes there and emplaced artillery to protect the pass.

After strafing the German positions at Faid Pass, my flight was to continue on to the Tunisian port of Sfax (sixty miles beyond the pass). We were to reconnoiter the harbor and the town and then turn southwest another eighty miles to the Tunisian port of Gabès. As at Sfax, we were to reconnoiter the area and then turn inland for the 155-mile return leg to Youks-les-Bains. As far as everyone was concerned, this appeared to be a suicide mission, but when Lieutenant Colonel Garman had finished explaining it to me, I accepted.

I asked three other pilots to accompany me, and they all accepted. Flying in the number three slot as element leader would be Lieutenant Jack Ilfrey, who had been my wingman and had shared in my first combat victory on November 29. My wingman would be 2d Lieutenant Robert Lovell, and Ilfrey's wingman would be 1st Lieutenant Richard McWherter. Naturally, when I went into combat, I wanted to choose the most competent combat pilots that we had. I chose McWherter and Lovell to fly with Jack Ilfrey and myself on that particular day because they were among the top-notch combat pilots in the 94th Fighter Squadron. And, in addition to having been my wingman on many missions flown during our stay in England and since our arrival in North Africa, Jack Ilfrey was well qualified to be an element leader.

We took off from Youks-les-Bains at 0645 hours on December 2, 1942, and flew a course of approximately 120 degrees to Faid Pass. My wingman (Lovell) was on my right, the element leader (Ilfrey) was on my left, and the element leader's wingman (McWherter) was on his left. This finger-four formation was highly maneuverable and could be changed very quickly. When we went into the pass, I was in the lead and Lieutenant Lovell was following in trail. Jack Ilfrey and Lieutenant McWherter followed us, also in trail.

We strafed enemy positions with the four .50-caliber machine guns and one 20mm cannon mounted in the nose of each P-38. Our single firing pass was conducted from low altitude and high speed, so the view was fleeting, but I saw strikes on many enemy bunkers and trenches, and the other pilots reported the same.

After the one firing pass, we turned a few degrees to the left to return to our course of 120 degrees, returned to our finger-four formation, and continued on a straight course on the deck to Sfax. It took us only ten minutes to cover the sixty miles at our flying speed of 360 miles per hour. The weather at that time was excellent—blue skies, no rain, and unlimited visibility. We continuously scanned the beautiful sky for enemy aircraft, but we saw nothing.

I could see Sfax some ten to fifteen miles before we reached the coast. The town looked peaceful and quiet, but there was a huge battleship in the harbor, about a half-mile offshore in the beautiful blue waters of the Gulf of Gabès. As we made our approach, Lieutenant Ilfrey called me on the radio and asked for permission to leave the flight to look more closely at the battleship. I gave him permission to do so.

At the time, the four P-38s in my flight were stacked between 100 and 300 feet. Jack pulled up to 500 feet, which I thought would give us away to the German radar and alert everybody to both our presence and our course. I was mildly annoyed at Jack, so I called him back to rejoin the flight, and he did so immediately.

Before Jack and McWherter had quite rejoined my element, I flew down along Sfax's wide main street with my wingman, Lieutenant Lovell, following in trail. The street ran north to south, parallel to the beach. I am sure we were flying all of three feet off the stone-paved street, which fortunately had no obstructions along its entire length. The props were just barely missing the ground. We had plenty of room on each side of our wingtips—the street was about half again as wide as a P-38.

The buildings were for the most part white. They were small and mostly two or three stories high. As I glanced to the right and left, I saw that the fronts of the buildings facing the main street had been removed. The buildings looked just like aircraft hangars. In fact, much to my amazement, I saw that Me-109 fighters and other German military airplanes were parked inside buildings on both sides of the street. All any of the aircraft had to do was taxi out into the street and take off.

There was absolutely nobody shooting at us. Our arrival had come as a complete surprise to the Germans—even to the crew of the battleship in the harbor.

After Lieutenants Ilfrey and McWherter arrived back in

formation, we turned south-southwest to parallel the coast-line of the Gulf of Gabès. Our next objective was the port of Gabès, some eighty miles from Sfax. We flew as low to the ground as we possibly could, usually no higher than treetop level.

About fifteen minutes later, as we were approaching Gabès from the northwest side of a forest, I saw Me-109s taking off from an airdrome to our southeast. The airdrome itself was about a half mile south of the town.

There were three flights of German fighters, four planes to a flight. I knew where to look because I had strafed Gabès Airdrome with Jack Ilfrey on November 29. But I also saw the Me-109s because they were creating a thin dust trail behind them; there were no runways at the airdrome, just packed earth. I could see other airplanes sitting on the ground.

I called Jack on the radio and said, "Jack, there are enemy airplanes taking off to the northeast. Let's get them!" Jack just said, "I see them."

The lead Me-109 was at treetop level, about fifty feet in the air. I opened the throttles of both my engines past the red stop, thus activating the water injection and giving myself a considerable temporary boost in power and speed. I would have no problem catching up with the 109s because they were still taking off and thus going quite slowly.

By the time I turned in to line up on the lead Me-109, he was only about 100 feet in the air. He did not turn to meet me or even try to evade; he simply continued his takeoff to the northeast. I doubt if he knew I was there. I banked to the left of the lead Me-109 and came around right on his tail. The whole body of the airplane appeared in my gunsight. I was not more than fifty yards away and gaining on him. My aiming point was dead on the entire stern section of the Me-109. He was a sitting duck and I was right on him. I was so close to him when I opened fire that, when his airplane exploded in front of me, pieces of the wings and other parts hit my plane.

I followed through on my sharp turn to the left and came directly up on the tail of another Me-109. In the brief

39

portion of a second, this Me-109 pilot tried to evade, but there was no escape. Again, I was not more than fifty yards—or maybe only fifty *feet*—from him when I fired. I was something like twenty to fifty feet away when he also blew up in midair. This airplane just disintegrated.

The battle was on. After I shot down two of the Me-109s, two of the others tried to attack me head-on. As I took snap shots at these and at other Me-109s that were pulling around in front of me, I noticed that one Me-109 had climbed up to about 1,000 to 2,000 feet above us and was just circling. Before I could go up to get him, however, the flak [antiaircraft] batteries at the airdrome opened fire. They cut loose with everything they had, firing at *all* of us, including the Me-109s. The bursting flak filled the air with a huge cloud of smoke, so extreme that it became necessary for me to fly on instruments when going through it, which I did two or three times while looking for more enemy airplanes.

Suddenly I heard a screaming, blood-curdling voice come over the intercom. It was Jack Ilfrey. "Robbie, I've been hit!" I did not know if Jack meant that *he* himself had been hit or if his airplane had been hit. I told him to get on the deck, which to us meant three feet off the ground, and head toward our base at Youks-les-Bains. Jack flew out of the cloud of bursting flak and headed in the direction of Youks with only one engine running. Jack's P-38 had been hit in the right engine, and the propeller was feathered, but he had full power on the left engine. I went down to escort him home, flying approximately three feet off his right wingtip and matching his speed of about 275 miles per hour. We were just three to four feet off the ground, with the propellers not quite hitting the vegetation.

To us, flying low was not a bad risk. In fact, it was the only maneuver in a case like this. Our being so low made it difficult for an enemy fighter to come down and shoot at us because the attacker would be in danger of running his own nose into the ground while he was trying to get his sights on one of us. Flying low for Jack Ilfrey and myself had never been a problem. We could strafe targets accurately with our props clicking over only a few feet off the ground. At that point in time, Jack Ilfrey was one of the Army Air Forces's best combat pilots.

I was keeping my eye on the Me-109 that I had spotted circling alone above the airdrome. As Jack and I began our race toward home, I glanced toward the German again, just in time to see him execute a half roll. He pulled his nose through, and, when he rolled out, he was right on Jack's tail.

I wanted to get a deflection shot at the Me-109, which was flying some ten to twenty feet to my left. From my position off Jack's right wing, I eased off my throttle and turned slightly to my left. I ended up about twenty feet in back of the Me-109. I wanted to shoot the pilot. I had the Me-109's nose in my sight, but when I pressed the firing solenoid nothing happened. I was out of ammunition.

I was helpless. I could see the German's bullets going into Jack's airplane, peeling the metal up as they penetrated. I could also see the German sitting in his Me-109. He looked around at me and *laughed!* I was so close that I could see his eyes were blue, he had blondish hair, and he had a light complexion.

You do things in combat on the spur of the moment, without thinking. You act instinctively. You don't wait, or concentrate, or try and make up your mind. It is instilled in a combat pilot to act automatically to save a comrade's life. In combat, you have a devotion to comradeship that very few people ever achieve at any other time in their lives. Anyway, it is *impossible* to think about the things you're going to do in intense combat—you just do them. What I did was start to ram the German airplane with my left propeller. When the German saw me coming, he immediately turned to the left. As he did, his tail hit my left wingtip. The collision demolished the Me-109's tail assembly, the pilot lost control, and the Me-109 dived into the ground.

I looked around, but there were no more Me-109s in the air. As Jack and I continued on to Youks-les-Bains, I flew close formation with him. After we landed, 268 bullet holes were counted in Jack's P-38.

I had definitely shot down two Me-109s as they took off from Gabès Airdrome, and I probably damaged several others in the melee that followed, but I had no confirmation of doing so. I did not claim the airplane that collided with me because I had not actually shot at it.

Lieutenant Lovell came in to Youks-les-Bains an hour or an hour and a half after Jack Ilfrey and I got there. When McWherter came in late that evening, he told us that he had landed his airplane on a road in the desert and filled it with automobile gasoline from an Arab-run gas station. Somehow, he managed to get the airplane back to Youks-les-Bains.

It is my belief that twelve Me-109s were destroyed in the air on that particular mission, but only seven were officially credited as destroyed. By my count, however, nine Me-109s were shot down in air combat, one was destroyed when I cut off its tail, and the remaining two were shot down by the enemy flak batteries. Officially, I was given credit for two Me-109s, Jack Ilfrey was given credit for two, Lovell was given credit for one destroyed and one damaged, and McWherter was given credit for two. Ilfrey and Lovell each also received unofficial credit for one Me-109 destroyed on the ground.

On December 12, 1942, Captain Newell Roberts and his wingman downed an Italian Cant Z.1007 flying boat near Philippeville, Algeria. He received a full credit for downing an Me-109 on February 7, 1943, south of Sardinia, and he achieved ace status with his fifth and last official victory credit, another Me-109, on February 9, 1943, near Kairouan, Tunisia, during a bomber-escort mission.

Roberts completed fifty-two combat missions amounting to 158 combat hours before he was ordered to return to the United States on April 7, 1943. He served as an instructor for the remainder of the war and was separated from the service on November 18, 1945. Roberts attended the University of California at Berkeley under the GI Bill, earning his bachelor's degree in zoology in 1948. He subsequently earned a medical degree at the University of Liverpool, England, in

1955, and completed a residency in psychiatry at Baylor University in 1960.

Thanks in large measure to lackluster generalship, the Tunisian Campaign bogged down for months on end. As one offensive after another failed to score a knock-out blow on the ground, the half-dozen Ninth and Twelfth Air Force Fighter groups committed to the campaign flew a grueling schedule of bomber-escort and air-superiority missions that wore down men and machines nearly to the point of extinction. The airfields remained crude and were often overcrowded, and there was no way for the overworked pilots to restore themselves. There weren't enough pilots in any case, and leaves were rare.

Air-to-air victories came almost daily in December and January, in penny packets of one to six victory credits per mission— if German or Italian airplanes could be found at all. An American fighter unit was as likely to be attacked on the ground, at home, as it was likely to attack German or Italian air units at or around *their* lairs.

The American fighter groups expended some effort on direct support of ground units, but the Army Air Corps had not developed a tactical air-support doctrine between the world wars, and it lacked trained pilots and dedicated equipment. Besides, the fighter groups were hard-pressed to fulfill their routine of bomber-escort missions. Fortunately, the RAF fielded a dedicated Army Co-operation Command, complete with well-trained and specially equipped units, and it bore the brunt of the ground-support role in Tunisia. However, two Army Air Forces fighter groups equipped with Bell P-39 Airacobras also found their way to North Africa in late 1942. Since, in the early Pacific defensive campaigns, the P-39 had proven to be utterly outclassed as a fighter, the P-39 groups—the 81st and 350th—were adapted to a ground-support role. One dedicated ground-support unit, the 27th Fighter-Bomber Group, which arrived in Algeria in late December, was equipped with A-36 light attack bombers, an American version of a British single-engine army-cooperation airplane called the Mustang. In due course—within a year—the A-36 Mustang would be adapted by American industry into the world's premier piston-engine fighter, the North American P-51 Mustang.

In November 1942 air action, Army Air Forces fighters had been credited with forty-six aerial victories. The total rose to seventy-two in December, ninety-seven in January, and seventy-five in February.

By the end of February 1943, several fresh fighter groups had arrived in North Africa, and the work could be more equitably split. Aces began emerging in several of the fighter groups, and other fighter pilots began the climb to acedom.

MY DAY FOR LUCK

1st Lieutenant JERRY COLLINSWORTH, USAAF
307th Fighter Squadron, 31st Fighter Group
Tunisia, March 8, 1943

J D Collinsworth was born in Dublin, Texas, on December 23, 1919. He graduated from flight school with Class 42-C at Luke Field, Arizona, on March 6, 1942, and was assigned with many of his classmates to a medium-bomber group in Louisiana to learn to fly North American B-25 Mitchell medium bombers. When a large number of the new pilots complained bitterly that they were not being allowed to fly fighters, volunteers from the class—the loudest complainers —were transferred to two fighter groups, also based in Louisiana. Thus, Lieutenant Jerry Collinsworth and a handful of his classmates found their way into the 31st Fighter Group.

Jerry Collinsworth flew his first combat missions from

England, across the English Channel to France. He was an escort pilot during the first U.S. Army Air Forces heavy-bomber mission in Europe, on August 17, 1942, and he flew over Dieppe two days later. Shortly after the 31st Fighter Group was taken off flight duty in England without explanation, Collinsworth was one of a handful of pilots sent by ship to Gibraltar to flight-test brand-new Spitfires.

I was in Gibraltar for about six weeks, and I test-hopped forty-some airplanes. At first, we didn't know what they were going to use the Spitfires for, or where we were going, or anything. We were told to just test-hop the airplanes. The British put them together, some Australian armorers fired the guns out into the Mediterranean, and we American pilots test-hopped them. After a successful test hop, the Spitfires were stacked against The Rock, and we'd proceed on to the next batch.

Along about the first week of November 1942, General Dwight Eisenhower and his staff came down to Gibraltar, and then the rest of the 31st Fighter Group arrived. The 52d Fighter Group came, too. They had been following us everywhere by about two weeks. They got Spitfires at Gibraltar, too. Then, on November 8, the 31st took off and went to Tafaraoui, but I had to stay in Gibraltar and finish test-hopping the Spitfires. It was a couple or three weeks before I finally rejoined the group at a real nice new base called La Senia. In December, we moved to Maison Blanche, which was near Algiers. Through January 1943, we mostly escorted C-47 transports from the 62d Troop Carrier Group, which were carrying cargo to the front.

In early February we proceeded down to Thelepte, Tunisia, to replace the 33d Fighter Group. This was the real thing. You don't know how you're going to react when the Real McCoy comes along. You don't know whether you're going to be brave, scared, or go to pieces.

The 31st Fighter Group saw no action in North Africa from the time we arrived until February 15, 1943. That day, twelve of us took off from Thelepte and went out to look for trouble. One of the pilots from my flight left early because of engine trouble, so I was the number three man in an oddball flight, the tail-end Charlie.

I was thinking that if we were attacked that day, those so and so's would attack our oddball flight; it was just like them. Sure enough, a little bit later, I saw some bogies at 4 o'clock high. I was wearing glasses at the time; my vision was corrected to 20/10. I called out the bogies.

We kept an eye on the bogies until, finally, when they got fairly close, I told the flight leader to break right. But the leader started to make what seemed to be a gentle Training Command turn. I *knew* his tail was in trouble, and that turn sure wouldn't hack it for me. *My* tail was in the *most* trouble! I made a tight, quick turn inside the other two Spitfires in my flight and faced the lead Focke-Wulf FW-190 alone.

By the time I got around, I could see the sparklers flying from the German airplane. That made me mad. This guy was *really* trying to kill me. The Focke-Wulfs had jumped our oddball flight, just like I knew they would. But I wasn't scared; I was angry. I thought, You so and so! If you can dish it out, I can, too.

With that, I pushed the firing button and squeezed the cannon trigger. I almost released them because nothing happened out there. The guns fired, but nothing seemed to happen. I was so green that I forgot it took a bullet time to go from Point A to Point B. Anyway, I shot him and he belly-landed into the desert. I was excited. I yelled, "I got him! I got him!" But when I got off the mike, this calm voice told me to shut up. There was a very good reason for that, and I did shut up. That was the 307th Fighter Squadron's first confirmed victory of the war, and other pilots on the mission damaged four other German fighters.

Two days after my first combat, the Germans threatened to overrun Thelepte, which they did a few days later. We pulled back to Tébessa, Algeria, on February 17. Tébessa was what the news reports referred to as a "prepared airdrome." It was a scraped-out piece of dirt that could be used as a runway. That was it. It was rainy and cold, and there was no shelter. At Tébessa, my buddy and I found scorpions while we were trying to dig a shelter in a gully. These were great big scorpions, but we never did get bitten. Next, we went up to Youks-les-Bains, which was also in Algeria, on February 21. Finally, around February 25, they moved us again, this time to Kalaa Djerda, Tunisia. This was a real nice base, with warm buildings to eat and sleep in. Pilots from the 31st Fighter Group got into a few little fights at the end of February and the first few days of March, but I wasn't involved.

March 8, 1943, was one year and two days after I had graduated flying school. It was the day of my scariest mission. Lieutenant Merlin Mitchell was leading the mission, which consisted of just one flight of four Spitfires. A fellow from the 309th Fighter Squadron was flying as Mitchell's wingman, and I was leading the second element with Lieutenant Woodlief "Woody" Thomas on my wing. We were supposed to just go out and find Rommel and the German Army. I guess we were to find out by being shot at.

We took off at 0915. The weather was miserable. The ceiling ran between 800 and 1,200 feet, and we were flying along at about 600 feet above the terrain, in a box. That is, Mitchell and I were up even with one another, and our wingmen were behind us.

Somewhere along the way, at around 0945, while we were flying in a generally easterly direction, I could see machine-gun tracers coming up just in front of us. Mitch made a tight left break to get away from it.

I was on Mitch's right. I rationalized that if I broke to my left, I would fly right through the wall of fire. I hesitated just a little bit, so I would pass the gunfire before I made my turn. Then, when we rolled to the left, Woody Thomas inadvertently pulled in front of me. He had cut inside me. When we rolled back into our box formation, Woody was now number three, and I was number four.

The accidental arrangement was fine with me. Woody and I had the same amount of experience. In fact, he had earned his wings one or two classes ahead of me. But Woody, being the good guy that he was, must have decided that his job was to be number four for the entire mission. He began to slip back. When he essed out to make way for me—I knew he'd chopped his throttle—I advanced my throttle.

Just as I got past Woody, I heard guns. I looked back. Woody's Spitfire had already rolled over on its back, and flames were coming out of it. Woody went in from 500 feet. His Spitfire just blew up. It exploded on impact.

I looked up and saw the Focke-Wulf that had shot Woody down. It was directly above me, trying to slow down. It had been on an overtake course when it had hit Woody. The pilot was rocking his wings, trying to keep me in sight.

It is my belief that a fighter pilot needs three things to be a *good* fighter pilot: He needs to believe in himself, be a good pilot, and possess good luck. That was my day for luck. That fellow had been coming up on *me*. If Woody Thomas hadn't decided that he was still number four, it would have been Woody telling you the story, and not me.

I hollered a warning to Merlin Mitchell. I had no idea how many German fighters there were, so I told Mitch, "Get into the clouds." But he answered, "Hell, no! I'm going to fight these so-and-sos."

I tried to get under the Focke-Wulf, but I couldn't. I finally made up my mind to fly into the clouds even though I didn't know how to fly instruments. When the Focke-Wulf pulled to the left to try to dump some of his overtaking speed and get behind me again, I flew into the clouds. We were about even when I went into the clouds.

The good old Spitfire was very stable. I took my hands off the controls and gently eased the left rudder—the downside rudder. Just gently.

I came back out of the clouds after only five or six seconds. As soon as I did, I saw two things, and I'm not sure which I saw first. Down below me, three airplanes were flying in a Lufbery circle, right on the deck. I figured that Mitch and his wingman from the 309th Fighter Squadron were chasing the tail of a Focke-Wulf—or that two Focke-Wulfs were chasing Mitch *or* his wingman. But I didn't have time to look harder. I also saw a Focke-Wulf off to the side. It was below me but higher than the three fighters in the

Lufbery. I assumed it was the same airplane that had just shot Woody Thomas down. It was heading toward the Lufbery.

Just as I saw the Focke-Wulf, its pilot saw me. I know he did because I could see black smoke pouring out of his engine. He had firewalled that plane. I made up my mind quickly that I was going after the guy who had gotten Woody. That was the only time I ever shot at an airplane with the intention of killing the pilot. I always shot at airplanes, not pilots—except in this one instance.

The Focke-Wulf proceeded to the deck from about 500 or 600 feet, and I went after him. The Spitfire had an emergency boost, which was activated by a little red knob on the left side of the cockpit, just in front of the throttle lever. You could run for about five minutes at emergency power before you would have to replace the engine. You had to break a little wire to activate the emergency boost. I broke the wire. I had to hold the throttle and the red knob at the same time. I had everything pushed to the firewall. We were headed in a generally southerly direction. I had no idea where we were, only that we were somewhere in Tunisia.

I had a little altitude on the German, and I was gaining on him. The German got nervous and racked that Focke-Wulf into a tight left turn. Friend, I thought, you ain't about to out-turn this Spitfire. I knew he couldn't. I cut inside of him and fired. One of my 20mm cannon jammed and the other cannon, in the other wing, gave my Spitfire a see-saw action. I don't know if I hit him or not, but he snapped over on his back.

I thought that if I passed over him, he'd do a split-S and come up behind me. I rocked the other way to keep him in sight. And then I saw him hit the ground and explode. He was doing about 350 or 375 miles per hour when he hit the ground. I was so scared that I'd forgotten we were only twenty or thirty feet above the ground. When he snapped, he rolled his airplane right into the ground. I don't know if I even hit him, but it doesn't really matter.

The adrenalin was flowing through this twenty-three-year-old. I had just seen my buddy hit the ground and explode a couple of minutes earlier. And now that German fellow had exploded and was on fire.

I didn't know where I was. I was still at full throttle, but I knew enough to turn in a westerly direction, because that's where the Allies were—somewhere out there. At least I had to get away from German territory. I calmed down, dropped down to about ten feet or so, and pulled the throttle, fuel mixture, and RPM back.

All of a sudden, from my 10 o'clock to my 12 o'clock, I saw this airplane flying along at about 600 or 800 feet. There were clouds above me, and I was in a light rain. I thought the other airplane looked like a Spitfire, that maybe it was Merlin Mitchell or Mitch's wingman. But I didn't say anything on the radio, and I stayed right where I was.

By the time the other airplane got to my 12 o'clock, I was close enough to see a swastika on the tail. It was an Me-109. I thought I could stay down where I was and stay directly underneath him. I could advance the throttle, mixture, and RPM, pull up, and just let him slide right in front of me. He'd never know what hit him. And that's what I proceeded to do—to *start* to do.

As I turned underneath him and advanced the throttle, he still hadn't seen me. I knew that by the time I pulled up to 500 feet I would be behind him and probably close enough not to miss. And that's when a Britisher back in England saved my life. You can call it luck if you want. But I remembered this Britisher saying, "Chaps, remember this always: Where there's one, there's quite often two." I didn't look back; I just did a 180-degree turn, while I was still on the deck. As I got turned around, the German's number two man passed right over me. Neither one of the Germans ever saw me. If I had pulled up on number one, number two would have had me as a beautiful sitting target.

The adrenalin was flowing again. I headed west. I was going to fly west until I ran out of fuel or found an airfield. I came across Thelepte. We didn't have it—Rommel had kicked us out—but I knew where I was. I picked up a northwesterly heading, flew back to Kalaa Djerda, and landed. Merlin Mitchell never made it back. He was shot down and spent the rest of the war as a prisoner in Germany.

Lieutenant Jerry Collinsworth next shared an Me-109 proba-ble with three other pilots on March 21, 1943, and he downed one FW-190 apiece over Tunisia on April 5 and May 6. On June 10, over the island of Pantelleria, Collinsworth damaged an FW-190 and probably downed an Me-109, and on June 11, also in the vicinity of Pantelleria, he definitely downed an FW-190. While flying from the island of Gozo, near Malta, Captain Collinsworth scored his sixth and last confirmed victory. This was an FW-109 that he brought down on July 12, 1943, near the airdrome at Ponte Olivo, Sicily. The next day the 31st Fighter Group moved to Ponte Olivo.

On July 21, 1943, two hours after moving with the 31st Fighter Group to Agrigento, Sicily, Captain Jerry Collins-worth led the effort to put out a grass fire that was threat-ening the group's newly landed Spitfires. While fighting the fire, Collinsworth was seriously wounded in the stomach and chest by a discarded hand grenade that cooked off from the heat. Collinsworth spent twenty-eight days in a hospital and then took unauthorized leave back to his unit to avoid being transferred to the replacement pilot pool. He flew from Sicily with the 307th Fighter Squadron for two more weeks, and then rotated home in early September 1943 with sixteen other pilots from the 31st Fighter Group. Jerry Collinsworth spent the rest of World War II training P-47 pilots.

Despite several appalling setbacks on the ground, the Germans charged with defending Tunisia were seen to be toppling inexorably onto the ropes. By mid-March, there was even the faint smell of a spring victory in the air. For the time being, however, the pace of the air war remained grueling.

Most of the American fighters in North Africa became shack-led to friendly bombers. Distances in the Tunisian battle arena were short, so the short-legged American fighter groups were able to escort many medium- and even heavy-bomber missions from start to finish. The American fighter groups had had little training in bomber-escort techniques, so learned on the fly, as it were. The flying was for the most part defensive because the bomber crews let out howls of protest every time the escorting fighters chased German or Italian fighters beyond the immediate vicinity of the bombers. The high commanders tended to side with the bomber crews when such disputes boiled over.

NO HITS, NO RUNS, NO ERRORS

1st Lieutenant HERMAN VISSCHER, USAAF
97th Fighter Squadron, 82d Fighter Group
Gabès, Tunisia, March 28, 1943

While growing up on his father's farm near Kalamazoo, Michigan, Herman William Visscher used to watch the Army Signal Corps airplanes that flew the mail from Chicago to Kalamazoo. The experience kindled his dreams of one day becoming an Army aviator—or at least gave him an excuse to leave the farming life. Visscher enlisted as a private in the Army Air Corps on November 1, 1939; he had graduated from high school in June and had not been able to find a job. He had been told that he would be given an opportunity to fly if he could pass the two-year college equivalency test. However, Visscher was only eighteen years old, which at the time was not old enough to fly military airplanes. Fortunately, he did qualify to become an aviation mechanic, and he was sent to the Aeronautical University in Chicago for nine months. After graduation, he worked on the flight line at Selfridge Field, Michigan, until, in August 1941, the aviation-cadet program was opened up to high-school graduates. Because Visscher was already an Air Corps enlisted man, the best the service would offer if he completed flight school was an opportunity to become a sergeant pilot.

Along with ninety-five other Air Corps enlisted men, Herman Visscher reported to Class 42-C in September 1941 and began an abbreviated six-month flying program. After earning their wings at Kelly Field, Texas, the Class 42-C sergeant pilots were trained to fly Lockheed P-38 Lightning fighters. During the P-38 training, sixteen of them were killed in accidents. In March 1942 the sergeant pilots were formed, along with a dozen officers, into the 82d Pursuit Group and sent to three airfields in the Los Angeles area to fly their P-38s against the feared Japanese invasion of the West Coast.

In September the sergeant pilots in the 82d Fighter Group were commissioned en masse and ordered to prepare for a move overseas. The whole group left Long Beach two days later to undertake an overland and sea journey that reached Ireland a month later. During a boring and seemingly pointless three-month layover in Ireland, the 82d Fighter Group pilots earned their flight pay and kept up their flying skills in borrowed RAF Spitfires. Suddenly, in mid-December 1942, the group was shipped to England and re-equipped with brand-new P-38s. Finally, on December 27—2d Lieutenant Herman Visscher's twenty-second birthday—the 82d Fighter Group undertook a nine-hour over-water flight from Land's End, England, to Gibraltar, and shortly thereafter it moved by way of Oran to Telergma Airdrome, near Constantine, Algeria, to begin combat flight operations.

On January 17, 1943, on only his second combat mission, 2d Lieutenant Herman Visscher downed a German Ju-52 tri-motor transport over the Mediterranean. On February 8, Visscher received credit for an Me-109 destroyed and an Me-109 probably destroyed during a bomber-escort mission to Gabès Airdrome, Tunisia. He was credited with another Me-109 probable on February 28, 1943, on a mission to Sardinia.

Telergma was just a dirt strip our engineers had bulldozed out of the countryside. The runway ran east-west; on the north side was a B-26 medium-bomber group, and our P-38s were located on the south side. We usually escorted that B-26 group.

The B-26s had been after the German airdrome at Gabès, on the Tunisian coast. Along with Sfax, Gabès was a hub for the German defense of Tunisia. The British Eighth Army was moving slowly along the coast to the south, and the Germans were staging their fighters and bombers through Gabès and Sfax.

Our bombers and fighters had been screwing up bad at Gabès, but they had a reason for it. They were supposed to go in and make their bomb run from the inland side of the airbase and then go out over the Mediterranean—stay away from the German flak and head back home. In other words, they were supposed to drop their bombs on the first pass. Well, the bombardiers couldn't get lined up for one reason or another, and, every time, they'd go out and make a big procedure turn and come back to make a second run. On each mission, the Germans just mauled the daylights out of the B-26s and P-38s.

After the B-26s had tried this three or four times around the middle and end of March 1943—and still hadn't hit the damned airport—Major General Jimmy Doolittle came down to Telergma. He wanted to find out what the hell the problem was.

The bomber people said the P-38s were always wandering off, trying to be heroes—getting into dogfights and stuff. That left the bombers unprotected, and the bomber crews got itchy about that and lost their concentration. And the fighter pilots complained that the bombers couldn't get lined up on the target the first time, and that they invited the Germans to attack or shoot them up on the second go-around.

Finally, after listening to us go on and on about each other, General Doolittle said, "We're going to go there one more time, tomorrow. I want the fighters to stop trying to win the war alone. Your job is to protect the bombers! There'll be some massive personnel changes in both groups if that target's still there when you get home." Well, when he said that, all the "professionals" in the 82d Group managed *not* to get their names on the flight schedule for the next day.

There were twenty-four B-26s and twenty P-38s scheduled to go—sixteen P-38s from the 97th Fighter Squadron plus a flight of four from one of the other squadrons in the group. *Someone* had to lead the fighters; they had to find a sacrificial lamb—and it was me.

That morning, at the briefing, I told the other pilots that if any of them got into a dogfight just to try to improve his personal score, I'd do what I could to get him an interview with General Doolittle. Our job was to stick with the bombers because that's what General Doolittle said it was.

We had two strokes of luck. That's all combat is—luck. Good and bad. In this case it was good luck.

The night before we flew, the Germans moved a lot of their stuff out of Gabès and up into the Tunis area, to the Cap Bon peninsula. That meant that the nearest German fighters to Gabès were 90 to 100 miles away. And *that* meant that any fighters they sent to get us couldn't fight very long because they had only a limited fuel supply and no auxiliary tanks. If the bombers damaged the runway at Gabès, there would be no place close for them to land, and they'd have to break off early to return to Tunis.

The second stroke of luck was that, for once, the bombers hit the target on the first pass.

The B-26s were twin-engine bombers, and they were loaded to the hilt. On takeoff, it seemed like they'd go forever before they broke ground. A B-26 looked just like a freight car going through the air. It was a good airplane, but if one engine quit, why they'd have to dump everything to keep it flying.

The bombers were to bomb from 10,000 to 12,000 feet. I had the fighters in close to them, over and behind them. We had to keep scissoring—criss-crossing back and forth across the bomber formation—to keep our progress down to their airspeed. I had one flight flying high cover, about 1,500 feet over the bombers; two flights were scissoring over the bombers by a few hundred feet; and two flights, including mine, were scissoring at about the same altitude as the bombers, right over them.

We had about a 75-minute flight from Telergma, and I'm sure the Germans knew about it the minute we took off and took our heading straight to the target. Their fighters showed up just 10 minutes before we reached Gabès, as we were completing our crossing of the mountains from Algeria to Tunisia.

Twelve or fifteen Me-109s came down from the north—our left—to intercept us. They were in a loose formation. When they started in after the bombers the first time, the nearest P-38 flights barreled right in after them, and the Germans pulled up and flew away from the bombers. As soon as the Germans broke off their attack, I called the P-38s back to the bombers. I wouldn't let them leave and chase the Germans until they caught them; I wanted them back scissoring over the bombers. Then the Germans returned and tried to get at the bombers again, but we chased them away again. And then we returned to guard the B-26s.

The Germans were not risk-takers. I can't blame them, though. With twenty P-38s pointing one way or another at the dozen or so of them, discretion *was* the better part of valor. I think the Germans by this time had a pretty healthy respect for the Allied air power. It was just common sense. We'd have done the same in their place if we had been outnumbered.

They weren't very well organized, either. They seemed to experience a lot of indecision about what they were doing. Sometimes, a half-dozen of them came down and made a try for the bombers, but, the next time, only one would come down and try. I think they hung around because of the luck they'd had during the three or four earlier attempts by the B-26s to bomb Gabès. Maybe they thought the bombers would have to go around again and that we'd get disorganized.

I chased the Me-109s a few times, but I never got close enough to shoot. I don't think any of us did; the Germans withdrew every time, just as soon as we got turned toward them. They'd break it off and go back upstairs again.

There was *lots* of flak over Gabès Airdrome, most of it 88mm. You could see it coming—a whole bunch of flashes, like someone was shining a flashlight on and off. It was extremely thick, but General Doolittle hadn't said "avoid the flak," he'd said "stick with the bombers." That's what he wanted, and that's what we did; we stuck right with the bombers. We kept scissoring over them right through the flak. That way, there was always someone watching the rear of the bombers, keeping the German fighters from getting in behind them.

Flak is funny stuff. When you see it, you're okay. It's mostly a puff of dust, and it's harmless then. It's dangerous when it hits you before you see it. It was very thick that day over Gabès, but no one in the B-26s or P-38s was wounded, and there was no damage to any of the airplanes.

The Germans stood off when we went into the flak. Coming out over the sea, the bombers turned right—south —and then continued on back to the west, straight toward Telergma. The German fighters tried to get at them. Maybe they were hoping to pick off a cripple that had been damaged by the flak, but there were no cripples, and the P-38s kept challenging the Me-109s, forcing them to break off their approaches.

The Germans never got up the nerve to press home an attack. After about another fifteen minutes, the Me-109s had to leave. They couldn't land at Gabès, and they were down on fuel.

When we got home, General Doolittle was waiting for us. He talked to the major who had led the bombers, wanting to know how it went. The major said they'd demolished Gabès Airdrome, and I agreed with him; I said there wasn't much left. The general reached in his pocket and pulled out a couple of Air Medals, which he pinned right on our flight suits.

This was my most gratifying mission of the war. The guys who wouldn't go—the "professionals"—were the ones who'd screwed up the first three or four missions. Then here comes some kid off the farm who did what he was told, who followed orders. That didn't set too well with some people, but we got the job done once and for all. We didn't shoot down any Germans that day, but we had no losses among the fighters or the bombers.

There's a moral to this story: So often in war, in my

experience, there are guys who get instructions, but the moment they get out of eyesight of a superior they do just about whatever the hell they wanted. An awful lot of our pilots and aircrewmen lost their lives in World War II that way—an awful lot of them.

Lieutenant Herman Visscher shot down an Me-109 on each of his next three confrontations—on May 13 and May 19, 1943, over Sardinia, and on August 28, 1943, near Naples. He returned to the United States in October 1943, but was back with the 97th Fighter Squadron within six months, and he stayed until the end of the war.

On September 15, 1952, while flying a jet fighter as commander of the 25th Fighter-Interceptor Squadron, Lieutenant Colonel Herman Visscher shot down a Chinese MiG-15 over North Korea. He retired from the Air Force in 1966, following twenty-seven years on active duty.

Of the ninety-six sergeant pilots who graduated with Class 42-C from Kelly Field in March 1942, exactly half survived the war—sixteen were killed in P-38 training accidents and thirty-two were killed in action in the war. Seven were shot down and taken prisoner. In all, the Army Air Forces pinned wings on 2,808 sergeant pilots before abandoning the program. Thereafter, all new pilots graduated from flight school as second lieutenants or warrant flight officers.

CHAPTER 2

The essence of the U.S. Army Air Forces campaign over northern Europe between October 1942 and the spring of 1943 was that, for practical purposes, there was no air campaign. The diversion of most of the small Eighth Air Force—fighters and bombers—to battle over North Africa as part of the new Twelfth Air Force left VIII Bomber Command and VIII Fighter Command virtually no assets with which to wage any sort of offensive battle.

From October 1942 until May 1943, only the 4th Fighter Group remained operational in the United Kingdom. The handful of other fighter groups that had reached the British Isles by October 1942 had been diverted or, in the case of the P-38–equipped 78th Fighter Group, stripped of its airplanes, which were needed as replacements by the Twelfth Air Force P-38 groups. During this period, 4th Fighter Group pilots accounted for all of sixteen enemy airplanes. (Between mid-March and April 8, the 4th was withdrawn from combat so it could transition from Spitfires to Republic P-47 Thunderbolts. The group's first aerial victories in the P-47—and the P-47's first victories, ever—were scored on April 15 over the Belgian coast.)

As was to emerge in time, the reason for the paucity of aerial victories—even the paucity of aerial encounters—had less to do with the scarcity of American-manned fighters than it did with American fighter tactics. The 4th Fighter Group was as aggressive and aggressively led a fighter unit as ever fought in a war. In better times, with better tactics, it became one of America's premier fighter units. But during the period it flew as the only American fighter unit in operation in northern Europe, and for several months beyond, it attained negligible results because it was hobbled by idiotic tactics.

The immediate culprit was Major General Monk Hunter, the commander of VIII Fighter Command, but it must be said that Hunter was a product of his training and, to a degree, a victim of poor technology. Both of these factors obliged him and his eager fighter pilots—Hunter was eager, too—to work apart, virtually in a separate war, from the Eighth Air Force's other combat arm, VIII Bomber Command. Indeed, the doctrines that defined bomber and fighter operations were so far apart as to obviate direct cooperation.

The bombers had been built and the bomber crews had been trained to attack enemy targets without protection of fighters. In part, this was the fault of the high-order strategic thinking of the inter-war decades. Altruistic European survivors of the carnage of World War I hoped to avoid the realities of ground combat by substituting the arm's-length strategies of aerial bombardment. In 1942, air strategists honestly believed that the war could be won by bomber campaigns alone. Since the mid-1930s, the Americans who bought this argument had been developing what they called the "self-defending" bomber. That innovation, however, had more to do with the fighter technology of the 1930s: fighters of the day possessed neither the range nor the speed of modern bombers. The fighter technology did improve, but by mid-1942 the self-defending bomber had taken on a life of its own. It was believed that Germany could be bombed into submission by long-range self-defending bombers that were capable of flying unescorted to industrial targets anywhere in western or even central Europe.

As with most self-fulfilling prophecies, fact came to match belief. In 1942, American heavy bombers (and their British counterparts) had the range to strike targets in distant Berlin and beyond. The British had attempted daylight raids against Berlin early in the war, and they had been trounced by German fighter and antiaircraft-gun defenses. They had switched to night "area" raids, nominally against industrial targets but, in reality, against whomever or whatever their bombs happened to hit. The U.S. Army Air Forces, on the other hand, had developed qualms against "terror" bombings. And besides, America's leading bomber enthusiasts believed strongly in the efficacy of both their precision daylight-bombing doctrine and their self-defending heavy bombers. Moreover, American fighters of the day, though powerful and powerfully armed, still lacked the range to accompany the bombers all the way to Berlin and back. The bombers could reach targets about 500 miles from their bases, but the fighters could fly 250 miles in one direction, and no farther.

Denied a role in escorting bombers to distant targets and blinded by a silly doctrine he had helped develop in the 1930s, Monk Hunter opted to send his meager fighter assets on "fighter sweeps" over those areas of France, Belgium, and the Netherlands that were within the meager operational range of any fighter type available to him by mid-1943. (This "operational" range was quite a bit less than 250 miles because the fighters needed some reserve for high-speed fighting, which consumed fuel by the barrel.) The longest-ranged operational fighter type the United States had during this period was the Lockheed P-38 Lightning, an airplane that had been designed as a medium-range bomber escort. But only three P-38 groups were in action against Germany and her partners in mid-1943, and all of them were in North Africa. Other P-38 units were in the Pacific and more were training in the United States. Some of the new groups were bound to end up in England, but the most immediate need was in the Pacific, because of the vast distances between island bases. For the foreseeable future, all Monk Hunter's VIII Fighter Command could possibly get its hands on would be short-legged defensive fighters, some Bell P-39 Airacobras, perhaps, or, more likely, a few groups of Republic P-47 Thunderbolts. The P-39 was an inadequate fighter by mid-1942, and the immensely heavy—seven-ton—P-47 did not have much range.

It was not Hunter's fault that he had inadequate airplanes (forget that there was only one group flying!), and he was not alone in his misperception of the role of fighters in World War II.

Hunter's failure to make a dent in the German fighter force—sixteen confirmed victories in seven months—also goes to the role to which the Army Air Forces both aspired and had been relegated by 1942.

The key to every decision Allied commanders made in 1942 and 1943 was the projected invasion of France. When the United States first entered the war, it was hoped that the invasion would take place in mid-1943. By late summer 1942, however, the North Africa Campaign—and a huge number of other factors—made it clear that D-Day was not going to take place until mid-1944. As the first symbolic raids and sweeps were undertaken over northwestern Europe by Eighth Air Force fighter and bomber units in mid-1942, there were two full years to achieve pre-invasion goals from the air. North Africa threw the margin into a cocked hat. If luck held, it would be mid-1943 before the strategic-bombing campaign could be resumed, with only one year left for cracking the German objectives.

The primary role of American and British air power in Europe from mid-1942 until the invasion was to be the defeat of the Luftwaffe. Operation POINTBLANK, the specific plan by which the Allies were to accomplish this feat, was promulgated in May 1943 following acceptance of the common goal by the RAF and the U.S. Army Air Forces. The defeat of the Luftwaffe was of primary concern to the Allies because, unlike the RAF or U.S. Army Air Forces, the Luftwaffe was a *tactical* air force. It had been developed in its entirety to support the German Army. Its bombers, for example, were light or medium models, and its bomber crews were trained to support ground troops at close or medium range. The Luftwaffe had *no* long-range capability—*no* strategic capability at all. Its role was tactical and, at most, operational. As such, it was of enormous potential danger to an invasion fleet or to a fledgling toehold on the soil of France. In order to assure a safe landing by tens of thousands of Allied soldiers, two things had to happen before the invasion began—or could begin: The Luftwaffe had to be seriously whittled down in strength, *and* it had to be pushed back as far as possible from the English Channel and North Sea coasts. Only by forcing German tactical and operational air units to operate at the extremity of their range and in the smallest possible numbers could the invasion be reasonably assured of success.

The goal of Operation POINTBLANK was to be accomplished in two ways: first, by simply shooting down German airplanes wherever they could be induced to fight and, second, by destroying Germany's ability to build airplanes. To accomplish the latter, the destruction of the German aircraft industry and related targets, the British and Americans opened the Combined Bomber Offensive. The RAF would undertake night "area" bombing raids against the German aircraft industry, and the U.S. Army Air Forces would undertake daylight precision-bombing raids against the same or similar targets. The simultaneous Anglo-American program of aggressive (but, alas, short-range) fighter sweeps over the French, Belgian, and Dutch coasts was aimed at engaging the Luftwaffe fighter wings in a battle of attrition that over time would destroy the bulk of whatever fighters the shattered German aircraft industry managed to produce. Further, by destroying German fighters, the Allies hoped to induce the German aircraft industry to switch over from the production of tactical bombers to the increased production of replacement fighters.

Sadly, while American fighters were being ignored or, at best, assiduously avoided by the crack Luftwaffe fighter units within their meager range, the "self-defending" daylight heavy-bomber groups charged with attacking strategic targets deeper inside France, the Netherlands, and northwestern Germany were being butchered. While the German fighters were side-stepping needless and avoidable attrition simply by ignoring the American fighter sweeps, the bombers were locked in a one-sided form of attrition that did not bode well for their survival.

Beginning in April 1943, the 4th Fighter Group's new P-47 Thunderbolts were joined over the Channel and North Sea coasts by the Thunderbolts of the 78th Fighter Group, and another P-47 unit, the 56th Fighter Group, was in training in England. Despite the doubling of assets, the results remained abysmal. Meanwhile, losses of American heavy bombers continued to rise. Major General Ira Eaker, who had replaced Tooey Spaatz as Eighth Air Force commander when the latter went to

North Africa, continued to believe in the efficacy of the self-defending bomber, but even he had to admit that there were not yet enough heavies available in northern Europe to make the strategy efficacious. Eaker asked Monk Hunter to provide fighters for escort duty to the extremity of their range—going into the Continent (penetration) and coming out (withdrawal). The bombers would be on their own a good part of the way, but *some* protection at the margins was better than none at all. From May 4 onward, nearly all VIII Fighter Command sorties were devoted to escorting the bombers.

Seven German airplanes were downed by American fighters over northern Europe in May 1943, and eighteen fell in June (seven in one day, June 22). Action during the first three weeks of July was sluggish, but an extremely aggressive new commander, Major General Frederick Anderson, had just taken over VIII Bomber Command on July 1, and he needed some time to make his new policies bite. On July 24, Anderson's VIII Bomber Command opened "Blitz Week" with the first of hopefully daily appearances over Germany. Weather shut down bomber operations on one of the seven consecutive mission days, but the other six days saw over 1,000 bomber sorties launched against fifteen targets all over northern and western Germany. Claims by bomber gunners were extravagant—330 victory credits were awarded—but there is no doubting that the German fighter forces were worn down somewhat, at least operationally, by the unrelenting appearances of the bombers.

The American day fighters put in fewer claims by far, but the fact that their claims were closer to reality made them startling in their own right. In July 1943, American fighter combat produced thirty-eight victory credits, of which thirty-three—nine and twenty-four, respectively—were scored during just two Blitz Week missions. Not coincidentally, the two missions in question were not only bomber-escort missions, they were the first *long-range* bomber-escort missions ever flown by Eighth Air Force fighters.

TRIPLE

Major GENE ROBERTS, USAAF
84th Fighter Squadron, 78th Fighter Group
Winterswijk, Holland, July 30, 1943

Eugene Paul Roberts was born in Wallace, Idaho, on September 12, 1917, and raised in Spokane, Washington. As soon as Roberts graduated from college in June 1940, he was accepted into the U.S. Army Air Corps flying-cadet program, and he earned his wings with Class 41-A at Kelly Field, Texas, on February 7, 1941. Lieutenant Roberts initially flew P-40s with the 20th Pursuit Group at Hamilton Field, California, but he was transferred to the 14th Fighter Group, a P-38 unit, in February 1942. When the 14th Fighter Group was split in two in order to create the new 78th Fighter Group, Roberts went to the 78th as the operations officer of the new 83d Fighter Squadron. In July 1942, Captain Roberts became commander of the 84th Fighter Squadron, which was based at the Oakland, California, municipal airport.

The 78th Fighter Group sailed to Great Britain aboard the Queen Elizabeth in November 1942. Once arrived, the group underwent two months of intensive training in its new P-38 fighters. In late February 1943, however, all of the 78th Fighter Group's P-38s were commandeered as replacement aircraft for units in North Africa. They were flown to the new battle zone by nearly all of the group's pilots, who were also commandeered. When the dust settled, the 78th had become a paper unit. The group commander, the three squadron commanders, and three flight commanders per squadron— and no airplanes—were virtually all that remained of the 78th Fighter Group. Most of the remaining command pilots were sent to all sorts of schools around the British Isles, to kill time until new airplanes and subordinates could be shipped to England.

The 78th Fighter Group was reconstituted at Duxford

Airdrome near Cambridge, England, in April 1943 with a full complement of new pilots, most of whom were fresh from fighter schools in the States. The group was also equipped with the Republic P-47B Thunderbolt fighter, a seven-ton monster that few, if any, of the 78th's pilots had ever seen before. On April 8, following a whirlwind familiarization course, twelve 78th Fighter Group Thunderbolts, along with twelve P-47 fighters each from the 4th and 56th Fighter groups, took part in the first-ever P-47 mission over France.

The 78th Fighter Group's early missions were unexciting and uncontested fighter sweeps over the coasts of France and Belgium. The huge 2,000-horsepower Pratt & Whitney R-2800 Double Wasp radial engine that powered the heavily armed and armored P-47B proved to be a gas guzzler, and there were no auxiliary fuel tanks available in England at the time. This severely limited the range and duration of the 78th's missions, so the missions proved ultimately fruitless.

It was not until May 14, 1943, that members of the group scored their first air-to-air victories in the war. Major Gene Roberts's first clash in the air—on his forty-sixth combat mission—took place over the coast of Holland on July 1, 1943. It resulted in credit for an FW-190 fighter probably destroyed.

On July 28, 1943, the 4th Fighter Group significantly increased the range of its P-47 fighters in an experiment with auxiliary fuel tanks. Two days later, the P-47s of the 78th and 56th Fighter groups were able to use for the first time what we referred to as "bathtub" belly tanks. The 115-gallon tanks—which were designed for use in long-distance ferry flights—were not pressurized, and they gave us a lot of problems, but they did give us a chance to add another 150 to 200 miles' range to our operations. Until then, I had taken part in as many as eighteen bomber-escort missions, but our cover was shallow; it reached no farther than, perhaps, Antwerp.

On July 30, the 78th Fighter Group was given the assignment of providing withdrawal support for our VIII Bomber Command bombers. The target that day was the

Focke-Wulf assembly plant in Kassel, Germany, and I would judge that 200 to 240 B-17s and B-24s took part in the mission.

At that time, only three Army Air Forces fighter groups were fully operational in England. The 56th Fighter Group gave the bombers penetration support, and the 4th Fighter Group was scheduled to provide late withdrawal support. The 78th Fighter Group's assignment was to provide initial withdrawal support. That means we were the first fighters to meet the bombers while they were withdrawing from the target. Our tactical plan was simple—protect the bombers and drive away the German fighters.

Though the new group commander, Lieutenant Colonel Melvin McNickle, was flying as my element leader, I was leading the group on this mission. We started with the usual forty-eight fighters—three squadrons of sixteen fighters per squadron. However, two of the pilots reported mechanical problems and had to abort. In each case, per our standard procedure at that time, I had to dispatch the aborting airplane's entire flight of four to provide an escort back to base. That left us with forty fighters for the mission.

At about 1000 hours, we dropped our belly tanks about fifteen miles off the Dutch coast. One of the reasons we did this was that we could not go higher than 23,000 feet; the tanks were not pressurized, and we could not get gas from the belly tanks higher than that. We then climbed to 29,000 feet and were at that altitude when we crossed the Dutch coast south of Hoek Van, heading east.

We arrived on schedule in the area where we were supposed to pick up the bombers, but we didn't see them initially, so we turned south. We sighted the bombers south of Raesfeld and turned ninety degrees to pick them up near Winterswijk. The B-17s were flying at 24,000 to 25,000 feet in typical protective "box" formations of thirty-six to forty-eight per box. As we approached the bomber boxes from ninety degrees off their starboard side in *our* usual escort formations—arranged in high, medium, and low squadrons—we discovered that they were being attacked by a number of enemy aircraft.

There was one B-17 beneath the main formation, and it was being attacked by as many as five German fighters. The bomber was pouring smoke and appeared to be in deep trouble. From my position in the lead of the group, I dove down on the enemy fighters that were attacking the cripple. However, the Germans saw us, broke away, and dove for the ground.

There wasn't much more we could do to help the crippled B-17, so I pulled up on the starboard side of the main bomber formation, about 1,000 yards out. I discovered on reaching this position that my second element—Lieutenant Colonel McNickle and his wingman—had broken away and was no longer with me. I had only myself and my wingman, Flight Officer Glenn Koontz. We immediately saw enemy aircraft ahead of us and above the formation. I judged that there were about 100 enemy aircraft in the area, as compared with our forty.

Dead ahead of me was a single enemy fighter, an FW-190. He was at the same level as Koontz and me, about 1,000 to 1,500 yards ahead. He was racing in the same direction as the bombers so he could get ahead of them, swing around in front of them, and make a head-on pass. The bombers were most vulnerable from dead ahead. The Germans referred to this tactic as "queuing up."

I dove slightly below the level of the FW so that the pilot couldn't see me, and then I hit full throttle. I closed to about 400 yards and opened fire from straight back off his tail. The P-47s at this time had the old ring-and-bead reflector gunsight, and the pilot had to calculate lead and deflection. Since I was directly astern the FW-190, I put the bead right on the fuselage and opened fire. I fired a three- to five-second burst and saw several strikes. The FW's wheels dropped and it spun down in smoke and flames.

It became apparent to me that the Germans were not in radio contact with each other. We seemed to be flying right along with them without their taking any notice of us. They weren't reacting to us in a way that would indicate they were communicating with one another.

After the first FW went down, I looked ahead and saw two

more enemy aircraft. They were about 2,000 yards in front of me, heading out to queue up in front of the bombers so they could peel off and come back through the bomber formation.

I used the same tactic as before; I dropped down a little, hit full throttle, and closed until I was within 400 yards of one of the enemy fighters—another FW-190. Then I pulled up a little to slow my P-47 down. (Actually, I was closing too fast and had to pull up to avoid running into the FW.) I opened fire from dead astern. I observed several strikes and, as before, the enemy fighter billowed smoke and flames, rolled over, and spun down.

I saw that Flight Officer Koontz was firing at the second FW, but I didn't see the results because both Koontz and the enemy fighter were beneath me. It turned out that Koontz did shoot the FW-190 down.

After the second engagement, we were about two miles ahead of the bombers, about 500 feet above them, and still well out to their starboard side. Koontz was on my right wing. About this time, I observed an Me-109 on the port side and ahead of the bomber formation. I dropped below the bomber formation, crossed over to the port side, and pulled up behind the Me-109, again at full throttle. I was closing once again, using the same tactics as I had twice before, but, from a distance of about two miles ahead of the bombers, this enemy fighter suddenly peeled 180 degrees to starboard to attack the bombers head-on. I followed it. I closed to within 400 or 500 yards and opened fire. He was in a tight turn, and that required deflection shooting. My first two bursts fell away behind the 109, but I continued to close. I fired my third burst as the German fighter straightened out to approach the bombers. I fired again as the 109 was getting to within 150 yards of the bombers, dead ahead of them. This was a straight-on shot from behind the 109, and I nailed it. The 109 fell down trailing smoke and flame.

I found myself at the same level as the bombers and approaching them from head-on. Koontz was still with me. I had no alternative but to fly between the two main formations, which were about two miles apart. Bless their hearts, they did not fire. After flying through the bomber formation, I pulled to the left out of their starboard side, heading parallel to them on their level, toward home. Ahead and above me, however, two enemy fighters were attacking a P-47.

The FWs and the P-47 were heading 180 degrees to me, so I could not close effectively to help. I did fire a burst at the leading FW, but without enough deflection. The P-47 dove and took evasive action. I didn't see him or the FWs again. I headed out and joined up with a loose element from the 84th Fighter Squadron, and we headed home together.

This action was the first in many respects. It was the first time the entire Eighth Air Force fighter force was equipped with auxiliary fuel tanks, and it was the first time American fighters engaged a large enemy fighter force and came away with an overwhelming victory. To my mind, these firsts were connected. The Germans apparently did not anticipate our presence that far inside Holland. Consequently, they were not geared up to confront us. The Germans didn't expect our fighters over Holland, and we did not encounter their best pilots or airplanes. I think that our deep penetration took us beyond their front line of antifighter defenses— their most experienced fighter pilots in their best and best-equipped fighter units. This is further evidenced by their apparent lack of radio contact with each other. I guess they weren't wasting radios on their second line of defense. I believe that the German pilots sent to shoot down the bombers were a conglomerate of new pilots who were being given on-the-job training. These pilots did not aggressively defend themselves or one another.

We were overmatched as far as numbers were concerned —we faced at least 10:4 odds—but we moved at will and came out of the operation looking real good. Though seven P-47s were lost (including our new group commander, Lieutenant Colonel Melvin McNickle), sixteen enemy fighters were destroyed by the 78th Fighter Group alone, and eight others were destroyed earlier and later by members of the 56th and 4th Fighter groups. Captain Chuck London, of our group's 83d Fighter Squadron, shot down two German fighters and thus became the first Army Air Forces ace in the European Theater. And I was the first VIII Fighter Command pilot to be given credit for three confirmed victories in a single action.

Gene Roberts flew eighty-nine missions with the 78th Fighter Group and eventually became the group deputy commander, with rank of lieutenant colonel. After breaking into the victory column with his triple victory on July 30, 1943, Roberts downed a Messerschmitt Me-110 twin-engine heavy fighter near Aachen, Germany, on August 17; an FW-190 and an Me-109 near Evreux, France, on August 24; an Me-110 and an Me-210 over Enschede, Holland, on October 10; and, his ninth and last victory, an Me-109 near Dinant, Holland, on October 20, 1943. At the time, he was the Eighth Air Force's leading ace and the recipient of a Distinguished Service Cross, the nation's second-highest combat award.

When Roberts was only five combat flight hours away from mandatory return to the United States, VIII Fighter Command's commanding general relieved him of flight duties as a ploy to keep him in England. Thus, Lieutenant Colonel Roberts spent six months with the VIII Fighter Command combat operations section, and then he served a six-month tour as the 67th Fighter Wing operations officer. In January 1945, Roberts assumed command of the 364th Fighter Group, and he flew 120 combat hours in the group's P-51 Mustangs by the time the war ended. Colonel Gene Roberts brought the 364th Fighter Group back to the United States at the end of the war, and he reverted to Reserve status when the unit disbanded in December 1945.

There it was—twenty-four confirmed victories in one day, on a single mission. The tactics and technology changed, and American fighters knocked down as many German airplanes in one mission as they had been able to knock down in dozens of fighter-sweep and even escort missions in the preceding two months.

The Germans knew there was no profit in attacking American fighters for the sake of engaging in dogfights that could go either way. Fighters, per se, were no danger to the Third Reich. Bombers were. Bombers were a threat to everything—to home, to loved ones, and to German morale and equanimity. American bombers, if allowed to get through to their targets, were a special danger to the Luftwaffe itself, for they had shown a propensity to concentrate on the industries from which German aircraft emerged—ball bearings, machine tools, and airplane factories themselves. German fighters would never attack American or British fighters unless there was an overwhelming opportunity to win. But bombers *had* to be attacked, no matter where or when they appeared over Germany or her satellites. And, so, if the American fighter enthusiasts wanted to disable the Luftwaffe through a strategy of attrition, they had to tie their fortunes to those of the bombers. To do that, better or much-improved fighters needed to be developed by the American industrial behemoth, better escort tactics needed to evolve, and better operational ranges needed to be achieved by the fighters.

THUNDERBOLT*

1st Lieutenant LUCKY TRULUCK, USAAF
63d Fighter Squadron, 56th Fighter Group
Borkum Island, Germany, September 27, 1943

John Hinds Truluck, Jr., was born in Clemson County, South Carolina, on January 8, 1918. While attending Clemson A&M College, Truluck participated in the Reserve Officer

---

John H. Truluck, Jr. And So It Was: Memories of a World War II Fighter Pilot (Walterboro, South Carolina: The Press and Standard, 1989). Excerpted and revised with permission of the author.

Training Corps program and, when he graduated in 1938 with a B.S. degree in architecture, he was commissioned a second lieutenant of infantry in the U.S. Army Reserve. In July 1939, John Truluck passed his state architectural examination and became the youngest registered architect ever to be licensed in South Carolina. It was while working on the construction of Shaw Field, in Sumter, South Carolina— while watching Bell P-39 Airacobra fighters take off and land—that Truluck became enamored with flight. Called to active duty on February 14, 1942, 2d Lieutenant Truluck served with an infantry unit until his application for flight school was accepted. On May 1, 1942, he reported to Kelly Field, Texas, for an abbreviated Pre-Flight course and, on June 1, he joined Class 42-K for Primary flight training. The transfer to the Air Corps cost Lieutenant Truluck his seniority and delayed for more than a year his promotion to first lieutenant.

Lieutenant Truluck received his wings on December 13, 1942, and reported to Dale Mabry Field, Florida, on December 18 to begin operational flight training as a replacement fighter pilot. His first solo in a Republic P-47 Thunderbolt took place on January 30, 1943, and from then on Lucky Truluck's fate as a warrior was inextricably linked with the huge, powerful fighter. From Dale Mabry, Truluck was transferred to the replacement pilot pool on March 25, 1943, and he was ordered overseas on March 30 with thirty-five other P-47 pilots. Following a five-day ocean voyage, Truluck and his fellow Thunderbolt pilots landed at Liverpool. From there, they made their way in stages to a training facility at Atcham, England, which had recently been transferred to the Americans by the RAF. At Atcham, the rookie pilots were to train for combat in the two or three P-47s that were then available and wait for vacancies to occur in the three P-47 groups then based in the U.K.

On May 6, 1943, I was fortunate enough to receive orders to report to the 56th Fighter Group, which was then stationed at Horsham St. Faith, near Norwich, in East Anglia. When I first arrived with the group, combat flying was still new for

American fighter pilots, except for the Americans who had flown with the Canadian and British air forces and had formed the 4th Fighter Group.

The 56th Fighter Group had tasted combat for the first time about three weeks before I arrived. The early missions were uneventful fighter sweeps over the coastal area of France, Belgium, and Holland. As an eager replacement at Atcham, I had wanted to hear details of combat flying, but very little information was available except through the British pilots who had been assigned to help train us. Given the British accent and slang, and their low opinion of the P-47 and American pilots, I began to have ambivalent feelings about the entire business.

The British were convinced that the P-47 was a hopeless case. We were told that our only chance of survival would be to stay above 18,000 feet because the Germans would easily destroy us at low altitudes. Additionally, as I learned when I joined the 56th Fighter Group, the manufacturer and the Air Forces technical staff at the Wright Field, Ohio, test facility had placed such restrictions on the plane that it would never have been successful if we had followed the tech manual. Flying according to the tech manual, we hardly had enough gasoline for a fighter sweep, and escort work would have been out of the question. After learning on our own that the plane would perform satisfactorily at low RPM and high manifold pressure, we were able to get increased mileage with our internal fuel supply. But, even with this, the range was severely restricted until belly tanks became available.

The 56th Fighter Group was never given the credit due for its role in the development of the P-47. In the United States, the group had been the first unit to fly the plane, and the group engineering staff and pilots had spent a lot of time at the Republic Aviation manufacturing plant working out the many problems that had arisen.

The P-47 was designed for high-altitude operation. The turbine supercharger provided enough air to the carburetor for good performance up to about 33,000 feet. Above that, however, the performance decreased. On one occasion over

Germany, I tried to climb up to engage a German above me. Above 40,000 feet, the performance was poor and at 43,000 feet I gave up since there was very little response to the controls and the engine was laboring. The German plane, which appeared to be an Me-109, was at least 1,000 feet above me when I gave up.

The engine in the P-47 was the largest manufactured at the time. It was an air-cooled eighteen-cylinder radial engine. It was rated at more than 2,000 horsepower, and it really guzzled gasoline. The internal tanks held approximately 300 gallons of fuel. That sounds like a lot, but 300 gallons would last less than an hour at full throttle. Allowing for takeoff, climbing, and a reserve, a normal mission was less than two hours in duration until auxiliary belly tanks became available.

Early in the war, an American manufacturer designed an abortion of a belly tank that snugly fitted to the contour of the P-47's belly in an attempt to maintain smooth air flow. With the tank in place, however, the plane looked like a pregnant whale. The tank was not pressurized and could not be used at high altitudes. The plane's flying capabilities were seriously affected, and the last straw was the fact that the tank was very hard to release and sometimes would literally be torn from the plane. A number of pilots could not effect release and had to return to base with the tank intact, since a pilot caught in actual combat with the tank in place would not have a chance of surviving. The first batch of successful auxiliary tanks were made of some type of fabric reinforced with wool and metal. I believe they were made in England. It was not until later that we received 75-, 90-, and 150-gallon wing and belly tanks made of steel.

The P-47s the 56th Fighter Group had when I arrived in May 1943 were far superior to the planes that I had flown in Florida at Dale Mabry Field. The difference was the servicing personnel, experience gained in actual flying operations, and the fact that planes were the new, improved "C" and "D" models.

The P-47 Thunderbolt was armed with eight .50-caliber machine guns—four in each wing. The magazines were capable of carrying 400 bullets for each gun, but after experiencing some problems with jammed guns, we loaded only 250 rounds per gun, or a total 2,000 rounds for the eight guns. The gun belts were loaded with three armor-piercing rounds followed by two incendiary rounds, and then repeating.

The British and Germans both used small-caliber machine guns and 20mm cannons with explosive shells. While a single hit with a 20mm cannon was effective, the eight .50-caliber machine guns in the P-47 were devastating. If the strikes from the .50-caliber guns centered on the target, a kill was assured.

My first flight with the 63d Fighter Squadron was on May 11, 1943. From then until June 20, I went on twenty-nine training flights, usually two each day if weather permitted and if a combat mission was not scheduled. Mostly, the training emphasized correct formations for takeoff, climb, and combat. Special emphasis was placed on the importance of a wingman staying with his element leader and being constantly alert to prevent attacks, especially from the rear. The wingman's head was to be turning constantly from one side to the other, and looking up and down, in order to spot possible attackers and give the alarm in time to meet the attack.

Horsham St. Faith, which had formerly been a permanent Royal Air Force fighter station, had excellent building facilities and a large grass field instead of paved runways, but it was not quite right for a P-47 group. Grass fields offer a slight advantage for landing since exact alignment is not required and the grass helps slow the plane, requiring less space. For takeoff, however, paved runways aid acceleration and are smoother. The British Hurricane and Spitfire fighters for which it had been built required only short take-off runs. Using a large grass field, an entire RAF squadron would line up abreast and take off as a unit. The P-47 did not accelerate as rapidly as the British fighters, and they needed to be going one hundred miles per hour to lift off. This presented a problem on the short grass fields. Even so, following the British custom, each squadron would take off in squadron formation.

On my first squadron takeoff from Horsham St. Faith—a training mission—I was flying in fourth position in the last flight of four P-47s. A wingman on takeoff concentrates on his leader's plane since the leader sets the speed, course, rate of climb, etc. For all practical purposes, when in close formation, the wingman is a mere mechanic who moves the controls and throttle as needed to stay in position with the leader. Just as I approached the hangar, I glimpsed the ventilator on top of it, and I was barely able to pull the plane over since I was flying only slightly above stalling speed. Following my complaints, I don't believe that I was ever asked to try this feat again.

There was much to learn about the airplane and about operational flying in general. On one of my earliest combat missions, we landed at an English base on the south coast to refuel before takeoff and again after returning from France. We landed about dark and without lights. Colonel Hubert "Hub" Zemke, the group commander, landed first and taxied back to the end of the runway to act as a controller. I came in and made a perfect landing, except I was twenty feet up in the air. My plane slammed into the runway, fortunately without damage. Colonel Zemke remarked on the radio, "Lucky boy." He was right; my tires had held.

Prior to each combat mission the pilots assembled in the briefing room, which had a large map of England and western Europe covering the front wall. Colonel Zemke, or whoever was leading the mission, would explain the mission and give us the course to follow, take-off time, etc. Intelligence would give us information about antiaircraft guns and escape routes in the event we were shot down. Then the weather officer, "Stormy," would tell us about weather conditions. And, finally, we would zero in our watches. After the briefing, we would return to our squadron, and our own Intelligence people would issue an escape kit with maps of the target area and a package of French and German money. Each kit had special compasses, saw blades, and other useful items. The parachute back-cushion was more than an inch thick, and concealed in it were "K" rations, fishing line and hook, maps, compasses, fold-up machete, cigarettes, matches, and first-aid kit. On top of the parachute was a collapsible dinghy with sail, flares, fishing line, and a bucket for bailing a life raft in case we had to ditch in the water. We also wore an inflatable life vest. Some of us carried the Army .45-caliber automatic pistol in a shoulder holster, but Major Dave Schilling, the 62d Fighter Squadron commander, wore a pair of pearlhandle .38 revolvers on a number of early missions. Naturally, behind his back, comments were made about the cowboy getup.

Our clothing usually consisted of long underwear or pajamas covered by olive drab trousers and shirt or coveralls, plus leather jacket, helmet, oxygen mask, and fur-lined flying boots. The boots were English-made. The top portions were sewn to the lowers so that they could be removed if we went down over Europe. The result looked like regular shoes. We wore three pairs of gloves: long white silk gloves, then short chamois gloves, and finally long leather gloves. I had a piece of Plexiglas, about two inches by three inches, sewn to the back of my left glove. The surface was sanded to obtain a texture for writing in ink the takeoff time, course in, course out, and other useful data. In the event of pending capture, the information could be licked off.

Weather conditions were constantly changing, and this created problems for flying. Seldom was the sky free of clouds, and frequently we were required to fly through thick and dense clouds. Instrument flying had been required during flight training, but we had all assumed that this would be necessary only for an occasional emergency. I doubt that any of us were really competent instrument flyers when we left the States. In England, the picture abruptly changed because the weather was bad so often that we had to fly instruments or "buy the farm." During my training at home, I had avoided all thick clouds if I could. But after a few months in England, I no longer attempted to dodge them. In fact, I'd even plunge through cumulonimbus thunderclouds instead of changing course to avoid them. On one mission, our squadron of sixteen ships assembled into tight formation below the clouds, which were less than 1,000 feet above the ground, and we set course for the Continent. We broke out of the clouds at about 25,000 feet over Holland—an excellent example of instrument flying.

My first combat mission was flown on June 20, 1943, only eight days after the 56th Fighter Group was credited with its first confirmed aerial victory of the war. The June 20 mission was a fighter sweep—an attempt to make the Germans intercept us over France with the idea of destroying the German fighter force. Initially, this was somewhat successful; however, it did not take long for the Germans to realize our purpose, and then they ignored us, leaving us alone to burn gas and wear out the airplanes. I was on a total of nine such missions and never saw an enemy plane.

The combat flying we did was primarily Ramrods—escorting the bombers. The bomber formations flew at an indicated speed of 150 to 160 miles per hour. However, our fighters cruised at 240 miles per hour. The bombers would fly a straight course, except for zigzags to confuse the German flak batteries, but our fighters would weave around in front, behind, and to either side of the bomber formations. Most of the time the fighters would be above the bombers. When the Germans attacked the bombers, our mission was to attack the Germans to prevent them from interfering with the bombing mission.

A fighter group consisted of three squadrons, and each squadron flew as a unit. The group commander or his deputy would lead the group by flying the number one position in one of the squadrons. (Usually, the group commander alternated from squadron to squadron.) Each squadron consisted of two, three, or four flights, and each flight was commanded by a flight leader. At first, each squadron flew a combat formation consisting of three flights, but then we started going out in squadrons of four flights. Pilots for each mission generally consisted of the squadron commander or the squadron operations officer leading White Flight, and a flight commander leading each of the Red, Blue, and Yellow flights. A flight consisted of four planes: the flight leader and his wingman, and the element leader and his wingman.

On each mission, two extra planes would follow the group as spares, to replace any plane that had to abort due to a mechanical defect. Unless needed to replace an aborted plane, the spares would usually follow until we were in sight of the enemy coastline, and then they would return to base. It is a tribute to my ground crew that my only abort was due to a broken wire in the headset of my helmet. Fortunately, on that mission, we were to land at a base in southern England to replenish our fuel before proceeding with our escort mission. The mission was canceled before takeoff for France, so I actually flew seventy-one missions without an abort.

In theory, the squadron commander would be the first to make the attack on German airplanes while covered on the sides by the other flights. Attacks were also to be made by each of the flight commanders, who was to be covered by the other three planes of his flight. The two wingmen in a flight were not supposed to engage the enemy, except to protect their leaders. From this, it is obvious that the squadron commander and all flight leaders should be aggressive, eager, and dead shots, for they were in the best position to engage the enemy.

The 56th Fighter Group was fortunate to have Hub Zemke as its commanding officer. Zemke had several years of flying experience; he had served as a liaison officer for a time in the Soviet Union instructing Soviet pilots, was an excellent pilot himself, and was very aggressive. There were other good leaders assigned to the group in those early months, but, unfortunately, during my early service, the 63d Fighter Squadron had a serious leadership problem. I imagine that poor leadership was experienced in numerous other commands of the Air Forces, as well as in the Army and Navy. In my opinion, strong aggressive leadership would have saved the lives of many Americans. Several pilots in my squadron were bitter about our leadership—and that is an understatement.

On an early mission near Wilhelmshaven, Germany, the

squadron was flying in front of and above the bombers when I saw a swarm of fighters attacking the bombers. I immediately reported this on the radio without any acknowledgement from our squadron commander. After not receiving a reply to my *third* report, I announced that I was going down to attack the enemy fighters. As soon as I peeled away from the formation, the squadron commander called to say that he would court-martial me if I did not return to the formation. I have always regretted the fact that I did rejoin the formation because I really did want an open hearing about our leadership. After we landed, a corporal came to pick up the squadron commander and me. As I started to get into the jeep, the squadron commander remarked, "Lucky, you planned on doing a little shooting up there, didn't you?"

"Major," I replied, "the first thing that I was taught when I went to fighter training was that a fighter was made for only one purpose, and that was to carry guns. And the guns were made to attack the enemy. If we are not going to use the guns, I suggest we take the ammunition and the guns out of the planes; then maybe we can get high enough in the air to protect you from the Germans." He did not offer any rebuttal and no court-martial charges were ever mentioned again.

Young pilots coming into the squadron as replacements were eager to learn about combat flying, just as I had been. They asked countless questions about all aspects of air-to-air fighting, including everything about German planes and pilots. Shortly after the Wilhelmshaven mission, just as I was entering the operations room, I heard one of the rookies ask our squadron commander, "Major, just how do you attack a German fighter?" The major started to reply, using his hands to demonstrate. "Well," he began, "if you are up here and the Germans are down here, you peel off . . ." At this moment, I remarked, "If that isn't a joke, I never heard one." The major looked at me, turned around, and went into his office. He left those three kids standing there, totally baffled.

My fourteenth and fifteenth missions were Ramrods, and they both occurred on August 17, 1943. On the morning mission, the bombers went after the ball-bearing works at Schweinfurt, Germany. We escorted the bombers going in on one leg, but we did not encounter any enemy opposition. To that point, the 63d Fighter Squadron had just one probable credit to its name.

As soon as we landed after the morning mission, we were hurriedly briefed while the planes were being refueled. Then we went right back out to escort the bombers on the homeward leg from a second raid, this time against the Me-109 factory at Regensburg, Germany.

We ran into a swarm of German fighters over Belgium. I was flying on the wing of 1st Lieutenant Gus Schiltz, and I just followed him into the fight, doing my best to stay with him and watch for German fighters that might pose a danger to us. Gus was like a wild man. While he was bouncing the Germans, I was constantly looking over my shoulder to cover our tails. Gus had destroyed two FW-190 single-engine fighters and was looking for another victim when he made a sharp turn to the right. At the moment he turned, I was looking behind us and did not see him until we were about to collide. I immediately hit the rudder and stick to break away, and went into a spin. When I finally pulled out at 12,000 feet, I was in a hornets' nest of German fighters.

Right in front of me, less than 100 yards away and moving across my path in what seemed like slow motion, was an FW-190. I saw another FW-190 at about 2 o'clock high—and another one at 9 o'clock low. Scattered around farther out, I could see countless other Germans.

I was petrified. While at the time it seemed like ten minutes, I probably was inactive for only a few seconds. By the time I decided that I should be using my guns, most of the German fighters had disappeared. I'm not sure how I did it, but I managed to destroy one of the FW-190s. Then I debated with myself: Should I hit the deck and go home or should I attempt to climb up and find some friendly fighters? I finally decided to try to find some help, so I started climbing. During all of this, the radio was constantly screaming; obviously, a lot of other pilots were occupied and probably as confused as I was. On my way up, I sighted a plane in the distance and made an attack. Unfortunately I was too green and I opened fire some 800 to 1,000 yards away. Nevertheless, the plane, an Me-210 twin-engine fighter, went into a spin with smoke trailing. I did not see it blow up or crash, so for this mission I was credited with one FW-190 destroyed and one Me-210 damaged. The 63d Fighter Squadron got eight confirmed kills (three by Gus Schiltz), and the group was credited with sixteen confirmed kills.

If this encounter had taken place even a few weeks later, after I had gained some direct combat experience and thus obtained a cooler outlook, I probably would have destroyed several more German planes. In fact, in a battle that took place only a little over a month later, I was far more composed than I had been on August 17.

For over two months after entering the 63d Fighter Squadron, I piloted planes that were permanently assigned to other pilots. When I was told that I was to get a plane of my very own—a week or two after the August 17 engagement—I was overjoyed. It was the latest model from Republic, a P-47D-6 with Serial Number 274750. Assigned to the plane was a permanent crew consisting of a crew chief, an assistant crew chief, and an armorer. They were not just good; they were super. When flying, I was literally alone; however, figuratively speaking, my crew was always with me and sweated out each mission, maybe more than I did.

We immediately started cleaning and sprucing up the new airplane. I made a stencil to spray paint *Lady Jane* in script, covering a large area on the left side of the engine cowling. Since wax was not available, we used $17.00 worth of brown shoe polish for waxing and tried to fill all recessed rivets until flush.

On my first trip to London, I visited a Rolls Royce automobile agency and bought a smoked-glass sun visor and a mirror. The mirror was placed to aid vision to the rear. With the help of the machine shop, we designed and made adjustable brackets so the sun visor could be moved into various positions inside the canopy to cover the sun. Most of the other pilots decided that the mirror was a good idea, so mirrors began to appear on other planes. About the same time, one of the crew chiefs rigged a mirror to see under the tail of his plane, and this was fitted to other planes.

Another problem was the cold at high altitudes, where the air temperature was fifty to sixty degrees below zero. The plane heater was inadequate for this low temperature, and I nearly froze. I managed to find some flexible metal tubing and had some "Y" fittings made at the welding shop. My crew chief renovated the heating ductwork by installing the tubing for discharge of warm air on each foot on the rudders and the throttle hand on the left side of the cockpit. Another outlet was installed under the gunsight to discharge warm air on the right hand while it was holding the stick.

My next direct encounter with German fighters was on September 27, 1943. I was flying *Lady Jane* that day. The 56th Fighter Group was escorting a bombing raid to Emden, Germany, by way of Borkum Island. I was flying the element lead in Postgate (63d Fighter Squadron) Blue Flight (Blue-3) when we left our base, but my flight leader had to abort, and he left with his wingman. I continued on as leader of Postgate Blue Flight with my wingman, Lieutenant Frederick Windmayer. I was flying between Postgate White and Yellow flights.

As we approached the bombers near Juist and Borkum islands, I was above their line of flight, at about 28,000 feet. Postgate Leader went to the rear of the last box of bombers and started turning to the left. I was zig-zagging over the bombers when I saw an FW-190 below and to my right. He was attacking the bombers from about 7 o'clock to the bomber formation. I reported the sighting and executed a couple of 90-degree turns to commence an attack on him. I then saw another FW-190 among the bombers—and another approaching the bombers from the rear. I called Windmayer and started down on the third FW, which was closest to us and by then quite close to the bombers.

Suddenly, another FW came out of the clouds from the same direction as the one we were after; it was also executing a 7 o'clock attack on the bombers. He was closest of all the FWs to me, so I went down on him. He was diving at a speed of 250 to 300 miles per hour. I closed to about 300 yards and started firing. I saw hits in his cockpit and left wing root, and several pieces flew off the FW-190. I continued to close and fire, and was about 75 to 100 yards away when this plane exploded. Pieces went flying off in every direction, and a wheel barely missed my wing.

I called my wingman and pulled up from about 18,000 to 24,000 feet. When I got there, I spotted an Me-109 about 1,500 to 2,000 feet below me. I called my wingman again and went down after the 109. The German fighter turned sharply to the right. I opened fire at about 500 yards and fired about fifty rounds per gun without hitting him. We were by this time in a tight Lufbery circle to the right. I stopped firing and tightened my turn to the limit, but I was in his prop wash and came near to stalling. I finally pulled in and got enough lead to fire a couple of short bursts. I observed several strikes on the 109, but I stalled each time or hit his prop wash. My excess speed was about gone, but I was gradually getting inside and nearer to him.

The 109 finally rolled over to go down. I rolled with him and started firing. We were both upside down when he practically disintegrated from an explosion. The plane went into a spin with smoke trailing from behind.

I was at about 17,000 feet and climbing up again when I saw another German on my wingman's tail. I yelled at Windmayer to break. As he did, I turned into the enemy airplane. I glimpsed four radial-engine fighters on the tail of this German. Thinking they were more FW-190s, I executed a tight chandelle and came down on the right side of the last one. As I started to close, I noticed that all four of the "FWs" were P-47s!

I turned to the left and saw the German fighter break downward. He was trailing smoke and all four of the P-47s were following him, so I broke off.

When I got home, I claimed one FW-190 and one Me-109

destroyed, and was given credit for both of them. I had used a total of 1,054 rounds of .50-caliber armor-piercing and incendiary ammunition.

First Lieutenant Lucky Truluck scored his fourth confirmed victory, an FW-190, over the Frisian Islands on November 26, 1943, and he achieved ace status on February 24, 1944, when he downed yet another FW-190 over Herford, Germany. Truluck's sixth victory was an Me-109 he downed on March 8 near Dummer Lake, Germany, and he scored his seventh and last victory, another FW-190, near Hanover, Germany, on March 15, 1944.

Captain Lucky Truluck returned to the United States in September 1944 and shortly thereafter married the real Lady Jane, a young Texas belle he had met during his flight-training days. Lucky Truluck served as an instructor until he was released from the service in July 1945. He immediately returned to South Carolina to resume his career as an architect.

VIII Fighter Command's three P-47 groups were credited with fifty-eight German airplanes in August 1943, all of them during bomber-escort duty. In stark contrast, the American P-47s flew 373 fighter-sweep sorties over France on August 15 and did not see a single German airplane.

Despite mounting pressure from his superiors in Washington to adopt changes, Monk Hunter continued to argue vehemently in favor of his ineffectual and discredited fighter-sweep tactic. In this, Hunter was supported by the Eighth Air Force commander, Major General Ira Eaker, who remained a vehement supporter in his own right of the self-defending bomber. Eaker was very close personally to the Army Air Forces chief, General Hap Arnold, so his job was safe. But, though Hunter was also an old friend of Arnold's, he had become an annoying relic from the past. Hunter was replaced as head of VIII Fighter Command on August 29 by Major General William Kepner, formerly the commander of the U.S.-based Fourth Air Force. A fighter pilot's fighter pilot, Kepner was, in a word, aggressive. Moreover, his outlook was in full accord with the reality of the air war over northern Europe. He simply wanted to do whatever worked.

In September 1943, only thirty-nine victory credits were awarded to the American P-47 groups (including the newly committed 353d Fighter Group), but, for various reasons, there were also few bomber missions flown that month. As if to confirm the lessons of the preceding months, VIII Fighter Command launched ninety-five fighter-sweep sorties on September 4 while RAF Spitfires escorted a large B-26 mission over France. The P-47s encountered no German airplanes, while the Spitfires destroyed nineteen of the German fighters that rose to challenge the medium bombers. On September 22, when no bomber strikes were launched, the P-47s clocked 395 non-escort sorties over Occupied Europe, but only two German airplanes were downed. Five days later, however, twenty-one German fighters were shot down when the P-47s escorted a heavy-bomber mission to Emden, Germany.

By the end of September, it was obvious to everyone concerned—not least the Germans—that Eighth Air Force had at last broken the code. The key to Allied air supremacy over northern Europe lay in the rigorous bombing of the German aircraft industry by heavy bombers and of German fighter installations in France, Belgium, and the Netherlands by both heavy and medium bombers. (The latter was a function of an inexorable program aimed at pushing German tactical air units back from the proposed invasion beaches in France. Incessant bombing, which at the least disrupted flight operations, would eventually render the forward airfields untenable.)

The key goal of the German day-fighter wings would be destruction of the American bombers, and the key goal of the American day fighters would be the destruction of the German day fighters that rose to challenge the bombers. As long as the bombers went out, the German fighters would attack, and thus the American fighters would have ample opportunity to *try* to destroy the Luftwaffe's tactical strength by means of attrition.

While the Eighth Air Force was feeling its way toward some sort of symbiotic relationship between its fighters and bombers, the air campaign in the Mediterranean had been forging ahead.

CHAPTER 3

On March 1, 1943, largely for administrative and political purposes, newly promoted Lieutenant General Tooey Spaatz, the commander of the Anglo-American Northwest African Air Force, officially superseded Major General Jimmy Doolittle as commander of the Twelfth Air Force. Spaatz had been in North Africa from the beginning, serving the Supreme Allied Commander, General Dwight Eisenhower, as deputy commander for air.

During his tenure at the head of the Twelfth Air Force, Jimmy Doolittle had served concurrently under Spaatz as commander of the combined Anglo-American Northwest African Strategic Air Force. On March 1, 1943, Doolittle moved down to head XII Bomber Command, from which post he could devote all his considerable energies to the maturing bomber campaign. In the same shuffle, the RAF's Air Marshal Arthur Coningham assumed overall command of the Northwest African Air Force's tactical units, including the U.S. Army Air Forces's XII Tactical Air Command and IX Fighter Command.

The moves at the top were made not so much to facilitate the North Africa air campaign—it was running smoothly enough—but with an eye to the future. Strategic planning was already being devoted to an assessment of possible moves across the Mediterranean from North African bases, and any such move would be preceded by an air offensive of some sort.

Meanwhile, as the day of reckoning drew closer, the air war over Tunisia rose in tempo and pitch. In March 1943, the monthly total of confirmed aerial victories awarded to Army Air Forces fighter pilots rose to 136, a record that included the best one-day total so far—twenty-one German warplanes downed in several big fights over Tunisia on March 22.

April was the last full month of the North African Campaign, and the air-victory credits more than doubled, to 336 for the month. By 1943 standards, there were several *really* big days. On the morning of April 5, P-38s of the 1st and 82d Fighter groups ambushed an armada of German transports between Marsala, Sicily, and Cap Bon, Tunisia, as the German aircraft attempted to bring in reinforcements. Including the victims of an afternoon shoot-out over a German airdrome undertaken by the 33d Fighter Group, a total of forty-seven German airplanes were downed that day. The 1st and 82d Fighter groups struck paydirt again on April 10, downing forty-six German aircraft—mostly Junkers Ju-52 tri-motor transports—also over the Cap Bon area. And, on April 11, the 82d Fighter Group alone bagged thirty-two German fighters, transports, and troop-carrying bombers—once again on the Marsala–Cap Bon run. The biggest day by far, however, was April 18, Palm Sunday. On that day, over the Gulf of Tunis, the P-40 pilots of the 57th and 324th Fighter groups shot down seventy-six Ju-52s and Me-109 escorts in little more than an hour. After that, the Germans stopped trying to fly ground troops and technicians in and out of Tunisia, and the air war cooled down considerably.

Finally, on May 13, 1943, on the heels of a crushing Allied ground offensive, the commander of the German ground forces in Tunisia surrendered the remnant of Army Group Africa to the Allies. With that, the North African Air Force seamlessly shifted its entire weight to a broad air campaign against German and Italian bases on Sardinia, Sicily, and a number of smaller Axis-held islands—any Axis base within range of Allied airfields in Morocco, Tunisia, and Algeria.

ACE CHRYSALIS

1st Lieutenant HERKY GREEN, USAAF
317th Fighter Squadron, 325th Fighter Group
Sardinia, May 19, 1943

Herschel Harper Green, who was born in Mayfield, Kentucky, on July 3, 1920, was five years old when he first went aloft in an airplane, and his future was fixed. He joined the Civilian Pilot Training (CPT) program in 1940, while attending Vanderbilt University, and he earned his private pilot's license the following year. Green briefly considered enlisting in the Navy flight program, but he was put off by the notion of having to find a moving aircraft carrier before he would be able to land. He therefore enlisted in the Army Air Corps in September 1941 with 200 hours of flight time recorded in his logbook.

Cadet Green joined Class 42-D for Pre-Flight training at the new Air Corps Elementary Flying School at Chickasha, Oklahoma, and he was in the middle of Primary flight training, also at Chickasha, when Pearl Harbor was attacked. Class 42-D's next stop was Randolph Field, near San Antonio, and, from there, the class was posted to Foster Field, near Victoria, Texas.

Green graduated from Victoria on April 29, 1942, and was immediately posted to the 57th Pursuit Group, a Curtiss P-40 unit based in Connecticut to guard a large stretch of the New England coast. Within a few weeks, however, the 57th was split in half, and Lieutenant Green was posted to the newly commissioned 79th Fighter Group. Next, in September 1942, the 79th was also split in two, and Lieutenant Green was posted to the new 317th Fighter Squadron of the new 325th Fighter Group.

Following several months of hard training, while guarding the Boston area against a feared long-range German bombing campaign, the 325th Fighter Group was ordered on

January 1, 1943, to proceed by rail to Langley Field, Virginia, for shipment to an active theater overseas. The group was reequipped with seventy-two brand-new P-40F Warhawk fighters and given a few days to learn how to take off from—of all things—an aircraft carrier. The P-40s were then flown to Norfolk Naval Air Station, where they and their pilots were loaded aboard the USS Ranger, *an obsolescent light carrier that two months earlier had played a major role in covering the invasion of North Africa.*

The Ranger *left Norfolk on January 8, 1943, and arrived off the coast of French Morocco on the morning of January 19. Though the Army pilots were dubious, the carrier's flight-deck crew provided the P-40s with 425 feet of deck space for their launches—and the entire fighter group got airborne without a mishap.*

When we arrived over Casablanca, we caused quite a shock because nobody knew we were coming. Imagine that! The only American aircraft carrier in the Atlantic, a tanker, two cruisers, and four destroyers had been put to use getting us to North Africa, and the Twelfth Air Force had no idea we were coming! Well, as soon as we landed at Casablanca, our group commander, Lieutenant Colonel Gordon Austin, contacted higher headquarters and set the record straight. Although the Twelfth Air Force hadn't expected us, they certainly knew what to do with our airplanes. It seems that the 33d Fighter Group, a P-40 group in action over in Tunisia, was short of aircraft, so we were ordered to dispatch twenty of ours right away. Two days later, another twenty-four P-40s were taken from us, also for the 33d. We did get some of these airplanes back after the North African Campaign folded up, but not all of them.

In the short run, we had to make do with whatever replacement aircraft we could scrounge in order to build our group back up to fighting strength. By early April, we had accumulated about fifty P-40s at Tafaraoui, and these were divided up among all three squadrons. However, the group was ordered to dispatch two complete twenty-four plane squadrons to Montesquieu, an airbase just south of Bône, Algeria, in order to begin flying combat missions. The three squadron commanders cut cards to see which of the squadrons would turn over its P-40s and stay behind. My squadron, the 317th, lost. When the other two squadrons and the group headquarters moved forward to Montesquieu on April 5, we remained behind at Tafaraoui, to wait until we had accumulated a full complement of replacement P-40s. While we were waiting, the North African Campaign came to an end when the Germans formally surrendered their army in Tunisia on May 13.

The 317th Fighter Squadron finally moved forward to Montesquieu on May 18, 1943. By that time, the 318th and 319th squadrons had flown two dozen missions. Most of them had been reasonably uneventful bomber-escort missions or fighter sweeps over enemy territory, but three enemy airplanes had been shot down and one of ours had been lost, fortunately without the loss of the pilot. However, even this minimal combat experience was sufficient excuse for the pilots from the other two squadrons to tell us how lucky we were to be coming in at that time—because the activity level was very low and we would have a chance to get our jittery nerves calmed down on milk runs against enemy-held bases on the Mediterranean islands.

How wrong they were.

The 317th Fighter Squadron's first operational mission—and the 325th Fighter Group's twenty-fifth—took place on May 19. We were to escort medium bombers against Decimomannu, a large enemy airdrome in the center of the large island of Sardinia, just north of the city of Cagliari. Our route would take us parallel to Sardinia's west coast, up to a point about abeam of the target. Then we were to turn east to strike the airdrome. The 317th Fighter Squadron was to be stacked close in on the left-hand side of the bomber stream in flights of four fighters, each deployed in the finger-four formation. My flight, which I was leading, was second from last. We were ordered quite specifically to maintain our position and defend the bombers unless we were directly attacked.

We made the run up to Sardinia without any difficulties and turned east toward the target on schedule. As we completed the turn over the Gulf of Oristano, the flight behind my flight was jumped by Me-109s. The four P-40s immediately broke toward the attackers, and a turning, swirling dogfight ensued. Moments later, two more Me-109s attacked the number four man in my flight, and all four of us immediately turned into the enemy fighters. Quickly, more pairs of Me-109s joined in the fight; they came at us from every direction.

It didn't take long for us new sports to become separated. The next thing I knew, it was me and about a half a dozen 109s yo-yoing all over the sky. I knew that my P-40 couldn't catch, outrun, outclimb, or outdive an Me-109. All I could do was outturn them, and that's what I tried to do. As soon as one 109 came in to attack me, I would break into him. But the Germans quickly got smart to my tactic and they began attacking me in pairs, simultaneously from each side. No matter which way I turned to evade one 109, I would set myself up for another 109.

The whole thing began to look dismal. Things just weren't going the way they were supposed to. Realistically, under those conditions, I knew I didn't have very long to live. I couldn't possibly exist in that environment, with German airplanes coming in from both sides. My dreams of achieving glory fighting for my country were evaporating.

Finally, I saw an Me-109 coming at me head-on. It was descending in a shallow dive. My reaction was to pull up and head straight for its prop. As the 109 pulled up, I pulled up. And as it nosed down, I nosed down. I guess I'd have flown through it if we had kept that up. I just bored straight at it, firing. Fortunately, however, I hit the 109, and I saw parts fly off. There was smoke, too. The 109 went spinning away, and another pilot in the squadron saw it crash.

Shortly after the 109 spun away, a bunch of tracers came zipping by. A lot of the tracers and other bullets hit my airplane. I executed a sudden snap roll to get off of that spot. All I wanted to do was get away from that piece of airspace filled with tracers. And that's what I did. When I spun out, I went down into an undercast we had drifted over. I'm sure the opposing pilot got credit for a victory.

By the time I recovered from the spin, I'd been running the engine at full bore, with the supercharger on, for some time. The engine was smoking from the strain! A 20mm cannon shell had exploded right behind my head, behind the armored seatback, making a big hole in the armor plate, and there was also a bunch of smoke from that.

I leveled out in the undercast and managed to recover. I stayed in the cloud as long as I could, heading south toward North Africa. I finally popped out and nervously looked all around, but I couldn't see any enemies. Eventually, I saw a speck way off to my left, and we slowly worked our way together. It turned out to be a member of my own flight.

He came up on my left side and looked at my airplane. He shook his head and then went under me to get on the right side. He was still shaking his head! We had no radio contact. My radio had been shot out along with some of the instruments. The other pilot looked right at me, drew his index finger across his brow in an exaggerated motion, and shook his head again. He escorted me back to Montesquieu and led me down to land because I didn't have an airspeed indicator.

The landing was uneventful, but after I was down they dragged the airplane off to the junk heap. When the mechanics went to work cannibalizing the engine, they found that a small piece of shrapnel had traveled down alongside the engine and clipped the top off a junction box before embedding itself in one of the cylinders. If that piece of shrapnel had been a tiny bit lower, it would have stopped the engine dead.

The 325th Fighter Group was flying at least one mission every day at that time. After that first mission, I was so shook up that I couldn't sleep. We knew every day whether we had to fly a mission the next day. That way, I could lay awake all night and think about it. I continued to fly because there just wasn't any honorable way out of it. But it was Hell.

After I'd flown a few more missions, I began to calm down

a little bit. And I got to the point that, once we were in the air, I felt okay and was really kind of hoping we *would* find some enemy aircraft, so we could have a go at them.

From that low on May 19, 1943—from being absolutely terrorized—I kept flying until I realized one day that everybody who fights a war can tell you about the time that, but for the grace of God, he would have been dead. I said to myself, "You've been through that a half dozen times." And a great light came on: *I wasn't going to get killed in the war!* So, from then on, I had no fear, no inhibitions. I could go tearing into a gaggle of enemy airplanes with just a wingman and not be worried at all about getting killed. My main concern was how many were going to get away before I could shoot them down.

We had an expression back in those days about fighter pilots: You don't have to be crazy to be one, but it sure helps. Perhaps I was a good case in point.

Herky Green was an excellent case in point, as his later career showed. His May 19, 1943, victory was the 317th Fighter Squadron's first of the war—and the 325th Fighter Group's fourth. Next, as a newly promoted captain, and despite his fear, Green downed another Me-109 on May 28, and a third one on June 28. He also was given credit for an Me-109 probable on August 28, 1943.

Captain Green experienced a long dry spell after the late August 1943 encounter, but it was during the closing months of the year that the 325th Fighter Group transitioned to big, heavy Republic P-47 Thunderbolt fighters. On January 30, 1944, on a low-level raid against a complex of German and Italian air bases in the Udine area of northern Italy, Captain Herky Green downed six enemy airplanes—four Junkers Ju-52 tri-motor transports that he got on a single pass, an Italian Macchi Mc.202 fighter, and a German Dornier Do-217 twin-engine bomber. Green was, for the time being, the Fifteenth Air Force's high-scoring ace, a man everyone called utterly fearless.

Still flying P-47s, Major Herky Green—who was by then the commander of the 317th Fighter Squadron—downed three German warplanes in March 1943, and another in early April. In the summer of 1944, after transitioning to North American P-51 Mustangs and maintaining his lead as the Mediterranean Theater's top-scoring ace, Green damaged four more German airplanes in air-to-air combat, and he destroyed one more Italian fighter and four more German fighters. When he was finally ordered to stand down from combat in late August 1944, Major Herky Green had eighteen confirmed victories to his credit. In the Mediterranean Theater, during the entire war, only one American pilot surpassed his achievement.

On May 18, 1943—five days after the German capitulation in Tunisia—Allied naval forces and the North African Air Force opened an intense bombardment campaign aimed at reducing the Italian defenses on Pantelleria, a heavily fortified island about seventy miles southwest of Sicily. The Allied commanders had decided to invade Sicily in July, and Pantelleria was to be seized early so its airfield could be rehabilitated and used to launch close air-support missions against Sicily and nearby Italian bases.

The air offensive focused against Pantelleria was part of the much broader campaign against all the Italian and German Mediterranean bases within reach of Allied airfields in North Africa. The entire striking power of the North African Air Force was devoted to softening invasion objectives and neutralizing other bases from which the Germans and Italians could support those objectives—or to confuse the Axis commanders as to what the Allied objectives really were. German and Italian fighter units did their best to fend off the Allied bombing raids, but the Allied fighters escorted every mission, and the battles of attrition worked to the advantage of the Allies. The more fighters the Germans and Italians lost defending their bases against bombing raids, the fewer there would be to challenge the invasion fleet off Sicily.

After 6,200 tons of bombs had been dropped in the course of 5,285 bomber and fighter sorties against Pantelleria, British infantry invaded the island on June 11, 1943—and walked right over the dazed defenders. The garrison surrendered without a fight and Pantelleria thus became the first objective of its type ever to be reduced solely from the air. The next day, following a night-long bombardment, British troops occupied the island of Lampedusa. Between June 6 and 12, American fighters alone destroyed eighty-nine German and Italian fighters over and in the immediate vicinity of Pantelleria.

On June 18, fighter-escorted Allied bombers opened the final pre-invasion air offensive against German and Italian bases and lines of communication on Sicily, especially against the city of Messina. On June 20, the airfield on Lampedusa was ready to support RAF warplanes and, on June 26, the 33d Fighter Group moved into Pantelleria's newly reopened airfield. On July 2, the focus of the intense Allied air attack on Sicily shifted to destruction of enemy airplanes and the neutralization of enemy airfields on and within range of the island. Between then and July 9, forty-three German and Italian airplanes—nearly all fighters—were destroyed by Army Air Forces fighters over and right around Sicily. On July 10 alone, while covering the invasion of Sicily, American fighters destroyed twenty-four German and Italian warplanes.

As early as July 13, the 27th and 31st Fighter groups began flying from several newly opened airfields on Sicily, and several other American fighter groups were scheduled to join them within the week. On July 14, the main weight of the ongoing North African Air Force offensive was shifted to closing the Axis line of supply across the narrow Strait of Messina. Naples also became a prime target of Allied air strikes.

On July 19, military targets in and around Rome were attacked by over 500 XII Bomber Command bombers, which dropped over 1,000 tons of bombs. Opposition to the Rome attack was negligible; only one Italian fighter was downed over the target.

Altogether in July 1943, U.S. Army Air Forces fighters were credited with 175 aerial victories. Given the enormous stakes involved—the continuing viability of Italy as an Axis partner—the Allied commanders found the overall reaction of the German and Italian air forces in the Mediterranean and Italy to be extremely disappointing.

On August 1, in a preview of things to come, 177 Army Air

Forces Consolidated B-24 Liberator bombers flew all the way from bases in North Africa to Ploesti, Romania, to bomb at very low level the huge Axis-controlled oil-refinery complex. The unescorted bombers succeeded in causing significant damage, but losses were prohibitive—forty-one B-24s were downed by flak and fighters, thirteen were lost to operational problems and accidents, and seven landed in neutral Turkey.

XII Bomber Command's second large raid against military targets around Rome was conducted by 106 B-17s and 168 B-25s and B-26s on August 13. Despite Italian fighter opposition that was described as "heavy," only two medium bombers and three Italian fighters were downed in the action. The very next day, the Italian government declared Rome an open city.

On Sicily, the offensive by the Allied 15th Army Group was nearing a successful conclusion. Several German and Italian divisions were fighting a dogged delaying action around the city of Messina while the bulk of their forces were evacuated across the three-mile-wide strait to the Italian mainland. Though the withdrawing Axis forces were highly vulnerable, Allied air interdiction was inexplicably feeble. At last, the German and Italian rearguard was withdrawn during the night of August 16, and Allied ground units entered Messina the next morning. Immediately, the North African Air Force launched preplanned sorties against the objectives of the projected British and American invasions of the Italian mainland—the toe of Italy and the Naples area, respectively.

Throughout August 1943, against opposition that remained maddeningly insubstantial, U.S. Army Air Forces fighters destroyed 131 enemy aircraft over Italy, Sicily, and Sardinia. All but a handful of the enemy airplanes were fighters, and nearly all of them were German fighters. On September 2, in what would be the largest aerial action of the month—and of the entire period—P-38s of the 82d Fighter Group brought down twenty-five German fighters over the island of Ischia during a bomber-escort mission to Naples.

Before dawn on September 3, 1943, the British Eighth Army crossed the Strait of Messina. By early afternoon, the military government of Italy had arranged an armistice. Axis aerial opposition to the invasion was negligible, and it remained so even when the U.S. Fifth Army landed at Salerno on September 9. On the day of the Salerno invasion, Army Air Forces fighters flew hundreds of aggressive sorties, but they met only one German bomber, one German observation plane, and one German fighter. The bomber was damaged and the other two were shot down. The next day, between dawn and dusk and more or less over the invasion beaches, American fighters downed four German fighters, probably downed one German fighter, and damaged two more.

SWEATING IT OUT

1st Lieutenant GERRY ROUNDS, USAAF
97th Fighter Squadron, 82d Fighter Group
Salerno, Italy, September 11, 1943

Fenton, Michigan's Gerald Lynn Rounds enlisted in the Army Air Corps in June 1940 and graduated from Aircraft Mechanics School in January 1941. After Rounds had served as a mechanics instructor for six months, his application for flight training was accepted. He earned his wings at Kelly Field, Texas, in March 1942 with Class 42-C and was assigned, with the rank of staff sergeant, to the 82d Fighter Group in California. Rounds was commissioned just prior to shipping out to Ireland with the 82d Fighter Group in October 1942.

Gerry Rounds's first confirmed victory was an Me-109 over Tunisia on February 8, 1943, and he shot down a second Me-109 over Tunisia on March 1. He was credited with an Me-109 probable over Gerbini Airdrome, Sicily, on May 21

*and an Me-109 destroyed over Sardinia on May 24. A fourth
Me-109 fell to 1st Lieutenant Gerry Rounds's guns over Sicily
on July 5, 1943.*

My guts hurt as I walked out to the dispersed P-38s, which
were scattered on the north side of the Gerbini-2 airstrip in
Sicily. Day after day of adrenalin pouring through my
system from the aerial combat had taken its toll. So far, I
had gone out to find a fight seventy-one times. And most of
the time I had found one. That day, September 11, 1943, we
were assigned to another patrol over the landing forces on
the Salerno beachhead, in southern Italy, looking for
German or Italian planes trying to interfere with the troops
below.

The crew chief had the engines checked and warm. Most
days our P-38s never cooled off between missions. The big
V-12 engines blurped, then roared to life. Once again this
friend and master mechanic waved me out with the other
nine fighters.

I led the squadron off the dirt field, two abreast, leaving a
pall of dust to clear before the next two could start their roll.
The fellows closed up quickly by "cutting across the pie" as
I made one large circle of the postage-stamp-size field. I set
the RPMs at 2,600 and manifold pressure at forty-five
inches, and switched the fuel-supply valves from the reserve
to the belly tanks. The two big 1,200-horsepower Alison
engines ran smoothly as they hauled me up over Mount
Etna.

At 12,000 feet, we were already over the Mediterranean
Sea with the boot of Italy drifting along to our right. The
gunsight rheostat was turned up and all the gun switches
were snapped up. My oxygen was set on Demand. The
Prestone cooler flaps were back to Auto, and the oil cooler
flaps also were switched to Auto. I synchronized the engines
at 2,200 RPM and ran the manifold pressure back to
thirty-five inches of mercury. The mixture control was back
to Lean. I kept checking the gyrocompass and compared the
reading with the magnetic compass. The coast disappeared

in the haze, and the swells of the sea provided no landmarks. I kept thinking, Gotta stay on course. You have nine fellows depending on you, with a million and a half dollars' worth of equipment.

The one hour and eight minutes I had calculated to the turn into land were up on the instrument-panel clock. I double-checked it with my wrist chronograph and began to turn right slowly so the other planes in the squadron would have time to maneuver under and over one another. I checked the heading. Nineteen minutes on the new course put us over the coast, in the "Apples" zone of combat. The fellows opened up the formation to give them more time to look around. Wings dipped now and then as the pilots looked below. We flew up the coast to the "Pears" zone. There, I checked in with the Navy controller aboard one of the ships in Salerno Harbor and then led the other P-38s out the peninsula of Capri, the "Peaches" zone. It was such a beautiful place below; I wondered why I was over it looking for someone to kill—or to be killed myself.

The earphones blasted me in both ears: "Meatball One, bandits over north end of Peaches. Angels ten. Over."

"How many?"

The kid on the ship said, "About eight." A quick 180 turned me inland, and a check of the fellows showed that they were out from under me. I quickly switched both gasoline valves to Reserve, snapped up the belly-tank switch, pushed the button, and felt a surge as a few hundred pounds of tank and fuel left the hanger hook. A check of the other planes revealed awkward tumbling tanks beneath them, also. They had gotten the message—"Ready for combat!" A 38 was not much in a fight while dragging around a big belly tank.

The beautiful city of Naples came into view in the haze about thirty-five miles to the northwest, but it was just another landmark that day. The kid on the ship said that the bandits were at 10,000 feet. We were at 12,000, but just to make sure I started a slight climb. I set my engines to 2,600 RPM and manifold pressure to forty inches. Coolant flaps were jammed forward and oil-cooler flaps were snapped to full open. I had to keep the engines cool. I also checked the gun switches.

"Look, look, look," I chanted to myself. "Where the hell are they? They have to be below." Then I spotted about a dozen sharp-nose single-engine devils at 2 o'clock high! How come they were above us? Damn kid!

I shouted "Two o'clock high!" as two or three of the fellows said the same. At the same time, I slammed in right rudder and aileron as I sucked the column into my stomach. We had to meet them head-on in order to shorten their firing time. There was a chance I might get a hit as they rocketed through our formation.

My chandelle was tight at the top to get on their tails. I hoped my number two man could stay with me; I needed a second pair of eyes. He was green at both combat and flying the P-38. That's why I'd assigned him to my wing instead of back in the formation, where he might have gotten caught alone.

I came out of the dive with sixty-five inches of mercury and 3,600 RPM showing. There was a 109 on a P-38's tail as I pulled out and cut back on the throttles. I put combat flaps down and banked left to get a lead on the little German fighter. Something disappeared under my right engine. A quick right bank showed it to be another 109 coming up from below. "What the hell!" We had *two* batches of the devils to work on. I couldn't understand why the controller hadn't seen this bunch on his screen.

I sucked it in tight to force the 109 to pull up into a vertical climb. He wouldn't want to do that for fear of a stall. Then something exploded under my seat armor plate! Damn! He'd hit me! I wondered, Will I get a Purple Heart for being shot in the ass? But the armor plate had stopped it. The little bastard shot up past me at 7 o'clock high. He was slowing fast in that climb. I thought maybe I could get him if I reversed fast, so I pulled back into the left bank and throttled through the stops for that extra 100 horsepower on each engine.

As I flattened out of the climbing turn I spotted him

headed straight and level, getting out of the fight. The sight pipper was just above his canopy, but it was a long shot. I clamped both buttons. The P-38 felt like it had hit a brick wall as the four .50s and one 20mm cannon all fired at once. They settled into steady hammering as the tight stream of tracers streaked to the target. I had a good armament man back at the base. There were flashes on the fuselage and wings of the 109. Keep hammering! You'll get him! There was a glint of sunlight as the 109's canopy flew off. Then the pilot tumbled out on the right wing. I quickly let off the buttons to give him the last chance, but I couldn't wait around to see if his chute opened.

A right turn put me back in the Lufbery the other fellows had formed, but it was too high. I thought, Gotta get this fight in the trees. Down there, the single-engine 109s couldn't turn tightly for fear of a high-speed stall, but our counter-rotating engines produced no snap roll in a turning stall. "Get down to the deck," I shouted into the mike. One more turn and I was all alone; the fellows had all heard. They were below me, slashing away at a flock of 109s.

I dived into the batch, lined up on a single-engine job, and was just about to give it to him when I saw he had elliptical wings! I had no idea what the hell a Spitfire was doing in that scrap. I brought back the throttles; I was being too hard on the engines.

Then I saw a 109 coming into the Lufbery. It was almost a headon shot. His wings were sparkling as he fired at one of my boys. I raked him with incendiaries, tracers, and armor-piercing .50-caliber bullets and 20mm explosive shells as he shot past me.

I pulled the throttles back again—I couldn't remember firewalling them in the first place. I was skimming through the trees above the gray sagebrush. My mind flashed, There's a devil up there! A quick right bank lined me up for a 90-degree shot. He slid through the devastation from my guns just as I saw another 38 chasing him from the rear. I had to suck the column in fast to clear the other 38.

I pulled the throttles back again to get the engines to stop detonating. As I did, I lined up on another airplane, but then

I saw those damn elliptical wings again. I wished that Limey would get out of our fight. He was liable to get hurt if we didn't identify him fast enough.

Another 109 was firing at a 38 above me. I yanked into a climbing turn and was about to line up when he stalled in his tight turn and snapped. He recovered just before he hit the brush. The 109 headed north for home, black smoke pouring from the engine as the pilot gave that V-12 all she would take. He'd had enough. Next time he'd know that a P-38 with combat flaps could turn inside him any day.

A quick check revealed only 38s in the sky, whirling around in the counter-rotating Lufbery circle. "Break for the Apples area," I shouted into the radio. They did and I was left behind. I set my cooler flaps to Auto, oil coolers to Auto, RPM to 2,800, and manifold pressure to fifty inches, but I wasn't gaining on the formation. What the hell is the matter with this bird? I checked on the hydraulic coolant flaps and saw that they were wide open on both booms. The flaps indicator showed one-quarter combat flaps. I actuated the hydraulic levers again. Nothing. A check of the hydraulic pressure gauge showed zero. Damn it! That explosion under my seat had been a hit on the hydraulic system.

I came up on a 38 with one prop feathered and I throttled back just as he dived for the emergency landing strip. I hoped he remembered how to make the difficult one-engine landing.

As I climbed up under the fellows and rocked my wings to tell them to close up on me, the radio shouted, "The commander says 'Well done, Fighters!'" I thought, *He* should have been up here!

Out at sea I cut the "dog leg" short for a more direct route to base. We needed to save gas. My plane was hurt and I thought some of the others might be, too. Manifold at forty inches and 2,400 RPM seemed to keep my cripple at 250 miles per hour, so the guys weren't running their "clean" birds too slowly, compared with my "dirty" bird. I checked the swells below again and they indicated a left wind. I corrected four degrees east to compensate.

The dirt field finally showed just to the right and past

smoldering Mount Etna. I radioed Meatball-2 to peel off and told the others to follow.

As the fellows landed, I switched to the landing gear emergency system. I had to pump down the gear by hand. But there was no resistance on the pump handle. I knew what it should feel like; I'd pumped gear down before. A pass over the field showed an observer on the ground that all doors were shut tight and there was an oil streak under the gondola. That and the sloppy emergency pump handle told me that the entire hydraulic system had been shot up. My fuel gauges showed less than a quarter tank.

I radioed the tower and explained the situation. A belly landing seemed to be the only out. The controller said to put it down along the side of the strip. I hated to do that. Old *CD*—"Chicken Dit"—was an honest machine. I asked if the engineering officers had any other ideas. "Nope," they said, so I approached and peeled up for a normal fighter landing, but I slid it off the runway so as not to block the field.

In debriefing, we agreed that there had been about twelve 109s above us and another dozen below. Five 109s were shot out of the sky. The 38 on one mill had landed safely on the Spit emergency field. *CD* was our only loss.

Back in my tent, I stripped off my sweat-soaked leather jacket, flight suit, dress shirt, and T-shirt. I flopped on the dusty GI cot and let the adrenalin in the pit of my gut subside.

I figured my clothes would be dry in time for the next mission.

Lieutenant Gerry Rounds's kill over the Salerno beachhead on September 11 was his fifth and last. He flew ten more combat missions, for a total of eighty-two, and was shipped home on October 4, 1943, to train new pilots. He did so until the end of the war and was discharged from the service on September 22, 1945.

Also on September 11, 1943, the Italian fleet formally surrendered at Malta and Axis troops began evacuating Sardinia by way of Corsica. Sardinia surrendered without a fight on September 18, and Allied fighter units were deployed there almost immediately. The Italian government formally capitulated to the Allies on September 29, but this largely symbolic move had no impact upon the German campaign to prevent the Allies from occupying Italy.

Fighting on the ground in Italy was intense—bitter in some places—but the air war remained desultory. During the entire month of September, American fighters accounted for only eighty-nine Axis aircraft. And October 1943 was even slower. Even though XII Bomber Command began to conduct long-range heavy-bomber raids over Italy's northern industrial heartland and as far away as Albania, the Luftwaffe and other Axis air forces refused to take the bait. Only sixty-seven Axis airplanes were destroyed in October. Of these, seventeen were downed in a single action on October 9, far from the main battle arena.

SEVEN STUKAS

Major BILL LEVERETTE, USAAF
37th Fighter Squadron, 14th Fighter Group
Dodecanese Islands, October 9, 1943

William Lawrence Leverette was born in Palatka, Florida, on September 5, 1913. He completed a degree in engineering at Clemson University in 1934 and worked in his profession until he enlisted in the Army Air Corps as a twenty-five-year-old flying cadet in mid-1939. After earning his wings with Class 40-A on March 23, 1940, Leverette was assigned to the 31st Pursuit Group at Selfridge Field, Michigan, where he flew the Seversky P-35 and other fighters. In June 1941, Lieutenant Leverette was assigned to the newly formed 53d

Pursuit Group, the first organization to be stationed at Dale Mabry Field, near Tallahassee, Florida. Early in 1942, the 53d moved to Panama, and the 338th Fighter Group, a pilot-replacement training unit, moved into Dale Mabry Field. Captain Leverette transferred into the 338th Fighter Group's 306th Fighter Squadron as a tactics instructor and operations officer, and he later was given command of the squadron. The 306th Fighter Squadron was equipped successively with P-39, P-40, P-47, and P-51 fighters.

By mid-1943, after shepherding hundreds of war-bound pilots through the intricacies of fighter-combat tactics, Major Bill Leverette and his colleagues were wondering if they would ever have an opportunity to put their years of finely honed tactical knowledge to direct use against their nation's enemies. Around that time, Leverette was ordered overseas, and he wound up in North Africa in late August 1943. An expert on single-engine fighter tactics with nearly 800 hours in single-engine fighters, Leverette was given command of the 14th Fighter Group's 37th Fighter Squadron, a unit equipped with twin-engine Lockheed P-38G Lightning fighters. Until Leverette joined the 37th Fighter Squadron, he had flown the P-38 just once, for about ninety minutes.

Major Bill Leverette's break-in period as a combat pilot took place through September 1943, coincidental with the invasion of Italy. He flew his first combat mission on September 3, the day the British Eighth Army landed on the Italian mainland, and his second mission was on September 5, his thirtieth birthday. Over the next three weeks, Leverette and the 37th Fighter Squadron flew a grinding succession of dive-bombing and beach-patrol missions over and around the Salerno beachhead, but Leverette did not even see an enemy airplane during that time.

Until nearly the end of the first week of October 1943, the 14th Fighter Group was mostly flying in support of our troops in Italy. At the time, however, British Prime Minister Winston Churchill had committed a squadron of Royal Navy surface ships and a small contingent of RAF fighters and bombers to harass the large Italian and German force that was occupying the Dodecanese Islands, which are in the Aegean Sea off the southwest coast of Turkey. It was Churchill's plan to invade the islands and somehow bring Turkey into the war on our side. Churchill pestered General Dwight Eisenhower into providing a force of American fighters to this side-show operation, and the 1st and 14th Fighter groups were selected. On October 4, we suddenly moved from our more-or-less permanent base at Sainte-Marie-du-Zit, Tunisia—30 miles south of Tunis—to a crude RAF satellite field known as Gambut-2, near Tobruk, Libya, about eight miles west of the Egyptian border.

On October 9, at 1030 hours, I took off with nine P-38s from the 37th Fighter Squadron. We were to cover a force of one Royal Navy cruiser and four Royal Navy destroyers that were bombarding the German and Italian garrison on the Isle of Rhodes. Shortly after takeoff, two planes were forced to return to Gambut-2 because of engine trouble. This left me with Red Flight, which consisted of four P-38s, and White Flight, which consisted of three P-38s. I was leading Red Flight and Lieutenant Wayne Blue was leading White Flight.

We flew all the way on the deck to stay beneath the German radar coverage from Crete. We sighted the British warships at almost exactly noon, fifteen minutes before we were scheduled to arrive. The ships were approximately fifteen miles east of Cape Valoca, on the Isle of Scarpanto (Kárpathos). I contacted them on their radio-control frequency and was told that they had *been* attacked. I misunderstood, however, and thought the controller had said that the ships were *being* attacked. I could see that the cruiser was smoking from the stern.

I led my P-38s up to 6,000 feet and began a counterclockwise circle around the ships just out of range of nervous antiaircraft gunners. As I reached 8,000 feet and was about halfway through the first circuit, 2d Lieutenant Homer Sprinkle, the number four man in my flight, called out, "Bogies at one o'clock!" There was a cloud of them in the distance. They were slightly higher and approaching the ships from the northwest.

I immediately added power to speed up the climb, and I changed course to pass slightly behind the bogies, in order to make a positive identification as to the type of enemy aircraft. It quickly became clear that they were Junkers Ju-87 gull-winged dive-bombers, probably out of Crete or the airfield at Scarpanto. There were twenty-five or thirty of them, in three flights.

Before we could get within firing range of the Stukas, several of them made dive-bombing runs on the British warships. At least one hit was scored on a destroyer, which broke in two and sank immediately.

As we closed on the Stukas—it was about 1215—I told Lieutenant Blue to hold up his flight momentarily in case there were more enemy aircraft, possibly fighters, following the Stukas. With my flight, I immediately closed on the left rear quarter of the Stuka formation. The obvious plan of attack was to get in close to the Stukas and clobber them with short, accurate bursts from our .50-caliber machine guns.

Before the Germans knew we were there, I attacked the nearest enemy airplane ahead of me. I fired a short burst with the .50s from about 20 degrees. Smoke poured from the left side of the Stuka's engine.

The Stuka pilots who still had bombs aboard jettisoned them as soon as the shooting started. Several of my pilots also reported later that a number of the Stukas jettisoned their fixed main landing gear as well.

As soon as I saw the smoke coming from the first Stuka, I broke to my left and attacked a second Stuka from its rear and slightly below. After I fired a short burst from about 200 yards, this airplane rolled over and spiraled steeply downward.

I broke away to the left again and turned back toward the formation of Stukas. As I did, I saw both Stukas that I had already fired on strike the water. Even though each Stuka had a rear gunner armed with twin 7.92mm machine guns on a flexible mount, I'm sure that neither of the rear gunners had fired at me.

I attacked a third Stuka from a slight angle off its left rear.

I opened fire at this airplane just as the rear gunner fired at me. The gunner immediately ceased fire, and I saw the pilot jump out of the airplane, although I did not see his parachute open. The gunner did not get out.

I continued on into the enemy formation and attacked another Stuka—my fourth—from an angle of 30 degrees. I observed cannon and machine-gun fire hit the Stuka's engine, and I saw large pieces of cowling and other parts fly off. The engine immediately began smoking profusely, and the Stuka nosed down.

I broke away upward and to my left, and then I reentered the enemy formation. Another Stuka was nearly dead ahead. I opened fire again with my cannon and machine guns from an angle of about 15 degrees. The canopy and various parts of this Stuka flew off, and a large flame shot out of the engine and from along the left wing root. The gunner jumped out of the airplane as I passed it.

Continuing into the formation, I approached a sixth Stuka from below and to his left rear, but on a crossing course that would take me over to the right rear, heading slightly away from it. I was closing so fast that the only way to bring my guns to bear was to roll the P-38 tightly left, to an almost inverted attitude. As my guns lined up on the Stuka momentarily, I opened fire at very close range and observed concentrated strikes on the upper right side of the engine. The engine immediately began to smoke, and I broke away slightly to my left. My element leader, Lieutenant Troy Hanna, saw this airplane strike the water.

I attacked the seventh Stuka from straight behind and slightly below. The rear gunner fired at me briefly, but he stopped as soon as I fired a short burst of my own. As the Stuka nosed slightly down, I closed to minimum range and fired a full burst into the bottom of the engine and fuselage. Some Stukas were known to have wooden propellers, and this one acted as though its prop had been shattered and completely shot away. The Stuka abruptly and uncontrollably pitched downward, and I was instantly looking broadside at a nearly vertical Stuka directly in front of me. I was already committed to passing underneath him, so I intuitively jammed the control yoke forward as hard as I could. I heard and felt a large *thump* as I went past him. Looking back, I saw a falling object that I at first feared was my left tail. But the tail was still in place. The falling object was probably the Stuka pilot or rear gunner, who had been catapulted out of his cockpit by the negative G forces that were exerted on the plunging Stuka.

After we landed, it became obvious that the jolt I had felt was from my left propeller cutting into the Stuka with almost two feet of all three blades. The damage to the leading edge of the blades was surprisingly light. We later reasoned, in view of the minor damage, that the prop most likely sliced through a light structure, probably the rudder and fin. This indicated that instead of passing underneath the Stuka, as I intended, I had actually grazed across the uppermost section of the steeply diving German airplane. Fortunately for me, the Stuka went down faster than my P-38, or I would have plowed headlong into it.

By this time, the surviving Stukas were approaching the south coast of the Isle of Rhodes, and all of my pilots had declared themselves out of ammunition. My own guns all had stopped firing—out of ammo—during my last pass. At about 1230, we made a 180-degree right turn around a lighthouse on a big rock off the southern tip of Rhodes and headed south.

In addition to my seven kills, Lieutenant Troy Hanna was credited with five Stukas destroyed, Lieutenant Wayne Blue got one airplane (a lone Ju-88 twin-engine type that had closely followed the Stukas), Lieutenant Homer Sprinkle (Hanna's wingman) got three Stukas and a Stuka probable, and Lieutenant Robert Margison (Blue's wingman) got one Stuka. That's sixteen Stukas and one Ju-88.

Bill Leverette was one of only three American pilots ever to down seven enemy airplanes in a single encounter. Only one American pilot, Navy Commander David McCampbell, beat that record, with nine kills in a single action. McCampbell and the other two pilots—Marine Lieutenant James Swett and Air Forces Captain William Shomo—all scored their victories in the Pacific Theater. For his feat, Major Bill Leverette was awarded a Distinguished Service Cross, the Army's second-highest combat decoration.

Leverette shot down four more German airplanes during his tour as commander of the 37th Fighter Squadron. While operating out of Triola Airdrome, in southern Italy, he destroyed an Me-109 over Greece on December 14, 1943; an Me-110 over Steyr, Austria, on February 24, 1944; an Me-109 over northern Italy on March 18, 1944; and an Me-110 over Weiner Neustadt, Austria, on one of his last combat missions, on April 12, 1944.

Lieutenant Colonel Bill Leverette remained in the service after the war and he earned a master's degree in aeronautical engineering from Princeton University in 1948. He was promoted to the rank of colonel in 1952, and he retired from the Air Force with that rank in 1966.

While the Allied fighters were looking—mostly in vain—for Axis airplanes to shoot down, big organizational changes were being implemented on high. Germany's ability to produce airplanes remained at the top of the Allied air forces' list of priorities, and the development of several large airbases in southern Italy brought aircraft factories as far away as Austria and southern Germany within range of XII Bomber Command heavy bombers. In order to capitalize most profitably from the new bases, it was decided to detach XII Bomber Command from the Twelfth Air Force and use it as the basis for a new strategic air force, the Fifteenth. The new Fifteenth Air Force was activated on November 1, 1943, under Major General Jimmy Doolittle, who had been serving for some time as head of XII Bomber Command. The new air force's mission was to bomb hitherto-unreachable Axis industrial and other strategic targets throughout southern Europe. The Twelfth Air Force—minus XII Bomber Command and six long-range fighter groups—remained in service as a tactical organization devoted to supporting the ground offensive in Italy. During roughly the same period—

October and November 1943—the headquarters of Major General Lewis Brereton's Ninth Air Force was shipped to England, where it would be reinstituted as a new tactical air force that would ultimately support Allied ground units in north-western Europe after the projected mid-1944 invasion of France. Next, on December 8, Lieutenant General Tooey Spaatz was alerted for a pending return to England to establish the new U.S. Strategic Air Forces in Europe, which would oversee and coordinate the strategic-bombing programs of the Eighth and Fifteenth air forces. Finally, on December 10, several weeks after the official inauguration of the Allied Mediterranean Theater of Operations, all theater air assets were combined under the aegis of the new Mediterranean Allied Air Forces.

The strategic bombing campaign in the south was inaugurated on November 2, 1943. Only one day after it was officially activated, the Fifteenth Air Force sent 112 heavy bombers against the Me-109 factory at Weiner Neustadt, Austria, outside Vienna. Thereafter, Fifteenth Air Force bombers and long-range fighter escorts raided far and wide across the hitherto-sacrosanct German satellites and slave states in southern Europe—northern Italy, southern France, Austria, Romania, Hungary, Greece, Albania, Yugoslavia, and Bulgaria. But, as far as the Fifteenth Air Force fighter pilots were concerned, it hardly seemed worthwhile to endure such grueling missions. In the entire Mediterranean Theater, only thirty-one Axis fighters were downed by U.S. fighters that November, and only a somewhat more heartening seventy-eight fell to the American fighters in December. The Luftwaffe, however, was far from dead in southern Europe. During the night of December 2, an estimated thirty German bombers struck Allied supply ships in harbor at Bari, Italy. Before escaping without loss, the Germans hit two ammunition ships with their bombs, and the resulting detonations sank fifteen other vessels.

January 1944 was the biggest month for American fighters since the invasion of North Africa, though that was in part due to the German reaction to the Allied landings at Anzio on January 22. A total of 203 German and Italian aircraft were downed by Twelfth and Fifteenth air force fighters in January 1944. The biggest day by far that month—forty-five confirmed victories—was January 30, when the heavy bombers flew to northern Italy to attack the Axis fighters in their lair.

SPECIAL SWEEP

Major BILL CHICK, USAAF
317th Fighter Squadron, 325th Fighter Group
Udine, Italy, January 30, 1944

In July 1937, less than a year before Lewis William Chick, Jr., was due to graduate from Texas A&M College, he left his studies in mechanical engineering to join the U.S. Army Air Corps. Shortly before the outbreak of World War II, Captain Chick was transferred to Panama, where he assumed command of the 24th Pursuit Squadron. Brief command stints with a fighter squadron and a fighter group in the United States in mid-1942 led to a transfer to the 4th Fighter Group in England. Following a five-month tour at VIII Fighter Command Headquarters, Chick briefly flew combat again in England with the 355th Fighter Group, this time in P-47s. He was transferred in December 1943 to the 325th "Checkertail" Fighter Group, and he assumed command of the veteran 317th Fighter Squadron just as it was being reequipped with P-47s in North Africa. Shortly after moving the squadron to a steel-matted former German airfield near Foggia, in southeastern Italy, Major Bill Chick scored his first victory, an Me-109 near Rome, on January 19, 1944. His second confirmed victory, another Me-109, fell on January 22, while his squadron was supporting the Anzio landings.

* * *

On January 30, 1944, the bombers were scheduled to bomb the Villaorba airfields, around Udine, in northern Italy, east of Venice, near the Yugoslav border. Since arriving in Italy a few weeks earlier, our job had been to escort the bombers until enemy fighters appeared, at which point we were to leave the bombers to the P-38s and attack the enemy fighters. While we were preparing for the January 30 mission, Lieutenant Colonel Bob Baesler, the 325th Fighter Group commander, and some of the other guys and I started talking about flying the bombers in high with no apparent escort while all the fighters flew below them, right on the deck. Then, as the bombers were getting in over Venice, we would pull up to their altitude and arrive over Udine as they were arriving. We'd be unexpected; the Luftwaffe wouldn't know we were going to be there.

The escort was a maximum effort, provided by all or parts of the 1st, 14th, 82d, and 325th Fighter groups. In fact, it was billed as a "special" fighter sweep. The other groups were flying P-38s, but the Checkertails were flying P-47D-15 "razorback" Thunderbolts with water injection. I loved the P-47. As far as I was concerned, if anyone got on my tail, I'd put the nose down and, by the time I hit 500 miles per hour indicated, I knew he wasn't back there anymore. Some pilots said the P-47 couldn't turn, but if you stayed above 250 miles per hour indicated, and made a nice easy turn, you were turning faster than other people thought you were.

I always took combat missions like they were big game hunts—hunting tigers, but with the tigers hunting back. I found the best thing to do was keep my eyes peeled all the way around. If I saw the other guy first, why, I had him. If he saw me first, I was in trouble. My idea was see him first, hit him hard, and get out of there.

We taxied onto the runway and took off two planes at a time. We had a full load of fuel plus two sixty-five-gallon wing tanks. We made one pass around the field to form up and headed out on course. There were twenty-two P-47s from the 317th Fighter Squadron, nineteen P-47s from the 318th, and twenty P-47s from the 319th. Our group commander, Bob Baesler, was leading the 318th Fighter Squadron. Early on, one P-47 from another squadron returned to base, which left an even sixty P-47s from the 325th Fighter Group.

We flew a course of 350 degrees, right over the Adriatic, right on the water. The visibility near the water was pretty damn hazy. I couldn't really see the airplanes ahead of me, but I could look down and see their prop wash on the water. When we were 75 miles out over the water, we turned to course 333 degrees for 225 miles, all the way to Venice. We all stayed below fifty feet, with complete radio silence. When we reached Venice at 1130 hours, we went to full power and started climbing. Villaorba was about forty-five miles away. It took us another fifteen minutes to get there and, when we arrived, we were coming up to 19,000 feet. The bombers were at 21,000 or 22,000 feet.

As we were on the way up over the target, my tent mate, the squadron operations officer, Captain Herky Green, called out that he had spotted some enemy planes way below. I told him, "Go get 'em, Herky!" and he went after them with ten of our twenty-two P-47s. The planes Herky saw turned out to be transports and bombers that had just taken off to get clear of Villaorba before our bombers started dropping their bombs.

I continued to climb up toward the bombers with the rest of the squadron. The enemy fighters—later estimated to be twenty Me-109s, twelve Mc.202s, and one FW-190—were nearing the bombers as we approached. There was also heavy and light flak exploding in the area from 19,000 feet to the deck.

When we got to Villaorba, it was every man for himself. In my squadron, when I'd taken over, I told the boys, "We're not going to fly in tight formation; we're going to fly in a gaggle. I want my wingman where he can see me and I can see him. I don't want him in there, nice and tight. I want him out there, looking around for the enemy. Whoever sees the enemy fighters first calls them out and leads the attack." Consequently, when we got in over Udine, we looked like a flock of barnswallows working over a field of bugs that had been raised up by a tractor. I saw the enemy fighters first and called them out. They were just about to get to the bombers and we were climbing in behind the bombers. A whole bunch of P-47s suddenly were going in every direction at every altitude. There was no rhyme, reason, or order to it. It was every fighter jock for himself.

I went after the first Me-109 I focused on. It was trying to get on the tail of a Thunderbolt which, I learned later, was being flown by my wingman, Captain Archie Hill. As I was coming in on that Me-109, a P-47 flicked past me, and an Me-109 was coming down on his tail, right in front of me, from my left side. I gave the Me-109 a quick squirt as it passed me, and he flew right into my bullets. It was a lucky snap shot. He just came apart right in front of me. Poof! There was no more airplane. I kept right on going after the first Me-109 that was trying to get on Hill's tail; I never slowed down.

I never bothered with deflection shooting. My philosophy was to get on an enemy fighter's tail, get close, and let him have it. I once got so close to an Me-109 before I fired that I missed him; the bullets converged in front of him. I had to move over to get some of my guns on him.

We had eight .50-caliber machine guns. The way I bore-sighted my guns was to take a five-gallon can, pace off a hundred yards in front of the airplane, and leave the can there. Then I jacked up the tail of the airplane until I thought it was to the level where I flew. Then I'd boresight all eight machine guns right on that five-gallon can, one at a time, firing one or two rounds from each gun to make sure they were on the can.

Most fighter units loaded four rounds of armor-piercing incendiary (API) and then one round of tracer, and so forth. The theory was that the tracer would mark where the API was going in, but that didn't really work because the tracer followed a different trajectory than the API. In the 317th, we loaded all API except for five tracer rounds after the first 250 API rounds. This told the pilot he had forty-five API rounds left in each belt to get him out of trouble and on the way home. Another good reason for leaving out the tracer was that a Jerry pilot wouldn't know he was being fired at until the API rounds started hitting his airplane.

I never believed in wasting ammunition. Besides, when I was firing the guns, it slowed the airplane down. After I shot down one Me-109 on another mission, I returned to base with only two bullets gone from each machine gun. That was enough; that Me-109 just came apart.

I finally got on the Me-109 that was chasing Archie Hill. When the German saw me, he stopped trying to get Hill and started trying to get away from me. He was doing all kinds of high jinks, trying to get away from me, but then he suddenly straightened out. I wondered why and I happened to look up. There we were, right under the B-17s. They had been coming in off my right wing when I started chasing the German, but he had led me in under them. Their bomb-bay doors were open and it looked like the sky was full of flyspecks. I knew they had loaded fragmentation bombs, so my thoughts were on passing that Me-109 and getting out of there fast.

We got out from underneath the bombers and I was still trying to catch up to the Me-109. I did, and I nailed him. I saw the airplane come apart. I didn't know what happened to the pilot—if he got out or not. All I wanted to do was hit hard and get out because I knew there might be somebody on my tail trying to do the same thing to me.

That day, my tent mate, Captain Herky Green, got four Junkers Ju-52 tri-motor transports, an Mc.202 fighter, and a Dornier Do-217 medium bomber. In all that day, twelve of our twenty-two 317th Fighter Squadron pilots on the Udine mission claimed twenty-four confirmed kills against no losses of our own. One of our pilots had to bail out over the Adriatic, but he was rescued.

Years later, when I was chief of the Air Force mission in La Paz, Bolivia, I flew to Lima, Peru, quite often. There was this German who picked us up at the airport and drove us to the hotel in Lima. He was a nice guy and I got to talking to him once. I asked him what he was doing during the war and he said he was flying Me-109s. "Were you ever shot down?" I asked. He said, "Yes, three times. Twice by B-17s and once by a P-47." I asked, "Where did the P-47 shoot you down?" and he said, "Over Udine." He named the date—January 30, 1944—so I told him the story of trying to pass the Me-109 out from under the bombers. He looked at me and said, "Sir, I think you shot me down."

Before concluding his tour with the 317th Fighter Squadron, during which he was promoted to lieutenant colonel, Bill Chick scored a total of six confirmed victories, all Me-109s shot down over Italy. He returned to the United States in mid-1944 after a total of four and a half years overseas. He served on the West Coast for the rest of the war, training a new fighter group that had not yet deployed when Japan surrendered in August 1945. Chick remained in the Air Force, mostly flying jets, until he retired with the rank of colonel in 1958.

While the air war on the southern flank had been grinding forward, what had come to be called the Combined Bomber Offensive—the strategic bombing of Germany by the RAF's Bomber Command and the U.S. Eighth and Fifteenth air forces —had at last achieved critical mass. The main show by far was the schedule of daylight heavy-bomber raids out of England.

CHAPTER 4

The American day-bomber offensive over northern Europe had tremendous—but inconclusive and certainly indecisive—results during the last quarter of 1943. On the plus side, six new Army Air Forces fighter groups got into action with the Eighth Air Force B-17s and B-24s between September 14 and December 28. Seven of the ten available groups were P-47 units; two of the new groups were equipped with very-long-range P-38s; and the last of the new fighter groups, the 354th, was the first in the world to go into action in the North American P-51B Mustang fighter.

In addition to the number of groups available, the Army Air Forces expanded the size of each group, and the groups themselves concentrated on breaking all records with respect to maintaining the highest possible number of battleworthy airplanes. The increased numbers of fighters available for duty escorting the bombers showed in the numbers of German fighters that were being reported as destroyed. And, within the stringent guideline set forth by the Eighth Air Force—"stay with the bombers"—many of the fighter groups were working on innovative tactics aimed at cutting deeper into the German fighter wings.

On November 4, 1943, the Eighth Air Force officially promulgated Operation ARGUMENT, the air campaign specifically aimed at destroying the Luftwaffe interceptor force over Germany. It consisted of official sanction and general guidelines for doing what was already being done. The ARGUMENT operations plan was little more than a policy statement; it left the execution phase up to the commanders, based at any given time upon whatever was occurring in the aerial battlefields of northwestern Europe.

In October 1943, the American day fighters were awarded seventy-five confirmed victories, every one of them over German fighters. In November, VIII Fighter Command fighters were credited with ninety-eight German fighters and six German bombers. And, in December, the American fighters downed five German bombers and eighty-seven German fighters. (The scarcity of bomber kills stemmed only in part from the Americans' focus on German fighters; the Luftwaffe was a tactical air force, and the vast bulk of its tactical bomber force was deployed on the Eastern Front, far beyond the range of the American fighters.)

The air battles over northern Europe became a race. Both sides were dedicating enormous resources to eking out incremental advantages by which they might counter the other. The Germans pulled the bulk of their day fighters back, closer to or right into Germany, but that was only in part because the unremitting Allied air attacks had made the forward airfields untenable. The Germans had other, more compelling reasons to pull back their day fighters. If the short-legged German fighters remained based at the margins of the battle arena, they would have only one crack at the American bombers as the heavies flew toward Germany with their bombs. However, if the German fighters were deployed closer to the targets and had a large number of secondary airfields available for fresh fuel and ammunition, they might get two cracks at the enormously long bomber streams before any bombs were dropped. And many of the German fighters would certainly have yet another crack at the heavies during the long trip back to England. So the Germans built scores of little airfields and manned them with trained armorers and mechanics who would wait for the single- and twin-engine fighters to drop in for fuel, ammunition, and minor adjustments.

The Germans also adopted the mass head-on firing pass as their preferred anti-bomber tactic. By late 1943, they were often able to assemble as many as 150 single-engine fighters in one or two big formations ahead of the bomber stream, and these were often capable of initiating head-on attacks that damaged or downed many bombers, especially those in the lead, which were manned by skilled bomber leaders. Often, just before the single-engine German fighters attacked from dead ahead, twin-engine German fighters launched stand-off attacks from the flanks, beyond machine-gun range of the bombers. The twin-engine fighters lobbed heavy cannon shells or 21cm rockets into the bomber formations, to break up the formidable (but *not* "self-defending") bomber boxes.

The trouble with the American fighter tactic of late 1943 was that it gave too much weight to the desires of the bomber crews. Naturally, as they had from the first mission onward, the bomber pilots and crewmen wanted the fighters to fly as close to the bomber stream as possible. The fighter pilots rejected this notion, but high and rising bomber losses seemed to argue in behalf of the close-in support. Thus, despite claims that they could do better on a longer leash, the fighters remained attached, limpet-like, to the bomber formations.

The close-in escort tactic made a certain sense when there were relatively few fighters, flying at the extremity of their ranges. But the availability late in the year of many more fighters, and much-longer-ranged ones at that, slowly negated the old arguments. Either more fighters could accompany the bombers, close in, for a longer distance, or the fighters could use their added range to work farther out from the bombers—say, to engage the massed German fighters well before the bombers arrived on the scene. Realizing that the German fighters used much of their limited fuel getting into position and forming up ahead of the bombers, the fighter tacticians suggested that head-on attacks could be obviated altogether if the remaining fuel aboard the German fighters could be expended in life-and-death struggles with freewheeling, aggressive, attack-oriented American fighters.

VIII Fighter Command—Major General Bill Kepner—was willing to give the new idea a shot, but Eighth Air Force—Major General Ira Eaker—shrank from the prospect. One reason for Eaker's demurrer might have been the highly inflated victory claims by gunners aboard the heavy bombers. While the awarding of confirmed victories to fighter pilots was controlled by several levels of confirmation, absolutely no limiting factors were placed on claims by or credits to bomber gunners. Perhaps this was a device to save the morale of sitting ducks, but, most likely, it was the work of wishful thinking. There was no gun-camera film, no requirement that victories be confirmed by fellow bomber crewmen, no requirement that an enemy airplane be seen as it crashed into the ground. Moreover, given the defensive arrangement of the bomber boxes and the sheer number of machine guns (thirteen .50-caliber machine guns per B-17, and ten per B-24), it was a rare German fighter that was not engaged by scores or even several hundred machine guns as it streaked through a bomber box. If the German fighter blew up—or if it didn't—everyone who fired a shot claimed a victory credit. So, while the fighters were turning in modest and highly regarded victory claims that numbered from one to less than fifty per mission, the bombers were "accounting" for scores and even a few hundred German fighters per mission. No wonder Eaker didn't want to end a good thing! With statistics like these to back him up, he *wanted* the German fighters to fly in close to the bombers—so the very effective bomber gunners could knock them down.

Once the loss of so many bombers and bomber crewmen could be rationalized in this manner, there was little incentive to change tactics. Nevertheless, the American day-fighter groups continued to advance their art. Their mechanics found ways to get more airplanes aloft per mission, everyone worked to eke out a few more minutes with the bomber formations, and tactics did change—because eager young fighter pilots simply did not care as much about penalties imposed from above as they did about destroying German fighters.

The fact of the matter was that Ira Eaker misunderstood the purpose of the day-fighter program over northwestern Europe. His early and ongoing enthusiasm for the "self-defending" bomber created a blind spot with respect to the potential of the long-range fighter. Unlike his thirty-eight-year-old bomber commander, Major General Fred Anderson, Eaker did not realize that the bombers had become bait for the German fighters, and that the American fighters needed to be free to exploit German vulnerabilities. Eaker's good friend, General Hap Arnold, had kept Eaker on at Eighth Air Force far longer than Eaker deserved, but Arnold had his limits.

On December 6, 1943, President Franklin Roosevelt ordered General Dwight Eisenhower to move from the Mediterranean Theater to England to head the new Supreme Headquarters, Allied Expeditionary Force (SHAEF). Within two days, Hap Arnold had closed a deal with Eisenhower over the establishment of a new U.S. Strategic Air Forces in Europe (USSAFE), which was to coordinate the strategic-bombing efforts of the Eighth and Fifteenth air forces against Germany. It was also agreed that Lieutenant General Tooey Spaatz, who had served under Eisenhower in North Africa and the Mediterranean, would head USSAFE. On December 18, the Eighth Air Force's Ira Eaker was ordered to assume command of the Mediterranean Allied Air Force as soon as his relief—the Fifteenth Air Force's Major General Jimmy Doolittle—could get to England.

Tooey Spaatz inaugurated his new USSAFE Headquarters at Bushy Park, England, on January 1, 1944. On January 6, Jimmy Doolittle formally relieved Eaker as commander of the Eighth Air Force. The old Eighth Air Force headquarters was renamed on January 6 to serve as Spaatz's headquarters, and, on the same day, the old VIII Bomber Command headquarters was upgraded to serve as Doolittle's. Unfortunately, Major General Fred Anderson had to rebuild his bomber-command headquarters from scratch. (After January 6, 1944, there was no VIII Bomber Command, per se. However, Anderson functioned as Doolittle's deputy operations officer for bombing, and he had an adequate staff for the purpose.)

At the outset, Jimmy Doolittle was made to understand what Eaker had failed to grasp, and he gave Bill Kepner a reasonably free hand to alter Operation ARGUMENT—mainly to unleash the escort fighters. At least he gave Kepner an opportunity to move ahead *prudently* with the destruction of the German fighter force over Germany. And Kepner and his eager subordinates indeed moved ahead.

One of the most important new American innovations was

phased escort, in which each escort group was assigned to a particular section of the bombers' route to or from the target. How the fighters reached their rendezvous point was up to the individual groups, but emphasis was placed on economical routes and fuel settings, so the fighters could remain on station with the bombers for as long as possible. At the extremity of the assigned sector, a replacement escort group was to join up, and so forth. Among other advantages, phased support ended the effectiveness of a particularly maddening German tactic, in which German fighters attacked the American fighters early in a mission, to get them to drop their auxiliary fuel tanks long before the tanks were empty. This tactic often forced the American escorts to turn for home before the main German attacks struck the bombers.

The first phased-escort mission was flown on January 7, 1944, and it made use of all eleven of the available escort groups. Three shorter-legged P-47 groups handled target penetration in rotation, the one P-51 and two P-38 groups traded off in sequence over the target, and then the five remaining P-47 groups handled target withdrawal. Though the American fighters downed only seven German fighters that day, the new tactic was deemed an overwhelming success, and it was adopted on the spot as the standard.

While VIII Fighter Command was working out phased escort, the fighter jocks themselves were laying the groundwork for a new "freelance" tactic. It had started by accident on December 20, 1943, when the long-range P-38s of the 55th Fighter Group arrived at their rendezvous on time and the bombers arrived thirty minutes late. The fighter leader asked for permission to use the wait profitably, and he was allowed to do so. The 55th scored no victories that day, but presumably its free-ranging presence ahead of the bombers had some effect on the ability of the German fighters to form up and deliver their attacks on the oncoming bomber stream. The experiment was repeated once or twice, when conditions allowed, but the tactic was not formally adopted until the ever-innovative 56th Fighter Group came up with a workable plan that freed up the equivalent of two small P-47 groups from bomber-escort commitments. By January

11, 1944, there were just enough other fighter groups available for escort duties to allow the 56th to undertake a pair of planned freelance missions.

OUR STANDARD TACTIC WAS "ATTACK"

Captain JIM CARTER, USAAF
61st Fighter Squadron, 56th Fighter Group
Osnabrück, Germany, January 11, 1944

James Richard Carter was born on May 2, 1919, and raised in Pullman, Washington. After graduating from high school in 1937, Carter majored in mechanical engineering at Washington State College for a year and a half, and then transferred into the pre-med program at the University of North Carolina. However, after his mother was seriously injured and his stepfather killed in an auto accident in 1940, Carter returned to Pullman to help run his stepfather's 2,200-acre farm. During that period, a neighbor's son, who was a colonel in the Army Air Corps, occasionally flew by in B-17 bombers. The example whetted Carter's long-held desire to fly and he applied for the Army's Aviation Cadet program. Carter qualified for the flight training in the spring of 1941, but he did not receive assignment to a Pre-Flight class until November. Lieutenant Jim Carter graduated from Kelly Field, Texas, with Class 42-F and was assigned directly to the 56th Fighter Group.

The 56th was the very first fighter group to be equipped with the Republic P-47 Thunderbolt. We had had the P-47 in the States and, as a result, most of us had 150 to 200 hours in the type by the time we started combat operations. However, all of our gunnery training was done in the U.K., at

Llandebr, Wales, and Goxhill, across the Humber River from Hull, England.

At first we had no external tanks, and despite its very large size, the P-47 had only a limited internal fuel supply. As a result, our first combat missions averaged only about ninety minutes each. Following the suggested trial-and-error method of our Republic Aircraft representative, I served as the guinea pig and proved that we did not have to use the Auto Rich fuel mixtures and the suggested 2,550 RPM while climbing out or while flying above 25,000 feet. In fact, we discovered that we could safely reduce the fuel mixture to Auto Lean and the RPM to 1,850 after we pulled the gear up. Finally, the test center at Edwards Field, California, sent a leading test pilot over to England. He helped us short-cut official channels and this allowed us to do our job better. We soon were officially permitted to use Auto Lean, 1,850 RPM, and manifold pressures of thirty-eight to forty-two inches of mercury on climb-out. When the P-47s were equipped with 108-gallon external centerline drop tanks— one per airplane—we were able to rendezvous with our bombers inside northern Germany.

The P-47D-2 model we were flying in January 1944 was still the older razorback version. It had a slim propeller. Of the D-model P-47, a German pilot once told me, "In the dive, she is fantastic." It had eight .50-caliber machine guns. We were still using the reflector gunsight, from which a visual ring was projected onto a glass plate behind the windscreen to help us in determining lead.

When we left Stratford, Connecticut, for England on January 6, 1943, we had twenty-five P-47s per squadron. This was increased to twenty-seven when we started combat operations. In late 1943, several new P-47 groups that had recently arrived in England were being reequipped with P-51s, and we received some of their P-47s. Also, our in-commission rate increased as our ground crewmen became more experienced. As a result, in the early part of January 1944 we were able to begin launching airplanes in the strength of two groups. Given the extra fighters we had available, we figured that, if we could launch sixteen aircraft per squadron to take care of the bombers, then we could also launch an additional twelve aircraft per squadron for strafing missions, to range around looking for German fighters, or to increase our escort on bombing missions. We also were able to use the two spare aircraft that were launched with each squadron to form another flight—if they were not used as fillers to replace other fighters that needed to abort.

I made captain in mid-December 1943 and was serving as the 61st Fighter Squadron's operations officer under Major Francis "Gabby" Gabreski. I had been credited with damaging an Me-109 on August 19, 1943, and with probably destroying an Me-110 on October 9. At the time, we did not have "overrun" in our gun cameras; the filming stopped with the release of the trigger so that the last few seconds' flight of our bullets were not recorded even if the target was hit. I believe this lack of camera overrun cost the 56th (and me) several victories, which were downgraded upon assessment of the film to probable or damaged. I am sure that the August 19 Me-109 was clobbered beyond a doubt, but no one saw it hit the ground or explode.

At that time in the air war, the Luftwaffe was achieving notable success in joining several fighter wings into large formations of 50 to 150 fighters and making concerted, massed head-on attacks on our B-17 or B-24 bomber formations. In early 1944, there were few guns on our heavy bombers that were able to fire forward. That made it safer for the German pilots to attack head-on, disrupt the close-knit bomber formations, and pick off the resultant stragglers. We tried to hit the German fighters head-on with the entire group in order to break up their large formations. Sometimes, our lead squadron was able to catch a formation of German fighters in their join-up climb to the bombers' altitude. If so, our fighters could disperse theirs by diving through them. The large German formations used up a lot of fuel just getting into position. If broken up in their climb to altitude, they were done for that mission. Even if we didn't shoot them all down and they could return another day, the bomber mission that day would succeed.

At the latitude of Germany, the sun was to the south

nearly the year around. As a result, on penetration of the Continent, we flew a squadron in the center and ahead of the rest of the group formation; a high squadron, which was down-sun and on the left of the lead squadron; and a low squadron, which was up-sun and on the right of the lead squadron. Each squadron consisted of three or four four-ship flights. Each flight flew the finger-four formation—tightly closed up on climb-out and in clouds, and spread out nearly abreast in combat formation. The lead section, consisting of two four-ship flights, was made up of White and Red flights. The squadron leader was White-1, his wingman was White-2, the second-element leader was White-3, and the element leader's wingman was White-4. Red, Blue, and Yellow flights were configured the same. Blue Leader was the leader of the second two-flight section, which backed up the lead section as required or acted as a small squadron of eight if the occasion suited. Yellow Flight was the backup to Blue. With twelve-plane squadrons, the order was White, Red or Blue, and Yellow flights. We attempted to maintain group, then squadron, then flight integrity, but this depended upon the engagement. Our rule, however, was to maintain element integrity no matter how hot and heavy the engagement became.

The January 11, 1944, mission was the 56th Fighter Group's first dual mission. We dubbed our two groups A and B. The 56A group was to proceed with the bomber force that was attacking an FW-190 aircraft factory at Oschersleben, Germany, and the 56B group was to escort a second bomber force that was attacking targets around Brunswick. Both groups of the 56th Fighter Group were tasked to freelance—sweep ahead of the bombers to each target area and search for and break up any massed formations of German fighters.

On January 11, Colonel Dave Schilling, the deputy commander of the 56th, led 56A—thirty-six P-47s—from Halesworth Airdrome at 1000 hours and began the slow climb to altitude. We crossed the coast of Holland at about 25,000 feet. We could tell that we had crossed in even if weather prevented us from seeing the coastline because the

German 88mm flak batteries always sent up a greeting. That day, there was a solid undercast which topped off at about 10,000 feet. It ran all the way to the target. Broken cirrus was above us, at about 27,000 feet. The cirrus had not been forecast, so it might have been formed from the contrails of the bombers.

We made rendezvous with the lead box of bombers north of Osnabrück at about 1055 hours, relieving the P-47s of the 78th Fighter Group. Before we arrived, we had heard reports of bombers in trouble. I did not see any bombers in trouble, but several of our fighter pilots later reported seeing large flashes in the formation, which would indicate that B-17s were being hit and possibly destroyed.

Our engagement started shortly after we joined the bombers. We were then north of Osnabrück, which is about halfway on a line between Frankfurt and Bremen. We were at 26,000 feet, about fifteen miles ahead, and 10 o'clock to the bomber formation. The 61st Fighter Squadron (Keyworth) had the group lead. Colonel Schilling was Keyworth White-1. I was Keyworth Blue-1, on Schilling's right, and Keyworth Yellow Flight was on his left.

The first bogies were called in above and 10 o'clock to our squadron and the bombers. They were then two to three miles from us. The Germans flew a much tighter finger-four formation than we did because they wanted to bring highly concentrated firepower to bear against our bombers. Our formation was spread out as a defensive measure to counter the German flak as well as to give us room to maneuver the wide-turning P-47. It also afforded us a wide field of vision so we could locate enemy aircraft before the German pilots located us. Because we were flying the same basic formation as the Germans, we always had to look twice to be sure if the formations we saw were friendly or enemy. In this case, the airplanes coming down at the bombers were in close flight formation and the flights were more in trail than our spread-out squadron formations. There were about twenty-five Me-109s coming in from above and head-on to us and the bombers.

Apparently the German leader had decided that he

couldn't get to the bombers without attacking us, or perhaps he thought it was safer to just mix it up. Our standard fighting tactic was to attack, so I followed Dave Schilling's lead as he went to meet the 109s.

There were enough 109s to go around, so, as we climbed into them, each flight leader and element leader chose his target and did his best to get into firing position while counting on his wingman for protection. Schilling went for the lead German flight and I went for the second. We both counted on Keyworth Yellow Flight to cover us.

As we reached the German formation, a general dogfight erupted. The neat formations appeared to explode into a swarm of individual aircraft. I was in a turn, trying to get to the leader of the second German flight, when a 109 from another flight rolled down in front of me. He was apparently heading for the bombers. I decided to dive after him, so I kicked hard rudder to follow. I got on his tail and fired while we both were going straight down. The German airplane went into a spin and then tumbled end over end.

I had never fired at a target that was in a spin or tumbling end over end and, thus, I was a bit puzzled as to the proper lead. I fired short bursts in front, directly at, and behind the center of the airplane. The ammo loads were not dictated, but at the time most of us used three armor-piercing and two incendiary rounds in succession. I saw the incendiaries hit both wings and the fuselage, but, as he tumbled, I also saw a great number of hits on the canopy and at the wing roots.

I thought then that I had waited to fire, as usual, until I was within about 200 yards, but film assessment later showed the opening to be nearer 400 yards. The hits I observed on the canopy convinced me that the pilot was done for, so I broke off and headed back up to the bombers. We still did not have overrun on our gunsight cameras, so the last two to three seconds of firing (80 to 120 bullets), if accurate, were not recorded on the film. The film showed hits, but not in the number I saw. Since I didn't follow the 109 to see if he burned or crashed, it was assessed as a probable.

I broke off at about 16,000 feet and zoomed back to

24,000, heading east to catch up to the lead bombers, which had passed my position. I found Colonel Schilling as we both were zoom-climbing back to the bombers at near full power. As my wingman and I joined up with the colonel and his wingman, Schilling spotted eight Me-109s climbing up to the bombers from 11 o'clock. Schilling flew head-on into the 109s, which scattered and dove for the deck before we had a chance to fire. The colonel broke off at about 14,000 feet and led us in the climb back to the bombers.

As we were climbing, Colonel Schilling reported that a straggling B-17 was about halfway between the first and second boxes. The bomber was at about 24,000 feet and there were clouds above it, at about 27,000 feet. There also were contrails coming off the lead box of bombers, so it was difficult to see the straggler until we got close to it. Until then, it was just a blur. I could detect no damage and all four of its props were turning. I have no idea why he was straggling.

As we got near the straggler, I could see six enemy aircraft around it. Five Me-109s were harassing the Fort from the 8 and 6 o'clock positions, and one FW-190 was flying formation off the bomber's right wing. I couldn't tell if they were firing or just trying to convince the B-17 crew to abandon ship or land. I was to the right (south) of the B-17, which was the sun side, so I climbed to get above the 190.

When my wingman and I got into position, I started to bounce the 190, but just then an Me-109 made a pass at the Fort. It crossed in front of the FW, turned right, and headed down. It was in a perfect position for me to get on its tail. I fell in behind the 109, closed to about 200 yards, placed the pipper in my reflector sight just below the 109, and opened fire from dead astern. I fired several short bursts down to 150 yards and saw many strikes on the fuselage and engine. Pieces were flying off. I was 150 yards or less behind the 109 when the pilot jettisoned his canopy. As the canopy passed just beneath me, the pilot bailed out. I pulled up over the wreckage and climbed back into the sun.

My wingman and I ended up southeast of the straggling B-17 and a few thousand feet below it, so I made a climbing left turn to get back to him. As we were leveling out, I saw two 109s making a rear-quarter pass at the B-17 from the bomber's 8 o'clock position. The 109s were out of gun range and our rate of closure was too slow. Even with full throttle, I was not going to catch them before they were in firing range of the B-17. Nevertheless, I shot at the trailing 109 at about 45 degrees deflection and about 700 yards range in the hope they both would see us and break off their attack. I fired again from about 600 yards and surprisingly got a few hits on the leading edges of the trailing 109's wings. At that point, tracers began showing from my guns, which indicated that I was down to less than fifty rounds per gun. The tracers, which converged ahead of the trailing 109, showed that I was leading too much, so I eased off and got a few more hits on the wings as I ran out of ammo. I pulled up over the 109 and told my wingman, Flight Officer Carl Hayes, to shoot while I covered.

Hayes, who was on his first mission, had stayed right with me, giving good cover. He pulled into a good position, but he got caught in the prop wash of the 109 or the bomber and was flipped on his back. When he recovered, the 109s were at too great an angle and too far away, so I told him to join on me. Hayes still had ammo following his aborted pass, but he was low on fuel from chasing after me. Wingmen always used more fuel than leaders. Also, our time was up and a P-51 group was arriving to take our place. We climbed to 24,000 feet and rejoined Colonel Schilling, whom I found quite easily because we both were focused on the vicinity of the straggler.

Our usual escort period lasted about thirty minutes. We thus left the bombers over the target at about 1120, having used a lot of fuel while chasing German aircraft. The wingmen were especially low on fuel. We always had a headwind on the return to base, and the wind velocity was seldom forecast correctly. At the time, we were just learning about the jet stream.

Schilling and I and our wingmen made the trip home as a flight. Return to base was about 1300. Most of the rest of the group had arrived at Halesworth before us, also in flight

133

formations. Our 56A group officially shot down eleven, probably destroyed two, and damaged five—against no losses on our side. The 56B group, which was an hour behind us, saw no enemy aircraft on its way to and from Brunswick.

Captain Jim Carter destroyed five more German fighters and was credited with one more probable during the course of his combat tour with the 56th Fighter Group. When his squadron commander, Gabby Gabreski, moved up to the post of group operations officer, Carter worked as his assistant. Owing to Gabreski's penchant for taking the hot missions and the group policy forbidding the operations officer and his assistant from flying on the same mission, Carter's score remained low while Gabreski's rose to twenty-eight confirmed victories. Nevertheless, though he saw few German aircraft during the course of his officially credited 137 combat missions and 435 combat hours, Captain Jim Carter never missed a target at which he fired. Colonel Jim Carter retired from the Air Force in 1968.

Over the next few weeks, freelancing became a way of life for many of the American escort groups. And it paid off handsomely, just as its advocates had been declaring all along. German fighter losses—and pilot attrition—climbed.

CHAPTER 5

The pressure was on. There were two sets of dates in mid-1944 on which the right combination of moon and tides would make the invasion of France most likely. The first set was in early May. If the Luftwaffe fighter force was going to be rendered moot before the invasion, only four months were left in which to do it. And, by mid-January, the American day fighters were still a long way from having their Luftwaffe counterparts on the run.

Despite the increasing tempo of bombings aimed at crippling the German aircraft industry, German fighter production was on the rise at the turn of the year. The Germans were producing more fighters eighteen months into the bomber offensive than they had been at the start. But, even if there were more fighters, the point at which the Americans were defeating the German fighter force was in the attrition of German fighter pilots. Many of Germany's top fighter pilots already had been consumed in the aerial conflagration over Germany's industrial heartland. Also, thanks to the ripple effect of the concentration by the American air forces on the Luftwaffe, the German pilot-training program was severely handicapped by a scarcity of training planes, instructors, and even fuel.

By late January 1944, the new team of American generals at the head of the daylight phase of the Anglo-American Combined Bomber Offensive was preparing to deal the Luftwaffe fighters a series of death blows.

Though the American day bombers were "bombing hell" out of the German aircraft industry, the Germans had succeeded in dispersing the bulk of the interlinked aircraft-production factories into penny packets throughout Occupied Europe. Many of the new, smaller targets either had not been located by the Allies at this stage of the war or they were not worth the attention of a long-range bombing mission. The net result was a rise in German fighter production that would not abate until nearly the end of the war. Also, as the Germans abandoned some of their forward bases in northwestern Europe—and unengaged rear bases elsewhere—they enjoyed at least a temporary late-January surge in available fighters over Germany. And, of course, there were more fighters covering fewer and fewer square miles of contested airspace. All of these factors conspired against the bombers, which suffered greater losses, even though the more numerous German fighter-interceptors were being flown by an increasing percentage of inexperienced and even ill-trained interceptor pilots.

The spiral of violence favored the American day fighters. There were growing numbers of American day fighters, and the range of the American fighters was improving. American pilots arriving in Europe were increasingly better trained, and the tactics they were employing were becoming more savvy and more aggressive by the day. Ironically, and unfortunately, the positive results of the campaign against the German interceptor force were partly masked by the appearance of many more American bombers in the skies over Germany. As a result of making more targets available to increasing numbers of German fighters, the real bomber losses rose even though the percentage of bomber losses went down.

The heavier bomber losses gave General Spaatz some pause in late January, but the claims for German fighters by American fighters was so high that Spaatz's aggressive subordinates—true believers, all, in the goals of Operation ARGUMENT—were able to talk the USSAFE commander into a redoubled effort. The result was Big Week, a master plan aimed at wearing down the German day-fighter force with a series of attacks against German aircraft and related factories on at least seven consecutive days in February.

The key to Big Week would be intentionally freeing the escort fighters as much as possible from close-escort work. Wherever possible, the escort fighters were to range ahead of the bombers to hit the German interceptors while they were still forming for their patented mass head-on attacks.

To conduct Big Week, the Eighth Air Force had at its disposal a daily in-commission force averaging 678 day fighters and plus or minus 1,000 heavy bombers. Spaatz and his subordinates were prepared to use every one of these aircraft as early as the first week of February—the bombers to goad the German fighters aloft and the fighters to knock the Germans down—but the weather was execrable. Almost-daily efforts well into the month resulted in total aborts or in very limited results. The Germans, however, were prime. They had an average daily in-service force of nearly 350 single-engine fighters and 100 twin-engine fighters with which to attack the bombers, and they had the desire to do so even in the face of the new and disturbing propensity of American escorts to range far ahead of the bombers. It is difficult to conceive of opposing forces more eager to get at one another; both sides would have fought more often had the weather been more amenable to the process.

Finally, with days of clear weather predicted, the British kicked off the Big Week operation on the night of February 19–20 with a 730-sortie night area attack against Leipzig. The Eighth Air Force day-bombing mission for February 20 was to be in three phases and would go after aircraft-industry targets in Leipzig, Gotha, and Brunswick. The American day fighters claimed sixty-one confirmed victories that day, against American losses of twenty-one bombers and four fighters. The Germans acknowledged the loss of fifty-eight fighters from all causes, including operational losses. (The German figures can be most accurately described as "writeoffs," for they include fighters that had to be scrapped after landing safely, usually because of damage inflicted by American machine guns.)

On February 21, 762 heavy bombers and 679 fighters went to Brunswick and several German airfields. The weather was marginal, however, and the German interceptors had a difficult time launching their attacks. Confirmed claims by American fighters amounted to twenty-seven German fighters against losses of sixteen bombers and five escorts. As usual, the German records differed—in this case, thirty-two losses from all causes.

February 22 was to see the first joint mission by Eighth Air Force and Fifteenth Air Force. A total of 1,396 heavy bombers and 965 escorts were to strike aircraft factories or related facilities in six German cities.

THE LUFBERY

2d Lieutenant FRANK KLIBBE, USAAF
61st Fighter Squadron, 56th Fighter Group
Lippstadt, Germany, February 22, 1944

Frank William Klibbe was born on May 30, 1920, in central Indiana. He enlisted in the Army Air Corps in October 1941, was accepted for flight training in July 1942, and earned his wings at Luke Field, Arizona, in April 1943. Following advanced training in P-47s, Flight Officer Klibbe was sent to England in September 1943 and joined the 56th Fighter Group's 61st Fighter Squadron as a replacement. Klibbe's first victory was an Me-109 shot down near Oldenburg, Germany, on November 26, 1943. On January 30, 1944, as a newly commissioned second lieutenant, Klibbe downed another Me-109 over Lingen, Germany, and on February 21 he shot down a third Me-109, this time over the Zuider Zee.

February 22 was a typical damp and dreary morning. As I rode my bike toward the flight line, to a small unattractive Nissen hut that served as the group briefing room, I had the feeling that the day would provide for plenty of action. As I sat waiting for the briefing to begin, I noticed that Colonel

Hub Zemke, Lieutenant Colonel Dave Schilling, and Major Gabby Gabreski were vigorously attempting to persuade one another that the day's mission was going to be nothing more than a milk run and that any one of the three would gladly volunteer to lead the group on this routine flight. This friendly banter confirmed my previous feeling, for when these three commanders began to jockey for the group lead position it could only mean one thing—the mission was going to be a hot one. It was obvious to me that each of these men had been privately briefed the evening before and was fully aware of the potential for heavy German fighter opposition. Each one was prepared to play the role of martyr as a favor to the others and lead this so-called milk run. I'm not certain how it happened or what diplomacy was employed, but Colonel Schilling, the group deputy commander, ended up as the leader for the mission.

As the briefing unfolded, it became apparent that this was indeed not a routine mission. The Eighth Air Force bomber command had been assigned to strike several strategic targets deep in the heartland of Germany. The paths of the bombers, as well as the target areas, were known to be heavily defended by German fighters. Our task was to rendezvous with the bombers over Belgium and escort them to the targets and on the return. This provided the setting for plenty of aerial activity, and the briefing room hummed with excitement and anxiety. As we were leaving the briefing room, my flight leader, Captain Donovan Smith, turned to me and said, "Today's the day, Klib. If we're lucky, we'll both get a kill. We'll exchange lead and you can get one yourself." We hastily established a set of visual hand signs to signal the exchange of positions, and then we went outside to complete our preparations for the mission.

Two hours later, forty-eight 56th Fighter Group P-47s were climbing on course over the English Channel toward the coast of Belgium. Just as we were approaching the Belgian coast, Don's wingman developed engine trouble and requested approval to return to Halesworth. Don acknowledged the request and added that my wingman should accompany the faulty fighter to ensure a safe return. With just the two of us now remaining in the original flight of four, Don and I gained some flexibility. However, we would be somewhat weaker on defense.

We continued our climb and leveled off at about 30,000 feet as we approached the German border. The group spread out in a wide combat formation as it continued on course to intercept our bomber force. As we approached the German town of Essen, we could see the bomber stream— our "Big Friends"—ahead in the distance. The sky was black with bursts of flak from antiaircraft guns below. Colonel Schilling called for a change in course to facilitate an earlier rendezvous, identify our particular box of bombers, and establish our position for escort. As we approached the bombers from 8 o'clock high there was a call that a group of enemy fighters was preparing to attack. Dave Schilling immediately called for everyone to go to full throttle, and we raced for the intercept.

The Jerries already had made their first attack on the lead box of bombers. Some of our fighters had spotted other bandits to the south, and still other Germans were to the rear of the bomber stream. Schilling dispatched a second section of our fighters to cover the rear boxes of bombers.

Don Smith and I were bringing up the rear of the second section when we heard repeated chatter from Schilling and the lead section, which by then had engaged one group of the enemy. As we listened, it became apparent that Dave and the guys were having a field day. Not only could I hear the occasional announcement of a kill, but I could hear the firing of .50-caliber machine guns as pilots depressed their radio mike buttons to speak. I was envious. Although I was not involved, I knew the Jerries were taking a licking. It made damn good listening.

As Don and I were pulling over the top of the last box of bombers, Don spotted a single FW-190 that was attacking a straggling bomber. Calling a bounce, he rolled his Jug over and began a screaming dive for his target below. I followed close on his tail. As we began to close in on the target, I could see that it was, sure enough, an FW-190 nibbling away at the crippled bomber. It was a sure kill for Don. Soon, smoke began to boil from his guns. I saw a strike or two on the left wing of the FW as the armor-piercing incendiary bullets began to find their mark. As Don continued to close, the number of strikes increased. Then the FW's right wing suddenly was engulfed in a flash of fire. The wing tore away and the FW-190 left a trail of smoke and flame as it plunged helplessly to earth 20,000 feet below.

Following Don's kill, we began to climb to a more comfortable altitude, 30,000 feet. There, we would again join our bombers. In complete radio silence, Don signaled for me to take over the lead. This was as we had planned; it was my turn to initiate a bounce. There was an ominous stillness in the air as we continued to weave back and forth over the top of our Big Friends. I continued to scan the sky, both high and low, as we escorted the bombers toward their target. I could see for many miles. The country below looked so peaceful. It was difficult to conceive that such a beautiful land could be engrossed in a totalitarian war.

Suddenly, I saw what appeared to be a single bandit at 3 o'clock low. I watched momentarily as it continued to climb in our direction. When the bandit reached approximately 6,000 feet, I knew I couldn't wait much longer: it was now or never. I had already rolled into the attack before I notified Don of my intentions. I never took my eyes off the target as I instinctively placed the gun switch to On and began to center the target in the gunsight. It was an Me-109. My plan was to continue in my dive, level out a mile or so behind the 109, and hopefully approach from the rear without being seen.

I leveled out as planned and began to close in on the enemy fighter. My gunsight was firmly fixed on the fuselage, and I impatiently waited to move into the effective range of my guns. Just as I was preparing to fire the first burst, however, a P-38 Lightning arrived from out of nowhere, slid neatly in front of me, fired, and destroyed the 109. Where this guy came from I shall never know, but one thing was certain—he was thirty seconds and 100 yards ahead of me.

I had no further business at such a low altitude, so I began a climbing left turn while looking over my left shoulder. I saw what I believed to be Don Smith's Thunderbolt as it attempted to join me for the climb. I relaxed for a moment, but then I was suddenly awakened by a realization of what I had *really* seen. There had been flashes along the leading edge of this aircraft's wings. My only chance was to immediately enter a Lufbery circle and pray that my opponent would be unable to bring his guns to bear. We were at approximately 8,000 feet and climbing into a tight Lufbery.

The Lufbery circle, in its simplest form, is nothing more than two or more aircraft in trail, flying at or near a vertical bank in a series of tight circular turns. When employing the Lufbery circle—usually as a defensive measure against an attacking aircraft—it is essential that the defending pilot maintain a constant tight circular path to prevent an opponent from gaining sufficient gunsight lead to bring his guns to bear. The success or failure of this maneuver is primarily dependent upon two factors: the maneuverability of the fighter aircraft itself and the precise skill and technique employed by a pilot to produce the maximum response of the aircraft.

How experienced a pilot was I up against? How would I gain any margin of advantage when he was already on my tail with speed, position, and a host of tactical maneuvers available to him? How would my P-47, *Little Chief,* perform against the very agile FW-190? These were a few of the questions that flashed through my mind as I tugged at the stick to tighten my turn. As my opponent came ever closer, I could see more fire from his guns. I ducked my head and awaited the impact of his bullets, which I believed was inevitable. Much to my surprise, however, it didn't happen. I continued to pull frantically on my stick to tighten the circle. My engine, with full supercharger on, purred like a kitten, but at the time it also sounded to me as weak as a kitten. Under the G forces imposed by my tight turns, my oxygen mask had begun to slip, which added discomfort to my already unpleasant situation. Despite the discomfort, I couldn't bring myself to release a hand from the stick in order to make an adjustment, for any loss of pressure on the controls would only result in a gain for my opponent.

I continued around in the Lufbery circle. The throttle was pushed forward to the breaking point and the control stick was in my belly as the FW-190 again came slicing inside and from above, firing all the way. One slip on my part was all he needed. If I reefed in too hard on the controls, I'd enter a stall and thus place myself in an even more critical position. I knew I was getting the very best out of *Little Chief,* for on occasion I could feel the first burble of a stall. Again and again, I glanced over my shoulder. The German attacked, his guns flashing and spitting destruction at me. During each attack, I instinctively ducked my head in case any of his bullets ripped into my cockpit.

I was wet with perspiration. Fear and tension were beginning to weaken me, and I wondered if I could maintain the strength to carry on. How much longer could I hope to survive the incessant and persistent challenge of my foe? Time was of the essence. Although I had managed to hold my own in the Lufbery, my fuel was rapidly being depleted.

If a friend spotted me, it would be easy for him to set me free. We were at approximately 9,000 feet when I noticed that two P-47s were flying nearly on the deck beneath me. They were headed east at about 2,000 feet when I began to scream over the emergency radio for help. I called the Jugs below to "come up and knock this bastard off my tail." Even though my slipping oxygen mask interfered with my transmission, I was sure they would hear my plea.

Between occasional glances at the FW-190, I watched the Jugs continue on course until I lost them in the contrast of the countryside below. Shortly thereafter, I looked upward and saw four other P-47s heading west at about 20,000 feet. I again screamed for help, calling for the four aircraft at 11 o'clock high to "get this FW off my tail." *Someone* heard me. I received a call asking for my position and altitude. I screamed back that I was "down here at 9,000 feet, in a Lufbery circle with an FW on my ass." How in the hell did I know my position except that I was directly below four guys passing overhead? A second transmission asked "What's the nearest town?" "I don't know," I yelled back, "but I'm right below these guys at 9,000 feet." I didn't realize it at the time, but my expectation of getting help with such vague and unintelligent position reports was asking for a miracle. Despite my pleas for help, I watched the four Jugs above me fade into the distance.

By then I had reconciled myself to the fact that my survival depended solely upon my own ability and initiative. By the time I began to shake some of my initial fear, we had been in the Lufbery well over six minutes. My opponent had made no appreciable gain. At least he had not hit me, which was some consolation. I watched over my shoulder intently, so I would be able to take advantage of any mistake the FW pilot might make. Slowly, I began to widen the gap between us until he was no longer in position to bring his guns to bear. Finally, I managed to secure a position 180 degrees around the circle from him. For the first time, I was no longer in a purely defensive position.

The odds were even and I had time to think about my next move. There were two options open to me: I could continue in the Lufbery to a position from which I could possibly destroy my attacker, or I could make a run for it. The first possibility was not at all appealing in view of my fuel supply. Furthermore, I wasn't sure I could secure a position to effect a kill, nor could I be sure that other German fighters wouldn't join the scrap. Making a run for it was my best bet. I'd soaked up enough combat experience for one day.

I'd made my decision, but as the nose of my aircraft was passing through a northerly heading, I saw my opponent roll his 190 over in a dive and head east, presumably his course for home. It was over.

My fuel supply was low, so I reduced power, reset the fuel mixture control to Lean, and set course for England. As I began to relax a bit, I took off my oxygen mask and pressed my lips to the canopy. *Little Chief* deserved a kiss for bringing me through.

What happened to Don? Why wasn't he on my wing when I made my attack? These were questions that naturally ran through my mind as my wheels touched the runway at Halesworth. As I taxied toward the hardstand, I could see Captain Smith waving his arm in greeting. Even before I cut the engine, Don was on the wing, throwing his arms around me and yelling, "Am I glad to see you, you little bastard. I thought you were a goner."

"What the hell happened to you?" I demanded as I climbed from the cockpit. "I thought you were with me when I made my pass. What happened? Where'd you go?"

As we walked toward the squadron operations hut, the answers to my questions began to unfold. Don had been with me, and it was a good thing he was. During my initial dive, Don told me, a Focke-Wulf came out of nowhere and slid in behind me. As I continued to dive, Don had called to me to break off the attack, but then he realized I couldn't hear him, so he pressed in and drove the FW off my tail. In the confusion that followed, however, Don mistakenly joined another P-47, which he thought was mine. From that point on, he had no idea of my position even though he could hear my frantic calls for help. He listened helplessly for the entire twelve minutes I spent in the Lufbery circle, but his attempts to find me were fruitless.

Lieutenant Frank Klibbe scored his fourth victory, an FW-190, over Steinhuder Lake, Germany, on March 8, 1944, and he achieved ace status on March 15 when he downed another FW-190 near Dummer Lake. Finally, over Celle, Germany, on the morning of May 8, 1944, Klibbe downed an Me-109 and an FW-190, thus raising his personal score to seven clean victories, all against German fighters. He flew a total of 201 combat hours in sixty-three combat missions in World War II. Frank Klibbe remained in the service after the war and retired from the Air Force with the rank of colonel.

Unfortunately, on February 22, deteriorating weather over Germany caused most of the bombers to return to base with their payloads. However, there was significant action through the day because several hundred bombers and hundreds of fighters pressed on to their primary or secondary targets despite the weather. Fighters from the Eighth Air Force turned in claims for fifty-nine confirmed kills, and the bombers claimed twenty-two. German sources admit to the loss of as many as fifty-two fighters over Germany from all causes.

The weather over northern Europe on February 23 was so bad that the Eighth Air Force was grounded. The Fifteenth Air Force put 102 B-24s over an aircraft assembly plant at Steyr, Austria, but there were not enough escorts on hand to beat back the German interceptors, and seventeen of the B-24s were lost against a claim of just one Me-210 destroyed by a long-range P-38.

On February 24, Ninth Air Force light and medium bombers went in ahead of the Eighth Air Force heavy-bomber force and thoroughly disrupted the German forward airfields in the Netherlands. Then, as several light feints were made in the north, the main bomber force went after aircraft factories at Gotha and the ball-bearing plants at Schweinfurt. The Fifteenth Air Force put a force of eighty-three B-24s and a group of P-38s over Steyr again. The Germans made their stand at Gotha and shot down a staggering sixty-six bombers and twelve escorts. The Americans claimed 155 German fighters downed for the day, but the German records indicate losses of just sixty-six fighters from all causes.

Hounded from two flanks, the Germans were suckered on February 25 into looking south. The Fifteenth Air Force heavies went to Regensburg, Germany, early in the day, and there they lost 39 of 159 B-24s, plus 3 P-38s. The Eighth Air Force then followed up with a second raid on Regensburg and additional raids against Augsburg, Fürth, and Stuttgart—639 bomber sorties in all. What set the February 25 action apart was the sudden upsurge in the number of P-51 Mustang fighters the Americans were able to get over the various targets from bases in England. Nearly 140 Mustangs from three groups took part in the day's action.

BREAKING THE WILD MUSTANG

1st Lieutenant BOB WELDEN, USAAF
356th Fighter Squadron, 354th Fighter Group
Mannheim, Germany, February 25, 1944

Robert Dexter Welden was born in Chicago on November 20, 1919, and raised in Lewiston, Montana. He entered the Army Air Forces on April 29, 1942, and completed flight training on May 20, 1943. Upon graduation, 2d Lieutenant Welden and a number of his classmates were immediately assigned as original members to the 354th Fighter Group, which was being formed as a Bell P-39 Airacobra unit at several bases around Portland, Oregon.

After about three months of training, the 354th Fighter Group was alerted for duty overseas and assigned to the Ninth Air Force's new IX Tactical Air Command. The P-39 pilots arrived in Colchester, England, without their airplanes on October 16, 1943. There was both immense surprise and elation when the first airplanes to reach the group turned out to be the very first P-51B Mustang fighters to arrive in the war zone.

Fittingly dubbed and known evermore as the Pioneer Mustang Group, the 354th spent its first weeks in England flight testing and, indeed, learning to fly and fight its modern and revolutionary fighters. The new fighter group and its hot new airplane were so urgently needed that, within only six weeks of reaching England, the group launched its intense and fruitful eighteen-month combat career with a withering schedule of daily bomber-escort and fighter-sweep missions over Europe. At the time of the first combat missions, most of the new Mustang pilots had only twelve to fifteen flight hours in the new fighter type. The group's first official victories were awarded almost at the outset of its actual combat service, in mid-December 1943. During that busy time, the new—and for a time the U.S. Army Air Forces' only operational—P-51

Mustang group was not only thrown straight into the heart of the air war over Europe, it had to break the untested P-51 Mustang to its critical combat role.

Second Lieutenant Bob Welden scored his first aerial victories—$1\frac{1}{2}$ Me-110 twin-engine heavy fighters—during a bomber-escort mission over the Kiel submarine base on January 5, 1944. He damaged an FW-190 over the Zuider Zee on February 10, and he was awarded another half-victory for an Me-109 that he helped bring down over Oschersleben, Germany, on February 22.

The P-51B was called the "Twelve-Month Miracle." Getting it in production—mating the airframe with the U.S.-built Packard version of the British-designed Rolls Royce Merlin engine—and getting it into combat took only a year. However, as a result of the rush to get the Mustang into combat as a long-range escort fighter, operational testing was never completed. This caused some problems when the 354th Fighter Group started flying the Mustang in combat. For instance, the P-51B's four .50-caliber machine guns each had to be canted about forty-five degrees in order to fit into the very, very thin laminar airfoil. The airfoil—the shape of the wing—was revolutionary for that time, but it did not match the only available armament. At the leading edge, where the guns were placed, it was too thin.

The ammunition belts and the trays in which the ammunition belts lay were positioned outboard along the wing. The belts had to feed over the tops of the gun breeches. Before feeding into the guns, however, each belt had to make a sharp inboard turn. Empty shell casings were ejected outboard. The feeding path of the ammunition belts resulted in a whole bunch of problems. When engagements occurred and deflection shooting was required—where you had to pull three or four Gs to get the gunsight on an enemy airplane—the ammunition belt crimped where it crossed the gun breech. This pulled the bullet linkages apart so that, many times, the guns would not fire.

This problem became so enervating that, on two separate

occasions, pilots in my squadron whose guns jammed, flew right up the tails of enemy fighters and ticked the enemy's rudders and fins with their props. Each of these Mustang pilots was credited with a kill, but there was no longevity in their solution! The gun problem had to be overcome another way.

The gun malfunctions caused all sorts of commotion up the chain of command, and North American factory tech reps descended upon our base to try to figure out what to do. The end result was that they went over to a B-26 base and looked at their ammunition belts, which fed a far greater distance than they did in a P-51. They acquired a whole bunch of boost motors, which was a contraption about the diameter of a D-cell flashlight and three or four inches long. On one end of the motor was a little cogged wheel that was activated by pulling the gun trigger. The cogs fed down between the rounds of ammunition, to the linkages.

Our mechanics and armorers stayed up the better part of two days and two nights installing the boost motors on all the P-51Bs we had at the time. The only problem was that, with the motors installed, it was a little crowded in the gun bays. Someone had to stand on the cover of the gun bay so someone else could get the lid fasteners tightened down. But it did solve the problem.

Offsetting the problem with the ammunition and guns— and aside from its absolutely outstanding engine—was the fact that the Mustang was the only fighter of the time in which you could drop up to a half flap at absolutely *any* speed. The airplane was designed for that purpose because, when you couldn't pull enough deflection on an enemy fighter, all you had to do was drop a quarter flap or a half flap. This increased the lift of the wing immeasurably and the nose of your bird would come right around so you could acquire the desired lead. The only problem was that you didn't enter into this kind of a maneuver without a great deal of manifold pressure on the engine. Also, you had to drop the flaps only momentarily, squeeze off the desired burst, and get those flaps back up. With the flaps down, speed really decreased in no time. The answer was to pull the flaps back up *and* run the engine at full RPM in order to maintain or recover airspeed.

The problem with the guns and the effective use of the flaps both came into play on our mission of February 25, 1944. That day, my flight commander was 1st Lieutenant Robert Goodnight, who was flying Starstud Green-1. Even though I was a first lieutenant and an experienced element leader, I was flying Starstud Green-4 that day on 2d Lieutenant Thomas Miller. Miller and I often flew together, and we alternated as element leader and wingman. It just happened to be my turn to fly the wing position that day.

The target of the Eighth Air Force heavy bombers on the February 25 mission was Fürth, Germany. The 354th Fighter Group's mission was to escort the bombers over the target and on the first leg of the withdrawal back toward England.

Each of the group's squadrons launched sixteen P-51Bs, for a total of forty-eight. Two spares were also launched; they would accompany us to the coast of Holland before returning to base. Our take-off pattern was a gentle turn to the left around the field in flight formations until all the squadrons were formed up. On command from the group leader that he was going to start on course, the three squadrons spread out at distances of between two and three turning radii. The four flights in each squadron stacked down and back from the lead flight, but very tightly to help us get through the overcast as a unit. Discipline was extreme. We always came out of the clouds in exactly the formation and nearly at the spacing in which we had entered it. It was something we had learned to do on our first mission, and had been doing on every mission since.

Once we were on top of the clouds, it was essential for the group to position itself so that it would be least susceptible to attack by enemy aircraft. The sun was always to our right (south) during target penetrations over or toward northern Europe. The group leader flew with the middle squadron. To its left and about 1,500 to 2,000 feet lower was the up-sun (or "low") squadron, and to its right about 1,500 to 2,000 feet higher was the down-sun (or "high") squadron. The reason for this arrangement was that the down-sun (high) squadron could see better and thus could better protect the rest of the group from enemy aircraft coming from the right, from out of the sun.

The 354th Fighter Group maintained this positioning of its squadrons throughout the flight to the rendezvous with the bombers. Usually, at that time of the war, our group rendezvoused with the bombers about thirty minutes before they reached the target. Then we escorted them to the target and back out. Once we made rendezvous, the group formation broke up and each of our fighter squadrons would pick up a box of twelve to sixteen bombers. Then the four flights of the squadron would position themselves so that one flight was about 1,500 feet above and forward of the box of bombers, another flight was above and to the rear, and one flight each to the left and right at the same level as the bombers. This was "close target support," and the fighters would be in pretty close to the box of bombers, usually no more than one or two turning radii.

Because the best speed of the bombers was slower than the slowest effective speed of the fighters, the fighters had to perform S turns to keep from getting ahead of the bombers. Other fighter groups in other types of fighters used different methods for matching speed with the bombers, but the Pioneer Mustang Group used S turns.

When the bombers got over the target, the flak usually became very intense. The fighters withdrew to a position outside the flak area and waited in the clear until the bombers had turned and were coming out of the flak.

However much enemy action other groups encountered as the bombers were penetrating to the target area, it was the 354th Fighter Group's experience that there was plenty of enemy action during target withdrawal because bombers damaged by flak over the target were easy prey for enemy fighters. At that stage of the war, our long-range Mustangs always flew with the bombers during the last twenty or thirty minutes of the penetration and during the first stage of the withdrawal, and we almost always had action with enemy fighters looking for crippled bombers.

The visibility over Fürth at 11,000 feet—the bombing altitude—was good. There was no undercast, but a ground haze hindered the B-17s and B-24s somewhat.

As Starstud Green Flight was coming off the target with a box of B-24s at approximately 1445, we spotted a lone straggling Liberator that was under attack by a lone Me-109. Lieutenant Goodnight, the flight leader, went down with his wingman, Lieutenant Homer Mitchell, while Lieutenant Miller and I covered them from above.

Goodnight closed to within about 300 yards of the Me-109 and opened fire. I clearly saw strikes. As the Me-109 turned sharply to the right, Goodnight followed and continued to fire. Unfortunately, Goodnight's airplane was brand new and the guns had not yet been outfitted with boost motors, so his guns jammed while he was turning sharply to the right to follow the 109. He pulled off and called for someone else to get on the 109.

The importance of mutual support had been drummed into us, so Miller and I had been closing in on the action the whole time. By the time Goodnight called for help, I was just to the right of his Mustang. As he and Mitchell pulled slightly up, back, and to the left to cover Miller and me, I pulled the nose of my airplane in toward the German. Right away I got in a burst that resulted in many strikes along the 109's right wing root. The Me-109 flicked to the left, but Goodnight and Mitchell were right there. Goodnight could not fire, but Lieutenant Mitchell got in a burst, and I observed strikes on top of the fuselage and around the tail.

We had been steadily losing altitude and were down to around 1,000 feet. One of the truly remarkable aspects of our fight this day was that there was no undercast. Usually, over northern Europe at that time of year, the undercast stretched thousands of feet between bombing altitude and a few hundred or a few thousand feet above the ground. But on February 25, 1944, in the area of our withdrawal, the air was clear to the ground. This was one of the few times we were able to stay with an enemy airplane; usually they evaded us by flying into the undercast.

The undercast problem was the reason we had learned to remain so rigidly in our two-ship elements. Not only was it the wingman's job to watch for enemy fighters, it was his job to help shoot down the enemy plane before it could escape. By bringing the eight guns of *two* Mustangs to bear, there was a lot better chance of blowing the enemy airplane out of the sky. And that avoided the usual questions back on the ground about whether there was enough of the right kind of damage observed or on gun-camera film to justify the award of a kill rather than a probable or only a damage credit. We were helping each other get higher scores. The way we saw it, half a definite kill was better than a whole probable.

As we continued to circle lower, Lieutenant Miller got into a good position on the 109, with about 5 degrees of deflection. I was flying slightly to the right and above the German. Miller and I opened fire almost simultaneously, which was something the pilots in our group had become good at. I could see Miller's bullets taking large pieces out of the 109's left wing and fuselage, and my hits were on the right wing and tail.

Miller pulled off after firing just one burst, but I continued to chase the 109 lower, to about 100 feet off the ground. I fired a very short burst from approximately 150 yards and got strikes on the right wing root. The 109 slipped to the right and crashed into a snow-covered field.

The entire flight pulled off and re-formed. We started to climb back to altitude and expected to follow the bomber stream toward home. Just as we were getting to about 11,000 feet, at about 1500 hours, Goodnight spotted a straggling B-17 under attack by one FW-190 and one Me-109.

Goodnight's guns were still jammed, so he stayed back with his wingman. Lieutenant Miller and I went after the Germans.

The 109 was nearest to us. We went straight in at it, and Miller, who was leading, shot it down. Then we went after the FW-190. We went straight in at this fighter, too, and we both fired from maximum range, about 300 yards. I observed strikes from both sets of guns on the 190's wing, fuselage, and tail. The German fighter broke to the right very quickly, and Miller and I were sucked into a rat race—a steeply banked circle to the right. The 190 was turning much more sharply than Miller and me, but I finally got my sight on him from above by applying thirty degrees of flaps and full RPM.

This was a perfect use of one of the P-51's best features. Dropping the flaps increased the lift of the wing and allowed me to come around more tightly so I could get the desired lead on the 190. But I had to leave on full RPM and suck the flaps right back up as soon as I could see strikes on the enemy airplane. If I'd let my RPMs drop, my airspeed would have dropped off drastically. And if I'd left the flaps down, I'd have kept turning past the desired point.

At the last possible instant before I fired, the German pilot tried to reef it in, but the 190 snapped and went into a flat spin. He had completed about two turns in the spin before I could lower my nose and fire a burst, which hit his cockpit from above. Instantly, the 190's canopy came off and the pilot jumped out. No one saw the German pilot's parachute deploy. He had jumped pretty close to the ground. He might have made it, or he might not have. However, Miller did see the 190 crash, so we were each given a half credit for it.

Miller and I rejoined Goodnight and Mitchell within five minutes of having first seen the 190 and the 109 going after the B-17. As we climbed to about 13,000 feet, Goodnight again spotted a straggling B-17, possibly the same one we had seen earlier. It was about a mile ahead of us and was being attacked by two Me-109s.

Lieutenant Miller and Lieutenant Mitchell went after the 109 on the outside. They damaged it and chased it away, but they did not see it crash. Meanwhile, I went after the 109 that was closer to the Fort. I closed to approximately 200 yards while the 109 was making a firing pass at the B-17. As the German broke away from the Fort, I fired a burst and saw strikes on the canopy and engine. Large pieces of the airplane flew off. The 109 continued a slow turn to the left, trailing black smoke. I was out of ammunition, so I rejoined Goodnight. Fortunately, Lieutenant Mitchell saw my 109 crash and I was given full credit for it.

Bob Welden next encountered a German fighter on April 9, 1944, over northern Germany, and he received a half-credit for its destruction. He achieved ace status (with $5\frac{1}{4}$ victories) when he destroyed an FW-190 over Saarbrücken, Germany, on May 11, 1944. Welden's last aerial victory was an Me-109 that he downed on June 30, 1944, near Le Havre, France.

Lieutenant Colonel Bob Welden retired from the Air Force in 1963. On December 11, 1990, shortly after providing the basis for this account, Bob Welden passed away.

There were signs on February 25 that the Luftwaffe fighter force had been worn down by the driving Big Week action. Despite the early opposition against the Fifteenth Air Force bombers over Regensburg, the total fighter-defense response was only around 100 effective sorties. The Americans claimed fifty-nine victories in all for the day, and German sources show forty-nine losses from all causes.

The next day, February 26, Big Week was called on account of weather. Despite sanguinary hopes and mighty efforts, the Eighth Air Force heavy bombers were all but grounded for nearly a week. When the Americans came back in force, however, they would be looking to break the back of the German fighter force once and for all. In order to accomplish that feat, Spaatz, Doolittle, Kepner, and Fred Anderson thought their offensive forces were ready for the ultimate target—Berlin.

CHAPTER 6

THE BIG B

Major TOM HAYES, USAAF
364th Fighter Squadron, 357th Fighter Group
Berlin, March 6, 1944

*Portland, Oregon's Thomas Lloyd Hayes, Jr., dreamed of
flight throughout his youth, but he saw no means for making
his dreams real until 1937, when he was a high-school senior.
Early that year, a Soviet airplane on a much-heralded flight
from Moscow to San Francisco was forced to end its journey
in Portland's neighbor, Vancouver, Washington. Young Tom
Hayes was one of the first civilians to greet the Russian
aircrew. Emboldened by his brush with reflected glory, Hayes
attempted to enlist in the U.S. Navy flight program as soon as
he graduated from high school that June. He was turned
away on account of his age and advised to earn a college
degree in order to qualify. Hayes dutifully matriculated at
Oregon State University, but all he really cared about was
qualifying for Navy flight school. However, in May 1940—
the month Germany invaded the Low Countries—Hayes
attended an Army Air Corps air show in Corvallis, Oregon.
When he learned at the show that he needed only two years of
college to qualify, he signed up on the spot.*

Within a month, Cadet Hayes was attending Primary flight training at Glendale, California, and he graduated with Class 41-A at Kelly Field, Texas, on February 7, 1941. Lieutenant Hayes was assigned to the 35th Pursuit Group. In November 1941, the group was ordered to the Philippines, but by December 7 one-third of the group—Tom Hayes included—had not yet shipped out. In January 1942, Hayes's group of pilots, crew chiefs, armorers, and P-40 fighters ended up on Java, battling the Japanese. On February 19, Hayes was shot down by a Japanese Zero fighter and severely injured. He was evacuated to Australia just as the American survivors of the one-sided air battles were being withdrawn. After recuperating from his injuries, Hayes helped to recommission the 35th Pursuit Group. He flew Bell P-39 Airacobras with the 35th in New Guinea until he was ordered home in October 1942 to help prepare newly trained fighter pilots for the rigors of combat flying in the Pacific.

After completing a month-long War Bond tour, Captain Hayes was assigned as a flight leader to a P-39 replacement training group in northern California. In May 1943, he was selected by the commander of the new 357th Fighter Group to replace a squadron commander who had been killed in a training accident. Hayes assumed command of the 364th Fighter Squadron in Tonopah, Nevada, and helped train the new P-39 unit. By October 1, 1943, the 357th Fighter Group was ready to ship out from its base at Marysville, California; it had been trained to perfection and was, in every respect, ready to go to war. Instead, the group was ordered to leave immediately for several bomber bases in Nebraska, Wyoming, and North Dakota.

We didn't know *what* was going on. It turned out that we had been scheduled all along to ship out to England on October 1. The new groups bound for England were scheduled to complete their phases of training every six weeks and then move on to new bases. But, as we eventually learned, we couldn't go straight to England because our base there was not ready. We were sent to the upper Midwest to mark time. As long as we were there, we kept up our flying skills by simulating German fighter attacks against heavy bombers. That helped get the B-17 and B-24 crews certified a little more quickly for deployment overseas.

The stopover turned out to be of great value. We quickly learned that the war-time shortage of small-arms ammunition had caused a huge increase in the local population of pheasant and other game birds, so fifteen or twenty of us sent for our shotguns. After we finished flying each day—sharpening our flying skills in aggressive, high-speed attacks that lacked only real gunfire—we went bird hunting. We shot so many pheasant that we were able to feed the entire squadron—300-plus people—every night. More important, we sharpened our shooting eyes.

After about a month, we left the P-39s behind and boarded the *Queen Elizabeth* for a high-speed run to Scotland. We spent Thanksgiving at sea. When we finally got to England and had been assigned to the Ninth Air Force, we were told that we were going to be the second fighter group in England to be equipped with North American P-51 Mustangs. We didn't know a thing about the Mustang except that it was a so-so dive-bomber with no high-altitude capability. We also didn't know that the 354th Fighter Group (our immediate predecessor in the Stateside training cycle) had been reequipped with an upgraded version of the Mustang when it arrived in England in mid-October.

The Mustang *we* knew about had been built by North American Aviation under contract to the RAF as a ground-support airplane. The early Army Air Forces version was known as the A-36, and it had been used for some time as a dive-bomber. There was also a fighter version known as the P-51A, but it and the A-36 were equipped with a 1,200-horsepower Allison engine that was inadequate. The P-51A and A-36 could not get above 17,000 feet.

Unknown to us, the Mustang had been the object of an intense development program beginning in late 1942. The key to that program had been the marriage of the Mustang to the 1,430-horsepower Packard Merlin engine, a licensed version of the Rolls Royce Merlin engine. Very late in the process, the urgent need for long-range fighters in Europe had resulted in the addition of an eighty-five-gallon fuel tank behind the P-51's cockpit, and this had led to some delays. The result, when all the bugs had been ironed out, was the P-51B, which the 354th Fighter Group was just about to take into combat when the 357th Fighter Group arrived in England.

Unfortunately, there were not enough P-51Bs for us or for the 4th Fighter Group, which was also supposed to be reequipped with the new type. The 354th had been suffering operational and training losses, and it was bound to suffer combat losses as soon as it began escort duty with the heavy bombers. The entire early production output had gone to the 354th, and all or most of the replacement Mustangs that arrived in England would be used to keep the 354th up to strength.

By the time we had been in England for a month, we still had no airplanes. All we did was slosh around in the mud and take classes in the morning *and* in the afternoon on aircraft identification. But we were doing no flying. I got checked out in a P-51, but only because I was a squadron commander. We eventually got a few of our own, but barely enough to check out the other pilots in the group.

Finally, on January 24, an important decision was made. Outside of keeping the 354th up to strength, all the available P-51Bs in England would be assigned to the Eighth Air Force. A few days later, the 358th Fighter Group, a P-47 group from the Eighth Air Force, was transferred to the Ninth Air Force, and the 357th Fighter Group was reassigned to the Eighth Air Force's 66th Fighter Wing. Within a few days, the 358th moved from its base, Leiston, to our base, Raydon Wood, and we moved from Raydon Wood to Leiston. That way, we would be in the north, about forty miles closer to the bomber routes to Germany, and the 358th would be in the south, closer to France.

The Eighth Air Force couldn't get us operational quickly enough. In a week's time, our group's strength in P-51Bs went from something like a dozen airplanes to seventy-five. It was busy. In addition to checking out the airplanes, we had to get all the pilots checked out. And, in the meantime, our command pilots—group, squadron, and flight leaders —started going out on missions with the 354th Fighter Group to learn about the war over northern Europe.

The 357th Fighter Group was declared operational on February 8, 1944. Following three relatively easy group combat missions over France—on February 11, 12, and 13—we went to Germany for the first time on February 20. It was the first mission of Big Week, and the target was Leipzig. The 362d and 363d Fighter squadrons posted their first victories on that mission. My 364th Fighter Squadron posted its first three victories during the February 22 mission, which was against the Me-109 factory at Regensburg, Germany, and the ball-bearing plant at Schweinfurt. We were grounded by weather on February 23, but on February 24, while escorting the heavy bombers to the Me-110 factory at Gotha, Germany, I received credit for an Me-109 probable over the target. We flew to Regensburg on February 25 and to Brunswick on February 29. I shot down an Me-109 on our March 2 mission to Frankfurt. In all, by then, the group had been credited with twenty confirmed victories, and we were sharp and confident.

By the close of Big Week, on February 29, people had been starting to talk about Berlin. Several times, we had flown close enough to the German capital to see it, but the Eighth Air Force had not yet flown a single mission there. Everyone was asking, "When the hell are we going to hit the Big B?" Before every mission, we'd go into the briefing hut, and they'd open the curtains that covered the map showing our route to the target. We were just waiting to see the red tapes marking the route to Berlin.

When we finally saw that it was going to be Berlin on March 3, our feelings sure changed. The bravado left us. The weather was terrible. Of the entire Eighth Air Force, only the 4th Fighter Group and one of the P-38 groups flew all the way to the target, but they never even saw the ground. All the bombers were recalled or went after secondary targets. The weather was so bad over England that we couldn't get the 357th together at all. We were finally recalled. I logged ninety minutes of flight time, all of it on instruments.

We lost two pilots on March 3, and nobody knows how. In my opinion, these losses were due to the weather. If the group lacked anything, it was instrument training. It is extremely easy to lose a sense of up and down in the clouds. Unless you overcome your instincts and force yourself to fly the instruments, you can easily enter an uncontrollable spin or even fly the airplane right into the ground. The weather over northern Europe that time of year was terrible, and I am sure that all the groups were losing pilots and airplanes because of disorientation or mid-air collisions in the clouds.

They sent about 500 B-17s and over 750 fighters to Berlin on March 4, but there were only a few holes in the clouds, and only a few German fighters could find us. Just one combat wing composed of thirty-eight bombers actually reached Berlin, and these planes bombed the holes in the clouds without knowing what was underneath them— residential suburbs. There was almost no fighter action. Only seven German airplanes were destroyed by our fighters that day, but pilots from the 357th got two of them.

On March 5, we escorted the 2d Bomber Division B-24s to Bordeaux, in southern France. On the way to the target, some of the B-24s dropped supplies to French Resistance fighters in the foothills to the French Alps. Over Bordeaux, our group encountered several FW-190s, which were shot down, and our pilots also got three four-engine FW-200 Condors that were taking off from a grass airfield. We had one airplane shot down, but the pilot, Flight Officer Chuck Yeager, eventually returned to the group by way of Spain. Unfortunately, on the way home, during a low-level strafing run, the group commander, Colonel Henry Spicer, was shot down by flak and captured. The group deputy commander, Lieutenant Colonel Don Graham, assumed command of the group when we got home.

On the night of March 5, all the smart money was on another mission to Berlin. I, of course, *knew* it was going to be Berlin when we received word that we would be going out on a "maximum effort." We were also told that the weather was supposed to be improving.

Maintenance said they could get only forty-eight Mustangs in the air the next morning—exactly what we needed, but with no spares. We therefore scheduled the first team, our very best and most-experienced pilots. There was no horsing around that night. We had a job to do, so everyone went to bed early.

The bombers had to take off hours before any of the fighters. There were hundreds of them, and they had to form up into their combat boxes, combat wings, and combat divisions. That took a long time. Also, the Germans had deployed a belt of 88mm and other flak guns along the Dutch and Belgian coasts, where the bombers usually crossed in. The bombers liked to pass over the flak guns at least at 20,000 feet, and that meant they had to circle higher and higher with their heavy bomb loads while they were still over England. Hundreds of bombers were circling long before it was time for us to get up. As usual, I was awakened by the drone of their engines. Because the bombers were overhead, I knew the mission was on long before it was announced officially. I also knew that, unfortunately, their contrails were creating an overcast through which we would have to take off later that beautiful spring morning.

I was going out as the deputy mission leader, so I met up with Don Graham early to go over last-minute arrangements for the entire group. This was Don's first mission as the group leader and my first as the backup. We arranged a few non-verbal signals so we could communicate off the air in the event one or the other of us ran into problems. We also decided what the group was going to do on the way home, depending on what happened before we were released from escort duty.

The pilots went over to the mess hall for breakfast, then we had the group briefing—the basic information that was going to get all of us to the target. The weather was good over England, but we were told that the front was moving east. The closer we got to Berlin the worse the weather was going to get. If it was clear, we only needed to follow the bomber stream out of England and overtake the lead bombers before they reached the target. But, if the weather was bad, we couldn't fly up the bomber stream for fear of colliding with the bombers in the clouds. Or, in the case of this mission, the bombers weren't even flying directly to Berlin. In an attempt to confuse the Germans—make them think the target was somewhere else—the bombers were flying along a route that would have been too long for us to follow anyway—from Münster to Meppen, Goslar to Uelzen, and Halle to Ratheneau. Halle was southwest of Berlin. In order to conserve our fuel, we were to fly practically due east all the way from the Dutch coast to Berlin.

As one of only three or four P-51 groups available for the mission, the 357th would, as usual, pick up the lead box of bombers at around 1300 hours and plus or minus seventy-five miles from the target. We were to sweep ahead of the bombers as they came in over the target, and then we were to hand the escort off to fresh P-47 or P-38 groups plus or minus seventy-five miles along the route home. On March 6, the bombers would actually be passing Berlin so they could make their bombing runs on different parts of the city from either west to east or south to north. That way, they would already be pointing toward home when they toggled their bombs. We would join them as they completed their run-up to the target from Halle, and we would leave them along the first leg toward England.

Following the group briefing, the pilots broke up for squadron briefings. Here, parachutes, oxygen masks, and escape kits were handed out, and the squadron leaders arranged the order of flights and made any necessary last-minute changes in flight and element leaders. Also, each squadron leader told the pilots what the squadron was going to do on the way home from the target, in case it was a milk run. After we had finished up with the escort part of the March 6 mission, my 364th Fighter Squadron was going to go home on the deck. If we had enough gas, we might go over into Austria to shoot up some of the German flying schools. If not, we would use up our ammunition strafing targets of opportunity on the direct course through Germany toward the North Sea.

We took fifteen or twenty minutes for the squadron

briefing, and then we went out to the flight line, to our airplanes. Each pilot checked his own airplane, strapped in, and went through the usual pre-flight routine with the crew chief. We started taking off at 1030.

We had a policy about aborts, and it was the same as all the other fighter groups in the Eighth Air Force. Ideally, we wanted to get to the target area with three squadrons of sixteen airplanes per squadron. On most missions, we took up to four spares most of the way across the North Sea. If there were any aborts, the spares could fill in. If there were fewer aborts than spares, the remaining spares went home before the group crossed in. If anyone thought he couldn't complete the entire mission—if there was any problem or if a pilot *thought* there was going to be any problem—he had to turn around and get the hell home while we were still over the North Sea. That way, we wouldn't have to send a *good* combat airplane to protect the airplane with the problem.

Just as we were approaching the Dutch coast, Don Graham porpoised his airplane—the signal that he was aborting. When I acknowledged, he immediately banked and turned for home. Shortly after Don left, a few others turned for home, too. When we made landfall over Holland, we were down to forty airplanes.

The problem was that we had been flying every day for six straight days, and we had no spares on March 6; we had exactly forty-eight planes in commission that day. The 357th Fighter Group was still in the learning process. I imagine some pilots were still, shall we say, queasy about flying in combat. And Berlin was thought to be an especially dangerous place. We still hadn't seen what the German fighters would do to protect their capital city. Maybe a lot of pilots had butterflies that day, or maybe the heavy schedule of combat missions—six in six days—had caused more wear and tear to the airplanes than we realized. Whatever the reasons, we kept losing airplanes *after* we made landfall. Altogether, *fifteen* of our forty-eight Mustangs aborted before we reached Berlin. My own section of two flights, which was supposed to be eight airplanes, ended up with an oddball five.

I had the group. I had to navigate us to Berlin and find the bombers in the overcast before they reached the target. I knew it was a matter of staying on course and getting where we were supposed to be on time. It was time and distance. The weather got worse and worse as we flew. We stopped flying the usual tight formation and spread the squadrons out between the two main layers of clouds. There was a thick layer of undercast that varied between 15,000 and 20,000 feet, and another good one started at about 28,000 feet. We flew between those layers, spread apart. We were flying along great, but I had no idea where the hell we were, no idea at all. I couldn't see any landmarks on the ground, and I had to *assume* that the wind was right, as stated in our briefing. If it wasn't, I could be way off course and never know about it. All I could do was fly the briefed heading and pray.

As I flew along, I switched over to the bomber frequency a few times, to find out what was going on. I was able to cross-check with them to at least see that my schedule was still okay. I might be off course, but if I was on course, I would meet up with the bombers on time. Around noon, I heard that German fighters were going after the bombers and that our P-47 groups were engaging them. But I was still an hour away from the rendezvous. I could only listen and hope I'd find the bombers.

I was getting concerned. I checked with Captain William "Obee" O'Brien, of the 363d Fighter Squadron, to find out if he thought we were on course. Some of the other pilots broke radio silence to needle me a little. They said things like, "Where the hell are we?" and "I bet we overshot the target." Just what I needed to hear! When someone said, "Christ, we must be over Russia!" I said, "Gowdy Red, here. Radio silence! Got it?" I knew their voices; I knew who was needling me. They didn't make it any easier on my frame of mind. I had to worry about making the rendezvous in that lousy weather, but I also had to worry that maybe the bombers would be *in* the damn overcast and that I'd find them by running into them. And I was really concerned that I hadn't made the course good, or that the bombers were ahead or behind schedule—or something.

Suddenly I was looking at a big break in the clouds. For the first time on the whole mission, since I'd left England, I could see the ground. And all I could see was a huge urban area. There were red-tile roofs as far as the eye could see. What with the time on the clock—1300, exactly—it *had* to be Berlin. Voices on the group radio net started coming up with, "Hey, that looks like Berlin!" and "Yeah, it must be." Then someone called out, "There're the bombers!"

I looked to my left, and there they were—B-17s. And then, right then, someone else called, "Bogies! Two and three o'clock!" It was a three-way rendezvous. I found out later that we were about twenty-five miles southwest of the city center. That meant we were a little behind schedule, or the bombers were a little ahead. But it was a perfect rendezvous anyway.

I had been flying at 26,000 feet all the way in. My high squadron was at around 27,000 feet and my low squadron was at about 25,000 feet. The bombers were stacked between 22,000 and 26,000 feet. There were clouds over us at about 28,000 feet and clouds underneath us at about 15,000 feet. It was hazy between the cloud layers, but the visibility was adequate.

There were German fighters stacked all the way from the level of the bombers to the upper cloud ceiling. They were still just specks when I saw them. They looked like a swarm of bees, maybe seven to ten miles distant. They were going flat-out head-on to the bombers. Thirty or forty twin-engine fighters were going in first to fire rockets in order to break up the bomber boxes. And coming up behind the twin-engine fighters were many single-engine fighters, Me-109s and FW-190s. Higher up was their top cover, thirty or forty Me-109s. Between all of them and the bombers was the 357th Fighter Group—thirty-three of us.

We had just enough time to change to internal tanks and kick off our drop tanks before the first Mustangs were close enough to open fire on the twin-engine fighters. There wasn't even time for me to call out any orders.

I was in the middle, leading what was left of the 364th

Fighter Squadron. The 362d and 363d squadrons were weaving above and below me, about a mile away on either side. If the Germans ignored us and continued on straight for the bombers, our standard tactic was for the high squadron, the 363d, to take care of their top cover while the middle squadron, the 364th, turned in to engage the Germans from ahead, and the low squadron, the 362d, turned wide to engage the Germans from behind. But the plan went to hell as soon as we saw the Germans; there wasn't any time to put it into action. As the Germans came in range, the 362d just weaved to its left, came in directly behind the first wave of single-engine fighters, and started knocking them down.

I no sooner kicked off my drop tanks than I was in a left turn to get in behind the Germans. Instead of going straight in for the bombers, some of the Germans turned to fight us. That was natural, but about half of the twin-engine fighters dove away into the lower clouds. These might have been night fighters that had been pressed into service to protect the capital. If so, this wasn't their kind of fight, and they were showing it.

We flew straight into the main German formation. We could have done more damage if there had been more of us, but we were apparently able to break up their main attack. Within seconds, it was just a hell of a mess. Everything was going in all directions at once. Individual dogfights were breaking out all over the place.

I managed to keep my section of five airplanes together. When the German twin-engine fighters turned into us or dove away, I left them for other P-51s and turned to engage the German top cover. By then, there were only eight or ten Me-109s above us, but they were coming down to hit us from our rear. I turned into the bunch of them and hollered out, "I'm taking the top guy!" I assumed he was their leader because the others were echeloned off him.

Things got blurred and happened fast. The next thing I knew, I had my hands full with that 109. We were turning and turning, but neither of us was shooting. We were climbing, descending, and climbing again, turning all the while. The 109 was ahead of me. He was after me and I was after him in a tight left-hand circle. The Me-109 was a good airplane at altitude, and the German pilot kept trying to climb, to get some advantage. Finally, I was able to gain on him. And then he split-essed out of it, heading straight down.

I was too far behind to fire, but I was closing the gap. From previous experience and lots of advice, I knew that all I had to do was follow the 109 and keep him in sight. If we ended up on the deck, a Mustang could overtake a 109.

There was no cloud cover in the area, but the Germans had smoke generators all around Berlin, and the smoke was up to 15,000 feet. Even though I was closing on it, the 109 became obscured in the smoke, and then it disappeared altogether. I pulled out at about 15,000 feet.

As I pulled around to look for the 109—or anyone else—something went by, straight down. Then, all of a sudden, something else went by, and this time I could identify it. It was a stick of 500-pound bombs. It looked like a ladder going straight down—all rungs and no rails. I was in the wrong place! I looked around, and there were plenty more ladders. I looked up, and all I could see were four-engine bombers. Holy God!

Bombers were over me and Berlin was under me! I was thinking, Which way do I turn? I kicked the airplane and snap-rolled straight down. At least now I was parallel to the falling bombs. I pulled out at 500 feet and must have flown between the bombs. Heading for the closest rural area off to the west, I started back up.

As I was getting back to about 15,000 feet, lo and behold, I picked up my original section of P-51s, plus Obee O'Brien, from the 363d. While I had been busy with my 109, three of these pilots had shot down two Me-110s.

I took the lead and climbed back up to help escort the bombers that were still approaching the city. We assumed a position on the west side of the bomber stream and patrolled back and forth, looking for German fighters. At about 1320, we found an Me-110 at low altitude. We all went down. The guy who'd called it out shot the 110 down while the rest of us covered him.

Next other fighters arrived to relieve us. We all had ammunition left, so we stayed at 500 feet, looking for targets on the ground. We took a heading of about 280 degrees, back toward the Dutch North Sea coast and home.

As we were coming up on Uelzen at about 1420, I saw a single-engine fighter ahead of us. It was at 500 feet on an opposite course and a few miles to my right. I thought it might be a P-51 whose pilot needed company, so I turned ninety degrees to my right to look it over. As I closed on it, I could see that it was an Me-109.

The German didn't see us as we continued to turn in behind him. The 109 was flying so slowly and I was approaching it so quickly that I was only 200 yards away when I opened fire. I no sooner squeezed the trigger than I had to drop my nose to duck underneath the 109. I don't think the pilot ever saw me.

The 109 fell straight into the ground and burst into flames. As it did, someone hollered, "There's an airfield!" It was nearly dead ahead. Apparently, the 109 had been coming in for a landing. That explained why he had been flying so slowly, but his approach was too long and he should have been looking for us.

There were He-111 bombers lined up along the edge of the airfield. I opened fire on them as soon as I saw them, and the other pilots in my section did the same as they followed me across the airfield. I hit at least one of the bombers, and the others shot up whatever happened to be right in front of them. We didn't get any of the He-111s burning, but I was sure we did a lot of damage. On the way out, I said over the radio, "Okay, enough's enough. Let's get out of here before they start shooting at us." We turned back on course for home. On the way to Holland, we shot up a few trains and trucks. We landed at 1600 hours. It had been a five-and-a-half-hour flight.

The thirty-three of us received credit for twenty of the eighty-one fighters the Germans lost to our fighters on

March 6, 1944. If we had been able to get more of our airplanes over Berlin that day, we could have done more damage. We suffered no losses.

Major Tom Hayes scored his third victory, an Me-410, on the March 8 mission to Berlin, and an Me-110 on the March 16 mission to Berlin. He was made group deputy commander on March 28, and he was promoted to the rank of lieutenant colonel shortly after he achieved ace status by downing an Me-109 on April 19, 1944. Thereafter, Hayes downed an Me-109 on May 28, an Me-109 and a shared Me-410 on June 29, and a final Me-109 on July 14, 1944. He rotated back to the United States in September 1944 to become deputy for operations of the training facility at Luke Field, Arizona. Tom Hayes retired from the Air Force as a brigadier general in 1970.

The bomber force stood down on March 7 on account of weather, and then they went back to Berlin on March 8. The ostensible target was a ball-bearing factory, but, as always, the object was to wear down the German fighter force. This was accomplished insofar as American claims of 155 German fighters were matched by German records indicating fifty-one actual losses from all causes.

The weather over Berlin was bad on March 9, but the heavies were able to bomb through the undercast by using their radar. The Germans barely put in an appearance and only one German fighter was both claimed and actually destroyed.

For all practical purposes, the Allies could count themselves the victors of Operation ARGUMENT, the battle for superiority in the air over Germany. One note of self-congratulation and confidence was posted on March 10. On that day, Major General Lewis Brereton's Ninth Air Force—which so far had been lending its assets to the offensive against Germany—was authorized to begin planning and executing its own program of pre-invasion tactical strikes in France and the Low Countries.

The American fighter pilots and bomber crews were exhausted by March 9—they were given the day off on March

10—but the German interceptor force had been laid low. The proof came on March 11, when the heavies went to Münster, Germany, in force. No German fighters appeared. By then, thoughts were racing ahead to the invasion. And, as it developed, there were even enough operational fighter groups available in England to strike a blow in the Battle of the Atlantic.

RAID ON ST. NAZAIRE

1st Lieutenant JACK THORNELL, USAAF
328th Fighter Squadron, 352d Fighter Group
St. Nazaire, France, March 11, 1944

John Francis Thornell, Jr., was born in Stoughton, Massachusetts, on April 19, 1921. He attended the county agricultural high school, from which he graduated in June 1939, and worked for a year before enlisting in the Army in July 1940. Thornell successfully applied for flight training right after the United States entered the war, and he graduated as a second lieutenant from Craig Field, Alabama, on February 16, 1943. After completing P-47 training, Lieutenant Thornell was assigned to the 328th Fighter Squadron of the newly formed 352d Fighter Group. The unit's personnel shipped out of Mitchell Field, New York, on July 1, 1943, and arrived in England aboard the Queen Elizabeth *on July 4.*

The 352d Fighter Group was assigned directly to flight operations out of Bodney, England. The pace was rugged, but the fighters were generally shackled to the bombers and not allowed to go off and hunt German aircraft. It was thus not until January 30, 1944, that 1st Lieutenant Jack Thornell scored his first victory, an Me-109, near Ruhlertwist,

Germany. He also damaged another Me-109 on the same mission.

The 352d Fighter Group's mission on March 11, 1944, was to strafe the German Navy's submarine pens at St. Nazaire, France, and then to shoot up targets of opportunity as we crossed Brittany and Normandy during our withdrawal to England via the Pas de Calais area. We were to fly straight in to St. Nazaire from the Bay of Biscay, continue across Brittany, and come out again over the Cherbourg Peninsula —over what would later become Utah and Omaha beaches. This was to be the first planned low-level strafing mission ever undertaken in Europe by P-47 fighters, and its purpose was mainly to learn about the intensity of the enemy antiaircraft barrage and other ground fire on and around what was then only a possible invasion site.

For purposes of this mission, the main body of the 352d Fighter Group moved from Bodney to Ford, an advanced RAF Coastal Command station in southern England. Our thirty-six P-47s—three twelve-ship squadrons—got to Ford on the afternoon of March 10. It had been decided to attack with only thirty-six P-47s, rather than our usual forty-eight, because the submarine pens were a very small target dug into the side of a cliff. There just wasn't going to be room for forty-eight aircraft to maneuver.

During the night, the RAF armorers armed our ships with 500-pound high-explosive bombs fitted with ten-second time-delay fuses. These fuses would give us time to skip-bomb through the doors of the pens—which we hoped would be open—and still have enough time to get out of the way over the top of the cliff. One bomb was mounted on the centerline shackles of each P-47, so we would not be carrying external fuel tanks.

The mission had to be timed almost to the second because the tides in the St. Nazaire area varied a great deal. The submarines could not enter or leave the pens at low tide, and the pen doors had to be closed at high tide to prevent flooding. We had to get there between the daily high and low, between 1000 and 1100 hours, in order to be reasonably sure of finding the doors open. Also, because our fuel supply was limited, we could not afford delays or detours once we were airborne.

We left Ford and flew on the deck all the way. The weather was not too good. The ceiling was about 1,000 feet and visibility was only about two miles. Our flight path to St. Nazaire from Ford took us around the western end of the Brittany peninsula, well off the coast from Brest, and then back east so we could approach St. Nazaire from south to north. The whole trip was about 200 miles, and it took us nearly an hour to arrive off the target. Leading the mission was Colonel Joe Mason, the group commander. He managed to get us just about on target and swung us in from the English Channel over the Bay of Biscay and directly toward St. Nazaire.

When St. Nazaire came into view, I could clearly see the submarine pens ahead of me. The doors were open! However, it became clear that the Germans were tracking us on radar despite our low altitude because some of the doors were just beginning to close when I got them in sight.

The group was arranged in three squadron formations abreast of one another with the 328th in the center, the 486th to the left, and the 487th to the right. Each squadron was arranged in a box formation, with the first flight in the lead, the second flight in the middle, and the third flight in the rear. Each four-plane flight was in line-abreast formation. Colonel Mason was flying squadron lead with the 328th Fighter Squadron. I was the element lead (second P-47 from the right) in the second flight, and 1st Lieutenant Bill Schwenke was flying off my right wing.

We went straight in. Each flight commander was to give the order for his own flight to release bombs. I lined up on one set of doors and, on my flight commander's order, I released my bomb. The idea was to skim it across the surface on one bounce, straight through the huge steel doors. It was like skipping a stone. There was no time to see where my bomb went. I had to concentrate on pulling up over the cliff, which was 200 to 300 feet high and dead ahead.

As I was pulling up, German 88mm and 37mm antiaircraft guns set in atop the cliff were firing down at us. As the P-47s topped the cliff, the German gunners elevated and traversed their guns to follow us as far as they could. We couldn't take evasive action because all the P-47s were pretty well bunched together; there was no room to maneuver. As a result, the group lost seven or eight airplanes to the antiaircraft fire. Four pilots were taken prisoner and the rest were killed.

During the recovery across the Brittany coast toward the Pas de Calais area, Bill Schwenke and I got separated from the rest of the group because of the confusion caused by the antiaircraft fire. Then we could not find the group again because of the poor visibility. As we tore inland across Brittany, the cloud ceiling lifted slightly and the visibility improved to about three miles.

Along the way, well inland, I suddenly passed over a B-17 that had bellied into a field. I could see that there were Germans around it, presumably trying to get it back into operation. I called Bill and told him I was going back to strafe the B-17 so the Germans wouldn't have the opportunity to put it back in commission. With Bill still on my right wing, I swung around and lined up on the B-17. I opened fire with all eight of my .50-caliber machine guns and set it on fire. Then we continued straight ahead.

As we neared the Normandy coast, it felt like I was flying through a hailstorm. Machine-gun and 37mm antiaircraft fire—and fire from German infantry, too—were coming up from the ground nearly the whole way. As we crossed the coast over the Cherbourg Peninsula, we were at only a few hundred feet. We were just getting out over the English Channel when Bill called and said he had been hit. I looked over at his P-47, which, sure enough, was covered with oil. He told me that he couldn't see out the windscreen or the canopy. "Okay," I said, "we'll climb so you can jump out."

The cloud cover was a little higher out over the water, 1,500 to 2,000 feet. We climbed to about 1,600 feet and Bill left his P-47. He got out okay. As I watched Bill descend in his chute, the airplane went into the Channel, leaving a big oil slick. Bill landed in the water. I waited around to make sure Bill inflated his Mae West and life raft, but he did not do either. I could see his chute in the water, but I couldn't see him. As I circled, I called the Air-Sea Rescue Service, and they said they'd be right out. Right then, my emergency fuel warning light came on, so I had to leave. I still didn't have England in sight.

Pretty soon, in the far distance, I saw the white cliffs showing up on the horizon. I was just about on course, south of Dover. About that time, a red warning light came on to tell me I had only three minutes of fuel left. Just then, I spotted an airfield, the RAF Spitfire base at Hawkinge. I put my gear and flaps down and made a straight-in approach. Just as I was crossing the end of the field, my engine quit; I was out of fuel. As I set the airplane down, a steamroller was crossing in front of me, hardpacking the grass runway. I couldn't evade the obstruction. I clipped the steamroller with the tip of my left wing, knocking off the pitot tube and tearing a hole in the wingtip. But I came to a stop right in front of the base operations building.

While I ate lunch, RAF ground crewmen fixed up my airplane, but they could not replace the pitot tube, which meant that I would not be able to gauge my airspeed. I called Bodney, told them my troubles, and asked them to have someone meet me over the base so I could land with him in formation. I got home fine that way, but we never saw Bill Schwenke again.

Following the St. Nazaire raid, Lieutenant Jack Thornell's air-to-air combat career began a meteoric rise. On March 15, 1944, he downed a pair of Me-109s over the Netherlands, and on March 22 he was one of four P-47 pilots who shared credit for downing an FW-200. Next, on April 10, Thornell destroyed an FW-190, and on April 19 he achieved ace status by downing a pair of FW-190s near Kassel, Germany. May 1944 was Jack Thornell's best month by far. He shot down three Me-109s in a fight around Nienburg, Germany, on May 8; bagged a pair of Me-109s over northeast France on May 27; got a single Me-109 over Magdeburg, Germany, on May 28; and rounded out the spectacular month on May 29 with another pair of Me-109s north of Neubrandenburg, in eastern Germany. On June 10, Thornell downed two more Me-109s over Bayeux, France, and he shared credit for yet another Me-109 on June 12, over St. Malo, France. His last victory before going home to the United States was a shared credit for an Me-410 twin-engine bomber destroyer, which was downed on June 21 over Germany. His total score was 17 1/4 enemy aircraft destroyed and two damaged.

After returning to the States, Captain Jack Thornell trained new P-47 pilots at Seymour-Johnson Field in North Carolina. He returned to Europe with a fresh squadron shortly after the war against Germany had drawn to a close, and he left the service in December 1945 to attend college at the University of California, Los Angeles. He was recalled to active duty in March 1948 and remained in the Air Force until he retired as a lieutenant colonel in 1971.

From March 9 to March 14, 1944, Army Air Forces fighter pilots claimed no aerial victories over northern Europe. There was no action at all on March 12, 13, and 14 because the heavies were kept from going out by extreme icing conditions at altitude. The weather was "marginal" on March 15, and so the Eighth Air Force went out to see if the Germans had recovered from the many shocks they had sustained over the preceding three weeks. The reaction was middling. The Luftwaffe launched 165 effective interceptor sorties as the American heavies bored in toward Brunswick. Of these, American fighter pilots claimed thirty-five confirmed victories, mostly by the 56th Fighter Group during the approach to the target.

Another big bomber raid on the German aircraft industry was launched on March 16, and the American escorts claimed seventy-five German fighters. On the next raid, on March 18, the claims were for thirty-eight German fighters. The bombers were grounded on March 20, but several fighter groups hopped over to France to beat up German airfields. They scored only three kills. The bombers flew to Bordeaux on March 21, and ten German fighters were claimed. And so forth. The German fighter force was ill, but it was alive, and it was capable of performing under circumstances advantageous to itself. Nothing much happened on the mission to Münster on March 22, but the Germans reacted on March 23, and the American fighters claimed twenty of them. Under the aegis of the Ninth Air Force, the Americans went to France on March 24, 25, and 26, and the American fighters claimed a total of seventeen victories. A big bomber raid to Germany on March 29 resulted in forty-six victory claims. This was to be the pattern for the remainder of the pre-invasion daylight air offensive over northwestern Europe.

CHAPTER 7

As early as February 13, 1944, the Anglo-American Combined Chiefs of Staff had issued an enabling directive aimed at the disruption of German lines of communication within reach of the Allied air forces in England and Italy. The directive left it to the air commanders to determine when it had become feasible to redirect significant forces against what came to be called "transportation targets." In late March, in light of what many analysts and senior air commanders perceived as the cumulative defeat of the Luftwaffe interceptor force over Germany in February and March, it became a matter of VIII Fighter Command policy—rather than individual group prerogative—to unleash the escort fighters that were returning home with full ammunition bays. The invasion of France was only a matter of weeks or, at most, two months away, and Occupied Europe was chock full of juicy German military paraphernalia that could be scrapped from the air. In fact, ranked just behind escort duties, the destruction of transportation targets—locomotives, railroad cars, barges, coastal vessels, bridges, and so forth—became the *prime* objective of the RAF fighter wings and U.S. Army Air Forces fighter groups based in Great Britain. As with many aspects of the air war in northern Europe, the formal plan for a campaign against transportation targets, set forth by the air commanders on March 25 and approved by General Eisenhower on March 26, codified and legitimatized what the fighter pilots had already been doing for some time on their own.

178

FREE TO ROAM

Captain JERRY BROWN, USAAF
38th Fighter Squadron, 55th Fighter Group
Lingen, Germany, April 8, 1944

Gerald Brown was born on December 2, 1917, in Globe, Arizona, and raised in Phoenix. He graduated from Williams Field, Arizona, as a second lieutenant on March 10, 1943, in Class 43-C, and was assigned directly to the 55th Fighter Group. Following training in P-38s, Lieutenant Brown was assigned to the 38th Fighter Squadron. The 55th Fighter Group was the first P-38 group to be assigned to the Eighth Air Force since late 1942. It shipped to England in August 1943 and was assigned to the base at Nuthampstead, from which it commenced combat operations on October 15, 1943.

Lieutenant Jerry Brown damaged a German Me-109 while escorting bombers over Bremen, Germany, on November 13, 1943, but it was not until January 31, 1944, that he scored his first confirmed victory, an Me-109 brought down over Venlo, Holland. On March 18, 1944, Brown added an FW-190 to his tally over Nancy, France.

The mission of the 55th Fighter Group on April 8, 1944, was to escort our heavy bombers to Berlin. The 55th Fighter Group, consisting of the 38th, 338th, and 343d Fighter squadrons, launched forty-eight P-38s, plus four spares, at 0730. The weather at the time consisted of broken clouds with tops at 4,000 feet. After joining up, we all set course at 0745 on 085 degrees in order to rendezvous with the bombers at 0930 at 25,000 feet near the Frisian Islands. Right on schedule, we located the two bomber wings consisting of 140 B-24 aircraft of the 2d Bomber Division. They were stacked from 22,000 to 25,000 feet. We were to take them all the way to Berlin and thence back to near the Kiel Canal. We encountered no opposition going to Berlin, but

179

the flak was very heavy in the target area. There was only minimal fighter activity near Berlin and none on the withdrawal.

Initially, during and after our first mission on October 15, 1943, our P-38 group was the only one capable of taking the bombers all the way to all of their targets in Germany. In December 1943, the 20th Fighter Group, which also flew P-38s, began similar operations.

I liked the P-38. I thought it a great fighter under 20,000 feet, but at some altitudes over that the Germans could pick a fight and break it off whenever they wanted. At those altitudes, the P-38 couldn't keep up with the German fighters. Also, while a P-38 equipped with external tanks had good range, we had to sweat our fuel consumption on the longer escort missions.

Our prime directive in late 1943 and early 1944 had been to stay with the bombers at all costs. This policy was good for the bombers, but it restricted the aggressiveness of the escorting fighter pilots and was a blow to morale. It also had resulted in excessive losses. To give an idea of the pace of operations we faced at the time, there were only about six fighter groups operational in all of England in October 1943, but by D-Day, in June 1944, there were fifteen groups in *each* United Kingdom–based air force, the Eighth and the Ninth. By D-Day, we could put up 1,500 fighters every day. By then, there wasn't any place that the Luftwaffe could go that we couldn't find it. But in October 1943 and for several months thereafter, the German fighters could find and attack us at will—and we could neither leave the bombers to search them out nor stray very far from the bombers even when the German fighters attacked. Finally, in February 1944, word came down to us that during escort missions we could actively pursue all enemy aircraft.

When the Eighth Air Force finally turned its fighters loose to go after targets of opportunity, it created huge problems for the Germans. All the transportation in northern Europe belonged to the Germans. So, whenever we could blow up barges, trucks, locomotives, boxcars—just about anything

—it contributed to the chaos. It was difficult for the Germans to defend the moving targets because we could come at them from all directions. However, strafing fixed targets such as bridges and airdromes was very hazardous because of the amount of flak protection the Germans had emplaced on the Continent. In fact, attacks on airdromes were extremely hazardous because they were always well defended by flak guns of all types. It was very seldom that we could surprise the Germans at their airdromes, even with a well-planned attack. We occasionally used a modified "droop-snoot" P-38, which was fixed up so that a bombardier could ride in the nose with a regular bombsight. We would formate a squadron on the droop-snoot, each plane with either one 1,000-pound or two 500-pound bombs. They all dropped the bombs on command from the bombardier. The other squadrons in the group provided escort. Then, after the bombs had been dropped, we all could seek targets of opportunity.

As a result of the new, more aggressive policy, we were free to roam on April 8 after we had returned to the Kiel Canal area with our bombers. As the B-24s headed out over the North Sea, our squadron, the 38th, headed back inland to look for targets of opportunity. I took my flight back to pick up any B-24s that might be straggling. I did this because stragglers stood a good chance of attracting German fighters. We were on the common frequency for bombers and escorts, but we hadn't received a specific call for help. We just flew back along the bomber stream and happened to find two stragglers.

As we swung back toward the last box of bombers, we were at about 25,000 feet. The two stragglers were about a quarter-mile from one another, roughly over the town of Lingen, Germany, near Dummer Lake. As we approached the bombers, I saw that a lone Me-109 was executing an attack on them. The 109 went through the rear box of bombers and headed straight for one of the stragglers, head on. It was at about 23,000 feet and off to the side of me about a quarter-mile.

You had to have some experience to be up there by yourself, and going through a box of bombers also showed the mark of experience. I believe that Me-109 pilot was one of the old heads.

After the 109 made his head-on pass at the straggling B-24, he split-essed and headed for the deck. He had seen us coming. By then, however, I was already turning toward him, dropping my external tanks, and pushing up RPMs and power. As the German headed for the deck, I split-essed my entire flight and we caught him at 5,000 feet. By then I had descended below him a little and thus could come up on him from about his 7 o'clock. I probably got lucky and caught him as he was looking up at the bombers he was shooting at. I hit him at the left wing root and cockpit area with the first burst, which was from about 100 yards. We didn't use tracers, but we had API for the .50-caliber machine guns and high-explosive rounds for the 20mm cannon. You could always tell when you hit something.

The Me-109 barrel-rolled to the left and descended to about 1,500 feet. The whole way down, I rolled with it and continued to hit it with short bursts. The pilot bailed out between 1,500 and 1,000 feet. We then proceeded on a course back to base, but on the way to the North Sea we strafed a number of trucks and two trains.

Captain Jerry Brown achieved ace status when he shot down an FW-190 fighter and an He-111 twin-engine medium bomber within five minutes on the afternoon of April 15, 1944. Days later, Brown's combat tour came to a routine conclusion, but rather than return to the United States, he volunteered to serve as the operations officer of a P-38 replacement training unit at a base in northern England. Right after D-Day, Brown volunteered to return to combat status and was thus assigned to the 4th Fighter Group, where he flew P-51s. Brown was forced to bail out of his Mustang on September 6, 1944, but he was picked up by the French Resistance and returned to England. He continued to fly combat missions until he was ordered to return to the United States in November 1944.

The onset of the Korean War found Major Jerry Brown in command of a fighter squadron based in Japan, and his unit was rushed into combat on July 3, 1950. Brown's fighter was shot down by enemy ground fire on November 30, 1950, and Brown was taken prisoner. He was released from captivity on September 6, 1953, and he remained in the Air Force until he retired as a wing commander, with the rank of colonel, in 1967.

Beginning April 13, the two U.K.-based tactical air forces—the U.S. Ninth and the British Second—were turned loose against a vast array of tactical targets in France and the Low Countries. Many of the planned tactical sorties—as distinct from opportunistic attacks on ground targets by returning escort fighters—were aimed at coastal batteries in Normandy, but, to avoid giving away the invasion objective, these had to be masked against a background of attacks on every other kind of tactical target almost everywhere that the impending invasion *might* take place.

The RAF Bomber Command night offensive and the twin daylight bomber offensives against strategic targets in Germany and Austria continued unabated during the spring run-up to the invasion. Vast fleets of heavy bombers were available to all three bomber forces, and the weather over the targets was clear more often than not.

With many Army Air Forces fighter groups devoting more time to escorting medium bombers closer to the deck, or conducting their own destructive free-wheeling hunting forays against ground targets of opportunity, the Germans and their Axis partners were pressed closer and closer to the wall. Somewhere, somehow, there were encounters in the air over the Axis nations and Occupied Europe nearly every day during the spring 1944 weeks leading up to the invasion.

On April 27, the Eighth Air Force was pulled off deep penetration over Germany for a day, and the heavies were sent to France to strike several transportation centers. The switch caught the Germans unprepared, and there was virtually no opposition. The test complete, however, the Eighth Air Force resumed the strategic offensive against Germany and left the tactical targets to the tactical air forces.

CRIPPLED

1st Lieutenant ED HELLER, USAAF
486th Fighter Squadron, 352d Fighter Group
Gifhorn, Germany, May 8, 1944

Edwin Heller, who had dreamed of being a fighter pilot from early childhood, was a twenty-three-year-old Pennsylvania state policeman when he enlisted as a U.S. Army aviation cadet right after Pearl Harbor. After completing flying school and P-47 transition school, Heller joined the 352d Fighter Group's 486th Fighter Squadron at Farmingdale, Long Island, in late March 1943 to replace a pilot who had been killed in a training accident. The 352d Fighter Group shipped out in June 1943 and, upon arrival in England, was assigned to Bodney Airdrome, in East Anglia. The group became operational and flew its first combat missions in September 1943. Originally equipped with P-47s, the 352d Group transitioned into P-51s in April 1944.

Throughout the period the 352d Group flew P-47s, Lieutenant Ed Heller took every mission assignment he could wangle—a total of about fifty. He damaged or destroyed several German airplanes on the ground, but as a wingman he was not able to fire directly at a German airplane in the air. By May 1944, Heller considered himself "experienced and good." He felt that his lack of aerial victories—and his survival to that point—had more to do with luck than skill.

Actual combat experiences were few and far between despite the grueling schedule, and being in the right place at the right time in those rare confrontations was easier imagined than accomplished. Heller's feelings were borne out over Germany on May 8, 1944, when luck and skill earned him his first victories and brought him home alive in his crippled P-51 fighter.

Our officers' club at Bodney had a traffic light prominently displayed above the bar. The red light meant no more drinking because there was to be a mission the next day; the yellow light meant headquarters had not heard yet if we had a mission the next day; and the green light meant we could go ahead and party because the next day's mission had been scrubbed. On the evening of May 7, 1944, the light was red, so, after supper, we went back to our Quonset huts and turned in.

The mission was an early one. We were awakened at 0400 hours. We ate breakfast at the officers' club and went to the group operations hut for our briefing. The mission for May 8 was a bomber escort, and our group of three squadrons of sixteen aircraft each was to rendezvous with a particular bomber group approximately halfway between the Channel and the target, which was in the vicinity of Magdeburg, Germany.

Bodney was a grass field. We always took off in four-ship flights, line abreast. I was flying Blue-3, the element lead in Captain Frank Cutler's Blue Flight. We were the last flight of the squadron to take off.

It was a typical English day in East Anglia. The clouds began at about 1,500 feet and went up to at least 20,000 feet. The group formed up underneath the clouds and climbed through soup with the flights in trail. The only person in the squadron who was flying instruments was Major Stephen Andrew, the squadron operations officer. He was leading the squadron that day. When we topped the clouds, the flights spread out a little bit, and we crossed out over the Channel at Lowestoft.

When we were about halfway across the Channel, my

wingman, Blue-4, called and said he had to abort. Blue Flight was then a three-ship flight and I was the 486th Fighter Squadron's tail-end Charlie.

We crossed into Holland at Haarlem and flew on to the rendezvous point without incident, located the bomber stream, and identified our bomber group by the symbol on the bombers' tails. They were at about 25,000 feet, heading toward the target. This particular group of six or eight bomber boxes was just a small part of the day's bomber stream.

As we relieved the previous escort group, we spread the flights out over the bombers, doing S-turns to match speed with them. We were flying two or three miles to every mile the bombers were flying. At the distance we were from Bodney and at the rate we were consuming fuel S-turning over the bombers, we expected to stay on escort station for only thirty-five or forty minutes, at which time we would be relieved by another fighter group.

I later learned that Luftwaffe fighters had been attacking elements of the bomber stream for well over an hour before our arrival, from about 0830 hours. The bomber stream was so long that it was possible for fighter pilots in one part of the stream to be completely unaware of air battles ahead or behind. Each fighter group used its own radio frequency, so we never heard from the other groups. We had not seen any signs of the battles and there was nothing going on when we assumed the escort for our part of the stream.

Though I was the third ship in a three-ship flight and did not have a wingman, I considered myself an element, so I did not fly right on Blue-1's wing. I stayed outside the lead element as if I were leading a two-ship element of my own. When the lead element essed to the left, I crossed over to its left, and when it essed right, I crossed over to its right, just as if I had been leading a complete element.

We had been essing over the bombers for about twenty minutes when someone called out a large gaggle of Jerrys. They were starting to come in on our boxes of bombers from ahead and slightly above. They reminded me of wolves attacking a flock of sheep.

We went after the Jerrys as they dove in to execute their head-on passes, but we didn't catch them before they reached the bombers. The German pilots were very brave. As they made their passes within 100 feet of the bombers, every angle into the bomber boxes—and out again—was covered by the bombers' own guns. I have no idea how the Jerrys flew through the bomber boxes without colliding with the bombers, but it was their standard tactic at the time, and they were good at it. They shot down several of the B-17s in that one pass.

As the Jerrys passed through the bombers, they wheeled around into sweeping 180-degree turns to set up beam attacks. They were all over the sky, but mostly level with the bombers. That's when we engaged them. Blue Flight bounced about thirty Me-109s and FW-190s from above as they were wheeling in for their second runs.

We attacked them randomly. Blue-1—Captain Frank Cutler—got in behind one of the Me-109s. Cutler's wingman was on Cutler's wing, but he was not checking Cutler's tail, or his own. As Cutler was getting to firing range on the Me-109, another Me-109 was lining up on Cutler. I was behind Cutler and his wingman. As luck would have it, I was in the perfect position to draw a zero-deflection bead on the Jerry closing on Cutler's element. I fired a one-second burst right up his six, from about 500 feet. It was an easy shot, and he obviously never saw me. I saw strikes all over the plane. I must have hit his engine, because he caught on fire, broke off to the right, and went down.

That plane was dead, so I forgot about it. The air was full of planes. I quickly jinked left and right to clear my own tail. Seeing that I was clear, I tried to find Cutler and his wingman, but they were not in sight.

I saw another Me-109 that I was in position to shoot at. He was about 700 feet away from me and flying from my right to my left 15 or 20 degrees to my line of flight. I banked off to my left and led him about three ship lengths. I fired and immediately saw strikes on him, in his engine and along his fuselage. His engine started smoking and he immediately peeled off toward the deck. I was right behind him.

I probably made a mistake following that Me-109 down. He was badly damaged, and there were plenty of Jerry fighters at altitude. I should have let him go so I could damage or destroy some of the others. More important, I deserted the bombers. But I wasn't thinking. There was too much going on to think things through.

It was a clear day inside Germany, with scattered cumulus clouds between 5,000 and 4,000 feet. I could see the ground from where we started down, from 20,000 feet. I was about 1,000 yards behind the Me-109, going almost straight down. I had clear visibility, and I might have been able to hit him, but I wanted to get closer to be sure.

He zapped right on down to the ground, pulled out at only twenty or thirty feet, and went through a village. He flew between houses and churches and haystacks and barns and orchards, jinking and turning so hard I could not pull a lead on him. If I had pulled deflection on him, I would have run into one of those obstacles. I had to play follow the leader until something happened. I was closing on him but still couldn't pull a lead.

It was hairy! We were twenty feet off the ground and flying at over 350 miles per hour through a huge obstacle course.

His engine was smoking, so I knew he couldn't go to full power. If he did, he was going to blow it up. Sooner or later, I'd get him.

I was about 500 yards behind him when he finally ran out of obstacles and came into a big clear space. He knew I was going to get him then, so he gave a real hard turn to the left and sucked it in. When he made the turn, his wingtip wasn't more than ten feet off the ground. I dropped my left wing and followed him. We ended up in a Lufbery—maintaining a hard, hard turn in one direction and continuously going around and around. In order to shoot at him, I had to turn inside him so I could get a deflection shot. But he was pulling it in so tight, I couldn't get my guns on him. All I could do was hold position across the circle from him. Inside the Lufbery, he was chasing me as much as I was chasing him. But neither one of us had the advantage.

The Jerry got so tight that we both had to slow to about

130 knots. I had to put about ten degrees of flaps down just to stay even with him. We started out eyeball to eyeball across the circle, but I was able to slowly increase my advantage. That was only because his engine was bad. When I finally dumped flaps to decrease my turning radius, he broke out. Maybe he had to break out because he knew his engine was going to go.

He didn't have any choice about where he was going. He just headed right for a little river and set up over it to make a belly landing. There was a little bridge in his way, and he was just lifting up to go over the bridge when I got in a last-second burst from 500 feet. I saw some strikes and then he pancaked it into the river. As I flew over him, I saw some people jumping off the bank of the river, going to rescue him. I zoomed up, shut my guns off, and did a wingover so I could take a picture of him.

Unfortunately, I still was flying right on the deck while maintaining a manifold pressure of sixty-two inches of mercury. Just as I took my pictures, my coolant popped—blew up in front of my face, all over the windshield. The loss of coolant was the death knell for a P-51's liquid-cooled in-line engine. I instinctively jammed the manual switch to open up the coolant door, which would cool the engine off a little bit.

As I started climbing, I radioed in the clear that, in all probability, I would have to bail out because I had lost my coolant. Major Steve Andrew wished me luck.

I had had no fear during the combat, which must have lasted all of five minutes. The adrenalin in my system overcame the fear. I had been so busy that I hadn't had time for fear. But after it was over, the shock hit me. It came on as a big ache in my solar plexus. I was all cramped up.

I leveled off at 10,000 feet and pulled the throttle back to 1,500 RPM, less than 200 miles per hour. I didn't want to labor the engine; I was sure it was going to quit momentarily. I decided to cruise at 10,000 feet because I thought it would be a little higher than small-arms' fire could reach and a little low for the big stuff. I knew that if anyone in the air saw me, I was a dead duck, for sure. I couldn't operate.

All I had to do to get the engine to seize up was go to full throttle.

I was just hanging in the air, flying on my outbound vector, about due west. In thirty minutes, I saw a large city—Hanover—right in front of me. As I banked left to go around to the south, the Germans began to fire their antiaircraft guns, but not at me. Way up at 25,000 or 30,000 feet I saw another P-51. The ack-ack got him—a lucky shot. The pilot bailed out and opened his parachute way up there. I would have free-fallen down to about 15,000 feet so I could get to the oxygen quicker. But he pulled his ripcord at around 25,000 feet. He must have been unconscious or dead by the time he got down to where it was possible to breathe.

I did not see any German fighters. Probably, they were all at their bases, refueling so they could attack the bombers during the withdrawal from Magdeburg. That was bad for the bombers, but it was good for me.

As I approached the Zuider Zee, I became very concerned. I was sure I wasn't going to get across the North Sea. I didn't want to bail out over the water, or land in it, but the alternative was to bail out over enemy territory, and I sure didn't want to do that. When I managed to raise the Air-Sea Rescue Service on the emergency channel, I told them I was crossing out over Haarlem in a bad airplane and that I might have to bail out over the water. If I had to give them a call, they would have their radar on me and could find me.

I let down through the soup before crossing out over the Dutch coast. When I broke through the fog, I was just above the water.

I made it. I crossed into England, where I had to dodge a few barrage balloons on the coast. The weather was very bad and the visibility was terrible, so I called Bodney's callsign and they homed me in. I flew another fifty miles and finally got the field in sight.

A normal landing involved approaching the field, zooming up, and making a tight, elliptical 360-degree turn around the field before touching down. I didn't do that for this landing because I was afraid my engine couldn't take it. I made a high, straight-in approach and set down real easy, almost a dead-stick landing. I was so glad to get home, I was shaking.

After I debriefed, I talked to the North American tech rep. He was absolutely amazed that I had been able to fly that P-51 for over two hours with hardly any coolant. He surmised that, when I opened the coolant door, I must have saved enough to make a steam coolant. This allowed me to fly as long as I didn't labor the engine.

To cap everything off, I returned to my Quonset hut and found that my seven roommates had figured I was dead or captured. They had already divided up all my belongings.

I got a few slaps on the back and I had a few drinks in the bar that night to celebrate my kills, but that was all. There was no sense of personal triumph. We were fighting a war and plenty of other pilots in the group scored that day. I did experience a brief inner glow, but that was because my success in the air had been a long time coming.

On May 8, 1944, members of the 352d Fighter Group accounted for twenty-two enemy fighters destroyed, four enemy fighters probably destroyed, and one enemy fighter damaged. The group was awarded the Presidential Unit Citation for this single day's action.

Having finally broken the ice with his two May 8 victories, Ed Heller downed another 2½ Me-109s during his regular tour. One of them—on June 21, 1944, over Brest-Litovsk, Poland—was the easternmost Eighth Air Force victory of the war to that time. Determined to gain ace status, Captain Ed Heller took two twenty-five-hour combat-tour extensions. He shot down an FW-190 and damaged another on March 2, 1945. In addition to the 5½ enemy airplanes he destroyed in the air and the fourteen he destroyed on the ground in World War II, Ed Heller was credited with 3½ aerial victories and two probables in the Korean War.

On May 9, the Eighth Air Force returned in strength to France and Belgium to pound seven Luftwaffe airdromes. By then, the date for the invasion of France—D-Day—had been firmly set for June 5 or June 6, and the various air forces based in Great

Britain were working their way down target lists designed to cripple the Luftwaffe, the German Army, and the decision-making powers of the German high command. By May 11, the Ninth Air Force target list had reached the Luftwaffe airfields within fighter range of the Normandy beaches, but that included targets in eastern Belgium, Luxembourg, and even the Saar region of far western Germany.

WITHOUT A SHOT

Captain MAURY LONG, USAAF
355th Fighter Squadron, 354th Fighter Group
Luxembourg, May 11, 1944

Maurice George Long was attending junior college in his hometown of Long Beach, California, when he decided to enlist in the Army Air Corps so he could select his branch of service. Because Long had only one year of college, he had to enter the service as a private and pass a competitive examination in order to qualify for flight school. Long signed up on July 16, 1941, but it was not until after the Japanese attack on Pearl Harbor that he was called up for Pre-Flight training at Moffett Field, California. Following Primary and Basic flight training at Cal-Aero Academy in Ontario, California, Cadet Long went on to Advanced flight training at Luke Field, Arizona, and he was commissioned there on September 29, 1942.

Lieutenant Long was first assigned to the 20th Fighter Group, a P-39 unit based at Paine Field, Washington. In mid-November 1942, the 20th was split in half to help form the new 354th Fighter Group, and Maury Long went to the

354th. After a year's training as a P-39 air-defense unit, the 354th Fighter Group personnel were shipped to England in November 1943 and the unit was equipped with new P-51B Mustangs.

I was given credit for a Junkers Ju-88 medium bomber probably shot down on our bomber-escort mission to Bremen on December 20, 1943. Then, shortly thereafter, I was assigned to the Eighth Air Force training base at Goxhill to help indoctrinate new P-51 pilots. This naturally led to a long dry spell between my first probable and my next score.

I languished at Goxhill until, on April 4, 1944, Captain Charles Gumm lost his life in the crash of his P-51 near the village of Nayland. His aircraft had engine failure. Chuck was a member of my flight and a very close friend. He had shot down the 354th's first German aircraft and was the group's first ace. The flight he was on at the time of his death was to Goxhill, to commiserate with me on my miserable assignment.

I felt so badly about the accident that I "borrowed" a P-51 from Goxhill and returned to the 354th Fighter Group's base at Boxted. I told the group commander that I was not going back to Goxhill, and I didn't. I was made the regular commander of the 355th Fighter Squadron's "A" Flight, and I was flying in that capacity on April 10, 1944, when I shot down an FW-190 near Denain, France.

On May 11, 1944, I was designated to lead the squadron for the first time because our squadron commander, Lieutenant Colonel George Bickell, was leading the group. The bombers' target that day was Saarbrücken, Germany.

The 354th Fighter Group launched fifty-two Mustangs on May 11—forty-eight primaries and four spares. On hand was the commanding general of the IX Tactical Air Command, Major General Elwood "Pete" Quesada, and a group of U.S. lawmakers he had brought to witness his pride and joy, the Pioneer Mustang Group, for the takeoff and return from a mission.

The weather was good and the launch of all fifty-two Mustangs went without a hitch. However, shortly after takeoff, Lieutenant Colonel Bickell said that he was aborting for some mechanical reason and that Captain Long would take the group lead! Imagine, if you will, this cocky, arrogant, scared-shitless captain getting *that* message!

It turned out that our course to rendezvous with the bombers was long and converging. There were 200 or 300 B-17s, and, as we converged on them from their left side, we could see them for some twenty minutes before we actually joined. Our altitude was 25,000 to 28,000 feet, and the weather at flight level was excellent.

The tops of the clouds in the target area were at about 12,000 feet. The bombers had not yet reached their IP when someone called out enemy fighters. There was a huge gaggle of a hundred or more of them high and at 12 o'clock to the bombers. When the German fighters were ready—as we raced to get into position—they suddenly started diving on the bombers from head-on. We were the only fighter group with the bombers at the moment, but our relief, another Mustang group, was racing to catch up.

The first Me-109 that I tangled with was just getting in position on the bombers. I was still lining up on him and had not yet fired when he must have seen me. He pulled in real tight and suddenly I saw pieces of cowling peel off from the underside of his engine. There was also a stream of vapor that was either coolant or oil. I would guess it all came about due to the heavy Gs he was pulling. The 109 immediately split-essed and dived nearly straight down into the overcast. I didn't follow it because the sky was full of Krauts in the vicinity of the bombers.

I climbed to rejoin the hassle and soon found another 109. Unlike the first one, this guy seemed rather disinterested in furthering Adolf's war objectives. He saw me quite early during my approach and immediately dived away. The last I saw of him he was also descending in a near-vertical dive into the overcast, but there were no pieces coming off this 109.

Due to our fuel supply, it was time to break away from the bombers and head for home. The bombers were over the target, our relief had arrived, and we had broken up the German attack. I waggled my wings and called on the radio for my flock of birds to join up. I wanted to gather as much of the group as possible in a single flight because our statistics were showing that marauding Krauts did their best to pick off single birds but generally left retiring fighter groups alone.

I believe we all returned to Boxted safely. By the time my group returned, however, my wingman was already in Operations being debriefed. Unbeknown to me, he was putting me in for two kills.

I had not even fired my guns, but I guess what my wingman had seen convinced him that I had indeed shot down those two 109s. General Quesada was still at Boxted with his VIP guests, and he was absolutely ecstatic about the results of the mission—eleven confirmed kills for the group. I was ushered into the august presence, and the general told George Bickell to write me up for a Distinguished Service Cross and he would make sure it got approved. I guess nothing was ever written up, because that is exactly what I got—nothing. But I did get official credit for the first 109 even though I had not actually fired at it. It was coming apart and losing oil or coolant when last seen, and that counted as a kill.

Shortly after the May 11 bomber-escort mission, the 354th Fighter Group was returned to the full operational control of the IX Tactical Air Command, and it began flying tactical missions aimed at softening the way for the impending invasion of France. Captain Maury Long downed another Me-109 on June 14, 1944, while on a dive-bombing mission to Amiens, France. On August 25, 1944, over Rethel, France, Long downed a pair of FW-190s and shared credit for an Me-109.

Following a tour in which he amassed over 250 combat hours, Maury Long returned home in the autumn of 1944. He

remained in the service after the war, flew combat in Korea,
and retired from the Air Force as a colonel.

By the middle of May 1944, the huge and growing Allied air
forces in western and southern Europe had achieved air superiority. The Luftwaffe and other Axis air forces remained forces to
be reckoned with in certain regions or under certain circumstances that demanded or favored strong defensive measures,
but the air belonged to the Allied air forces. Where they went
and when they flew had become largely a matter of conve-
nience.

THE HUNTER

1st Lieutenant DAVE THWAITES, USAAF
361st Fighter Squadron, 356th Fighter Group
Brunswick, Germany, May 19, 1944

David Franklin Thwaites enlisted in the U.S. Army Air Corps
on September 15, 1939, only two months after graduating
from high school in his native Conshohocken, Pennsylvania.
By taking required mathematics courses at night school, he
qualified for communications school in 1941. There, a pilot
who befriended Thwaites urged the young enlisted man to
apply for flight school, and Thwaites passed the test. He
earned his wings at Luke Field, Arizona, on July 28, 1943,
and was posted to Tallahassee, Florida, to train in P-47s.
Lieutenant Thwaites reached England as a replacement pilot
in December 1943 and was assigned to the 356th Fighter
Group. He flew his first combat mission over Occupied
Europe on December 31, 1943.

Thwaites's first score was a half share in a Ju-88 twin-engine bomber over Cambrai, in northern France, on January 21, 1944. On February 13, he destroyed an FW-190 southwest of Paris, and he received credit for another Fw-190 in a high-altitude air battle over Hamburg, Germany, on May 13, 1944.

The mission on May 19, 1944, was, as usual, a bomber escort. Getting up, eating breakfast, riding our bikes to the squadron operations hut, finding the position we would be flying, and trucking over to the 356th Fighter Group operations hut was much the same as before any other mission. After filing into the group briefing room, we viewed the tracks of the bombers we would be escorting. It looked like it was going to be an exciting mission because we would be escorting B-24s to Brunswick, Germany. It is possible that the Brunswick raid that day was a diversion because, at about the same time, Berlin also was to be bombed. Most of us were still fired up from our action during a raid against Berlin on May 13. Then, the 356th Fighter Group had broken up three gaggles of enemy aircraft in the Kiel area, destroying six, probably destroying two, and damaging seven with only one loss. On May 13, we had prevented the Germans from even engaging the bombers. Today's raid looked like it might provide the same type of action. I would be flying as the Blue Flight element leader.

Going out on a mission was no guaranty of action. I had scored two and a half victories before May 19, 1944, but I had seen enemy aircraft on only one other mission—on March 6, when my flight commander shot down an Me-109. I used to get pretty mad when I was not on a mission and the group ran into the enemy. But those were the breaks. We had twenty-five pilots in the squadron, but normally only sixteen went on each mission, and even one less when the group commander or group operations officer flew with us. I was one who wanted to go out and *hunt* the Germans, but our mission required us to stay with the bombers so the enemy could not attack them. Some fighter groups, like the 56th, flew double groups, which allowed them to do a little hunting while flying bomber-escort missions. However, the 356th Fighter Group was never allowed to do that.

The bombers typically numbered in the hundreds. They were also based in our area of East Anglia; we could see them forming up for hours before we took off. The bomber formations were huge, miles and miles long. There were usually several fighter groups with the bomber formation at once, high and low and in different places. Each escort group was normally relieved by another group, but that sometimes occurred later than scheduled. We usually spent much more time getting to the bombers and coming home than we spent *with* the bombers. On the May 19 mission, for example, we were probably scheduled for thirty to forty-five minutes at the most with the bombers. If the enemy attacked during the escort relief, then we would be low on fuel and might not be able to defend the bombers for long, or even defend them at all. Everything depended on fuel.

On these missions, the fighter pilot's biggest problems were a sore butt from being strapped in a hard seat for four to five hours at a time, and difficulties involved with using the relief tube. To accomplish the latter, one had to completely unfasten the safety belt, shoulder harness, and parachute. At altitude, it took forever to get yourself going. Then, someone calling bogies at 8 o'clock high had a tendency to cause you to tighten up and stop the flow!

The climb-out from Martlesham Heath on May 19 was almost pleasant because we had only a minimum of overcast to fly through. The weather was better than the briefed 4/10 cumulus from 2,500 to 10,000 feet. Visibility was good. We usually were subjected to flak when we made landfall over the Netherlands, but the fire was very light this day. For once, I didn't wonder if I would see holes magically appear in the wings and other places in my airplane. The join-up with the bombers was breathtaking, as always. There were light contrails streaming off each airplane. The bombers were a little lower than usual, flying at about 20,000 feet. My squadron, the 361st, was high on the north side of the bombers, the 360th was ahead of us and south of the bombers, and I believe the 359th was higher than us and also south of the string of bombers.

The 361st Fighter Squadron—or Chinwag, after our radio callsign—was flying at about 22,000 feet a little to the north of the bombers when three formations of enemy fighters were called in. The high ones were Me-109s, which the Germans were using as top cover for the FW-190s and other Me-109s that would be attacking the bombers from ahead in two groups of about forty aircraft each.

The enemy did not fly a recognized formation, like we did. They were just a gaggle. They never directly attacked our fighters, and they usually even stayed away from the bombers when we were nearby. Usually, when they did attack our fighters during this period of the war, they did so only with their top cover. As soon as our fighters arrived they usually headed for home in order to minimize their losses.

On May 19, one of the enemy gaggles in front of our bomber formation attacked the bombers. While our fighters were responding, these Germans made a pass at the bombers from 10 o'clock level. The 360th Fighter Squadron went after them.

Another gaggle, below us, was turning into the bombers to make an approach from about 10 o'clock to them. We were quite a distance from them, but we should have been able to catch up after we turned to the right. However, we made such a wide turn that we came in quite far behind the enemy, to the east. Once behind the Germans, we gave chase as they continued on through the bomber formation. Chinwag Leader followed them through the bombers even though he knew that we probably were going to be shot at by the bomber machine gunners.

As our leading flights were passing through the bomber formation, my wingman called me to say that he could not keep up. I slowed up to stay with him, but of course that caused me to get quite far behind the rest of the squadron. I was thus alone with my wingman when I saw that a gaggle of FW-190s was coming in head-on at the lead box of bombers. I estimate that there were twenty-five to thirty of the

FW-190s. I thought these were the same FW-190s my squadron was then chasing, so I headed toward them.

As I chased after the German gaggle, I saw a B-24 spin out of the formation. It was burning. Another B-24, still in the formation, was smoking, and a third B-24 was diving out of the formation as its crew was bailing out.

After attacking the B-24s, the 190s I was chasing turned and headed back to attack the bombers once again from head-on. By then, there were several other P-47s in my vicinity—other stragglers. Once an attack began, everything tended to spread out and it was easy to get down quickly to smaller units and individuals. The four-plane flights and two-plane elements were supposed to stay together so the wingmen could protect their leaders, but in actual practice I often found myself alone when we were involved in fighter action. I noticed then that I'd lost my wingman altogether.

I was a little higher than the German fighters and slightly above and ahead of the bombers, on their right (south) side. I pulled up slightly and did a partial split-S to get on the tails of the Germans as they approached the bombers again. I stalled during the maneuver due to my speed and the altitude. It was what we called a high-speed stall—the air is quite thin at 20,000-plus feet, and it is easy to stall while going 300 to 400 miles per hour. Anyway, I ended up just slightly above and about 350 yards behind the nearest German fighter. He turned to the right and I followed him. When I opened fire, I could see that I was getting hits on his wings and fuselage. I had a 30-degree deflection on him; I was at approximately his 5 o'clock position. I fired a short burst and saw strikes. There were no tracers in the burst; we only had tracers toward the end of our ammo to tell us when we were running out. It would have been nice to have them then as an aid, but we did have API rounds, which flared when they hit something solid. The API was belted every fifth round, so when you saw a strike it meant that four additional armor-piercing rounds were going in, not only the API round you could see.

The German dove away, so I applied full power and raced to join the small group of P-47s, which was still chasing the other German fighters. As one of the P-47s closed on the German group, one of the 190 pilots doglegged quickly out of the formation and cut throttle to get behind the P-47. This brought him directly behind the Jug. The 190 pilot immediately opened fire and got some hits.

As I caught up, I got behind the 190 and took a deflection shot from about his 7 o'clock and slightly high. My bullets hit him in the fuselage and one wing. He rolled over and dived for the clouds below us. The P-47 that had been hit looked okay, so I continued ahead to catch up with the small group of friendly fighters, which was still following the main body of FW-190s. I did not see where the damaged Jug went.

I noticed then that flying all out, at full throttle, was just keeping me even with the other 47s. I could not gain on them. From my position to the rear I observed that another attempt by several German fighters to get behind us was foiled by a lone Jug that attacked the other side of the German formation. However, the lone Jug continued to chase one of the enemy aircraft down toward the clouds. I kept at full throttle, which helped me stay above the highest enemy airplanes, and to the rear of them. I slowly pulled ahead of the other P-47s.

Suddenly, one of the FW-190s cut out to the right, as if to try and get behind us. By putting on emergency power, I was able to close on him and get a good deflection shot. (The emergency power water injection was applied by flipping a toggle switch on the throttle. The injection of water allowed much higher manifold pressure readings, but it also dramatically increased fuel consumption and the possibility of engine failure.) I got hits on both wings and the fuselage from above and behind him. Then he straightened out, which gave me an even better shot that produced more hits. With that, the 190 flipped over, the canopy flew off, and the pilot bailed out just before the ship passed under my wing.

By the time the German pilot bailed out, my extra diving speed had carried me beneath the German gaggle. With my throttle still wide open, I pulled up into the 190s, watching for an opportunity to take another crack at them.

There were only five P-47s left in our little group. Two

were rednosed 56th Fighter Group airplanes, and two were from my group's 360th Fighter Squadron. We were behind fourteen to sixteen enemy aircraft. All this time, we had been heading east, away from home. The Germans had the advantage, and I wondered why they didn't turn and fight us. The only advantage we had over the FW-190s was firepower and maybe the ability to outdive them. We had eight .50-caliber machine guns and they each had one 20mm cannon and two 7.7mm machine guns. But by then there were many more of them. I guessed they were under orders to attack the bombers and that they had left after only a couple of passes at the B-24s because of our heavy fighter support.

The Germans were leading us down toward the clouds. I fired at two more FW-190s even though they were out of range, at 500 yards or more. I nevertheless saw strikes on one of them. As these two 190s went into the clouds, which topped out at around 5,000 feet, I tried to close on another one. I used my water injection again, but I lost the Focke-Wulf in the clouds. When I popped out below the clouds, it was hazy and the visibility was considerably worse than it was above the clouds. I could not see any enemy aircraft, so I headed back up.

When I climbed up through the lower clouds, heading for home, I saw several red-nosed 56th Fighter Group P-47s, but the two Jugs from the 360th Fighter Squadron were gone by then. I guessed that the 56th Fighter Group had arrived to relieve us while we were fighting off the Germans. I couldn't speak with the 56th Fighter Group pilots to find out because each group had its own frequency. Even forty-eight planes on one frequency was too much. I was sure, however, that my group was well on its way home by then. Certainly, the time to leave the bombers had passed. I climbed to 20,000 feet and turned for home, all the while looking for more targets—or, rather, looking around to make sure that *I* wasn't a target!

We had 305 gallons of fuel in the internal tanks and, on May 19, we had 100-gallon tanks on each wing. Generally, we flew the wing tanks until they ran out because we had no gauges and no warning except a drop in fuel pressure, which, unless you were looking, was tough to catch. I kept a record of what fuel I used on each mission and compared it with other pilots who had been on the same mission. We always worried about fuel because we never knew when we would get into a fight and use fuel like crazy. We had to get all the way back to England or the war would be over for us, one way or another. If you could make the external tanks last to maximum penetration then, discounting wind effect going west, you could get home with 100 gallons if you didn't have to fight. Two hundred gallons going in, 200 going out, and 100 to fight with—an oversimplification, believe me!

I knew I was way over the norm for fuel consumption. Running a Thunderbolt at full throttle with some spurts of water injection really used up fuel. The usual rate of consumption was approximately 275 gallons per hour at full throttle, but it went well over 300 gallons per hour at war-emergency power. So, if I was going to get all the way home, I had to cut back to minimum RPM with a Manual-Lean fuel mixture.

The sky around me was completely empty of other aircraft, and I did not see anything in the air until I was crossing the Zuider Zee. There, I picked up a B-24 with a smoking engine. I escorted him to landfall in England, but he went into a cloud and I lost him. I crossed back out over the North Sea near Egmond and did one orbit to try to pick up the B-24. I could not find him, so I set course for home. The fuel light was glowing slightly when I landed at Martlesham Heath a half-hour later.

I claimed one FW-190 destroyed, which according to our squadron intelligence officer was confirmed by two different sources, someone in the 360th Fighter Squadron and someone else in the 56th Fighter Group. I also claimed three damaged FW-190s. I logged four hours and ten minutes on the mission, and fired 1,839 of my original 2,400 rounds of .50-caliber ammunition.

It was a good mission for the 356th Fighter Group. We

tallied eleven German fighters destroyed and six damaged, but we lost three pilots. Fortunately, after the war, we found out that all three of them survived as prisoners of war.

On May 25, 1944, his very next time at bat, 1st Lieutenant Dave Thwaites downed an Me-109 near Neufchâteau, France. Thwaites became the 356th Fighter Group's first ace (and its only purely P-47 ace) on August 4, 1944, when he shot down another Me-109 near Bremen. Finally, on September 5, 1944, Captain Dave Thwaites received a half credit for an He-111 medium bomber downed near Enschede, Holland. This brought his final tally to six. After Captain Thwaites returned to the United States in the fall of 1944, he trained P-47 pilots at Dover, Delaware, for the remainder of the war. The Air Force sent Thwaites to college in the mid-1950s and he earned a degree in electrical engineering. Lieutenant Colonel Dave Thwaites retired from the service in 1965 following twenty-six years of continuous service.

CHAPTER 8

There is only one fair way to measure the success of Operation POINTBLANK and its many related phases and strategies: How much opposition was the Luftwaffe able to muster over the beaches and invasion fleet when the Americans, British, and Canadians invaded Normandy on D-Day, June 6, 1944?

On D-Day itself, two German fighters appeared over the invasion beaches. Two. No German fighters rose to challenge the hundreds of fighter-escorted transport aircraft that dropped divisions of paratroopers behind the Normandy beaches, and no German airplanes—not one—got within sight of the invasion armada. On June 6, twenty-six German airplanes—fighters and light bombers—were destroyed over France by Army Air Forces fighters, but none of these came within sight of the Normandy coast. The Luftwaffe never contested the invasion in any meaningful form. On June 6, 1944, and on every day of the war that remained to be fought, operations by the Luftwaffe's tactical bomber force against the Allied armies in northwestern Europe were ineffectual nearly to the point of nonexistence.

LOW-LEVEL JEOPARDY

1st Lieutenant JIM STARNES, USAAF
505th Fighter Squadron, 339th Fighter Group
Central France, June 8, 1944

*James Roy Starnes was born on March 24, 1924, and raised
in Wilmington, North Carolina. He was a high-school senior
on December 7, 1941, but his long-standing dream of becoming an Air Corps fighter pilot was brought much closer to
reality when, in early 1942, the Army began accepting
high-school graduates for flight training. During the final
months before graduation, young Starnes spent much of his
spare time at the local airport, watching an operational
fighter group conduct training and the defense of the local
coastal area and sea lanes.*

*When Starnes finally graduated and reported for his induc-
tion physical, he was three pounds underweight. Rather than
seek a waiver, which would have taken months, he talked the
doctors into allowing him to return in a week. Starnes gorged
himself in the interim on ice cream and bananas—and
gained over five pounds in the process. He was sworn in on
July 8, 1942, but had to wait until February 3, 1943, to be
called to duty because the flight schools were full.*

*Cadet Starnes passed through Pre-Flight at Maxwell Field,
Alabama; Primary at Carlstrom Field, Florida; Basic at
Cochran Field, Georgia; and Advanced at Marianna Field,
Florida. He was commissioned on November 3, 1943, but
was nearly retained as an instructor because his commanding officer felt that, at nineteen years of age, Starnes was too
young to fly a fighter in combat. Lieutenant Starnes successfully argued his way past that hurdle by suggesting to
his superiors that instructors should be more mature than
he was.*

*Following advanced training with a P-47 replacement
training unit, Starnes volunteered for early deployment with
the 339th Fighter-Bomber Group, which was then learning to*

fly P-39s in a close-support tactical role. Two weeks after the group arrived in England on April 4, 1944, it was outfitted with P-51B Mustangs and assigned to the Eighth Air Force's 66th Fighter Wing for bomber-escort duty. The 339th Fighter Group flew its first combat mission on April 30, 1944, after the pilots had completed an average of only two check flights in their factory-new P-51s.

On May 19, 1944, on the 339th Fighter Group's first mission to Berlin, 2d Lieutenant Jim Starnes received a half-credit for an FW-190 that was downed over Güstrow, Germany. Two days later, on May 21, the entire VIII Fighter Command was sent to Europe at low level to destroy as much of the rail system as possible. On that mission, Starnes received a half-credit for a German trainer that he found near Leipzig. On May 29, Lieutenant Starnes downed an FW-190 over Stettin, Germany, during a bomber-escort mission to Poznan, Poland.

The air war in Europe became a maximum effort for our forces in support of the invasion of Normandy beaches on D-Day—June 6, 1944. On June 6 and 7, the 339th Fighter Group flew three missions per day. All were dive-bombing missions except for the first D-Day assignment, which was a patrol over the invasion fleet in the English Channel. I flew the first and third D-Day missions. The latter, my first dive-bombing missions with live bombs, went in against a small rail bridge in France. On June 7, I flew only the second mission of the day—another dive-bombing mission, this time against rail targets in France.

I received my promotion to first lieutenant on the morning of June 8. After breakfast and our mission briefing, we took off one hour before daylight on another dive-bombing mission to France. Each airplane carried two 500-pound bombs instead of the 250-pound bombs we had carried on all of our previous dive-bombing missions. I do not know why the field order for this mission called for these bombs because the P-51 flew a bit more sluggishly with the larger bombs.

Our airfield at Fowlmere, which was eight miles south of Cambridge, had no lighting, so we had to use the lights of several jeeps to help us line up with the runway. After assembly into flights of four, we climbed out on a course of about 150 degrees—southeast—to our target area, which was in the vicinity of Dreux, France. At about 1,500 feet, we entered the overcast, and I soon lost sight of my element leader. Since I was on his left wing, I went on instruments and took up a heading of 140 degrees to avoid a possible mid-air collision with other members of the flight. When I broke out on top of the clouds at 5,000 feet, it was still totally dark. I saw no other aircraft. I resumed a course of 150 degrees, continued climbing to 15,000 feet, and proceeded to the target area alone.

Each fighter group that was flying that morning had been assigned a specific rectangular area, about fifty miles wide and seventy-five miles long. Our job was to isolate the Normandy beachhead area by attacking the German lines of communication and resupply. The 339th Fighter Group's area was about 250 miles from base.

When I arrived in the group's area of responsibility, I descended to about 5,000 feet and began to search for a suitable target. Just as dawn was breaking, I spotted a steam locomotive moving through a rail yard near a small French town, and I decided to attack it. I circled once to look the area over. Using the cockpit arming switches, I armed the nose and tail fuses of my bombs. This locked the arming wires of the bombs to the bomb rack, which would allow the bombs to fall without the wires. When the wires were pulled free, small propeller-like vanes on the bomb fuses were free to spin as the bomb dropped, and that armed the fuses. I also turned on the gunsight.

Our bombing technique consisted of flying to the right of the target so that it appeared halfway out along the left wing. My bomb run was made parallel with the tracks in order to minimize the chance of hitting French civilians. As the locomotive started to disappear underneath the left wing, I rolled left and down at an angle of sixty to seventy degrees. I had to fly smoothly to keep the gunsight pipper (a dot in the center of 100-mil reticle) on the target. As my speed was increasing, I adjusted rudder trim to avoid slipping or skidding. I let the aircraft's nose rise slowly. As the target disappeared underneath the nose, I pressed the pickle button on the control stick and immediately began a hard pullout to avoid going below 1,000 feet.

I felt the concussion from the bombs as I pulled up, and I circled left to see where they had hit. I had missed the locomotive, but apparently I had cut the tracks ahead of it.

I turned on my gun switch and made two broadside strafing passes at the steam engine. I estimate that I expended thirty to forty rounds from each of my four guns on each strafing pass. In the dim dawn light, my .50-caliber API bullets really flashed brightly when they hit. The strikes caused steam to billow up. I felt relief at being rid of those heavy bombs and elation at having hit the target alone.

Radio chatter indicated that other members of the squadron were bombing targets in the same general area, but I could not see them. The chatter was excited because one pilot, Lieutenant Philip Ewing, had released his bombs too low and damaged his aircraft to the extent that he had to bail out.

After I turned northwest to return to base, I was climbing through 4,000 feet above a large patch of ground fog when I spotted an Me-109 below and several miles to my left. He was at tree-top level, barely skimming the fog bank. I shoved the power up to 2,700 RPM and fifty inches of manifold pressure and began a diving tail chase. The Me-109 continued south on the deck, unaware of my presence. He was going faster than I initially realized, and my main concern was overtaking him before I ran low on fuel. I was in range after several minutes of pursuit, but I was being buffeted by his prop wash and could not fire.

We passed over a small French village—I think it was Fougères—and it crossed my mind that the French residents were probably cheering at the sight of my P-51 on the tail of an Me-109. I pulled slightly to the right to avoid his prop wash, then I rolled back left and gave him two five-second bursts with only a few degrees of deflection. He never knew I was there until my bullets struck the fuselage and right wing root. The Me-109 fishtailed briefly and nosed down into the thin layer of ground fog. I pulled up to the right and watched as a plume of smoke boiled up through the fog.

Since I was now fifty miles farther from base and low on fuel, I did not take the time to record the smoke plume with my gun camera; I headed straight back toward England. I was really pleased with myself because I had located and shot down an Me-109 while flying alone. The trip home was uneventful and I had enough fuel left when I arrived over Fowlmere to execute a victory roll over the field before landing. Flying time on this mission was three hours and forty-five minutes, and the gun-camera film helped me get this kill confirmed.

The afternoon mission on June 8 was another Normandy beachhead-support mission. This time, the group was to attack targets of opportunity south of the Seine River, in the same general area as our morning mission. We were carrying two 250-pound bombs, and I was flying Red-2 position— wingman to our squadron commander, Major Donald Larson.

Shortly after takeoff, Larson's radio became inoperative. An inoperative radio was normally the basis for an abort, but Major Larson really hated to miss out on a combat mission. He not only remained with the squadron, he remained in the squadron lead.

The weather was clear as we descended to about 5,000 feet in the area of responsibility and began a search for suitable targets. In a few minutes, not far from the town of Rennes, we located a German truck and armor convoy of about twenty vehicles that was headed west toward the beachhead. The vehicles were well spaced and moving very slowly. About one-third of them appeared to be armored personnel carriers, but from 5,000 feet we could not be certain.

Major Larson dipped his right wing, which was the signal to go into an echelon formation. The second Red Flight element moved farther out and I crossed under to take my position on the major's right wing. Larson then fishtailed his aircraft and turned left, so we took up spacing in trail formation at about 800- to 1,000-yard intervals in a loose snakelike formation. We armed the nose and tail fuses of our bombs.

The area was typical French agricultural countryside—cleared fields interspersed with many trees and hedgerows. The road on which the convoy was traveling was not a major highway, but it was paved. It looked crooked because of the slightly rolling terrain.

We were a few miles south of the road, preparing for the attack, when I looked to the right at about the 2 o'clock position and saw we were about to be attacked by eight to ten FW-190s. They were slightly above our level and had already fanned out to pick out individual targets in our loose string formation. I called out a break to the right, jettisoned my bombs, shoved on full power, and turned into the lead FW-190, which was preparing to attack Major Larson. Because his radio was dead, the major was unaware of the attack.

The lead 190 pilot saw my intercept angle and turned to his left, toward me, nearly head-on. I was unable to turn back to the left sharply enough to fire on him. As we were making maximum-rate left circles, another FW-190 came in on my tail. Red-3—Lieutenant Bill Jaaskelainen—was on this 190's tail, another FW-190 was behind Bill, and Red-4—Lieutenant Peter McMahon—was behind him. We were all in a descending spiral to keep from stalling out in our maximum-rate turns.

Since I was using maximum power and ten degrees of flaps to assist in my turn, I was easily outturning the FW-190 ahead of me. After three or four circles, I ended up on his tail. I did not look back, but I assumed that I was outturning the 190 on my tail, or at least preventing him from drawing enough lead to hit me with his guns.

I fired intermittent bursts at the 190 in front of me. I was pulling all the lead I could without blanking him out under my nose, but most of my bullets went behind him. As we approached treetop level, however, I began to score some hits. The FW-190 was pulling wingtip streamers [condensation vortices] in his desperate low-altitude struggle. Finally, he reversed his turn, which was a fatal mistake. I hit him hard during the reversal. The pilot decided to jump out at minimum altitude, and he jettisoned his canopy and jumped over the side of his cockpit. I continued to fire at the 190 in order to record its crash on my combat film. There was no time for the pilot's chute to open, and he fell into the burning wreckage of his aircraft.

This was my fifth and most exciting encounter with enemy aircraft—a dogfight at low altitude in which neither aircraft started with a significant altitude or position advantage. The fight lasted between five and ten minutes, and I had fired so many long bursts that my guns overheated. As I pulled up to rejoin the others, a round occasionally cooked off in the gun chambers. The noise frightened me because it sounded like my aircraft was taking a hit.

Bill Jaaskelainen had shot down the 190 that had been on my tail, and Peter McMahon shot down the next one. McMahon claimed that he also had fired on my FW-190 before it crashed. Since our squadron had a generous policy of sharing credits, he was given a half-credit for the kill. Altogether, the 505th Fighter Squadron downed five FW-190s in this encounter. Our only loss was the P-51 flown by Lieutenant Joseph Sawicki. His aircraft was last seen going down smoking with an FW-190 on its tail.

Major Larson had somehow discovered the various dogfights in progress and had held off his attack on the convoy. We joined up on him and strafed the German vehicles, which had pulled off the road at various points by the time our attack began. I made only one firing pass because my ammunition was just about gone. The two 250-pound bombs from Major Larson's aircraft—he was by then the only P-51 with bombs—were not enough to cut the highway, but we did shoot up many of the trucks and armored personnel carriers.

Jim Starnes shared credit in yet another Me-109 on July 29, his first victory in a new P-51D fighter equipped with six .50-caliber machine guns, and he achieved ace status on August 4, 1944, by downing an Me-109 near Hamburg.

Though Starnes was the first member of the 505th Fighter Squadron to qualify for a return to the United States, he volunteered to extend his tour for another fifty combat hours. He did go home in October 1944 but returned to the 505th Fighter Squadron after taking only a thirty-day leave. He flew combat missions until the end of the war. His last aerial victory—the eighth German airplane he was involved in downing and his sixth aggregate victory—was an Me-109 that he destroyed in the air on March 2, 1945, near Magdeburg while escorting B-17s bound for Berlin.

When Germany surrendered, Captain Jim Starnes was twenty-one years old and had flown 113 combat missions amounting to 520 combat hours. The 339th Fighter Squadron was ordered to move to the Pacific Theater, but the war against Japan ended before it could. The group was shipped home, but, in order to remain in the service, Starnes elected to stay on occupation duty in Europe, an assignment that lasted for fourteen months and netted him a Regular Air Force commission. He flew in combat again in 1968, from bases in Vietnam and Thailand, and he retired as a colonel in November 1974 after thirty-two years on active duty.

There were German warplanes to be destroyed in the air—hundreds upon hundreds of them—but the gravest peril faced by most Eighth and Ninth Air Forces fighter pilots during early and mid-summer of 1944 was gunfire from the ground, for the use of fighters at low level to keep the German Army at bay was utterly relentless. Pilot and airplane losses in this type of air tactical warfare would have been unacceptable but for two factors—the sheer numbers of airplanes and pilots available to the fighter wings in England and the sheer scope of the losses the American day fighters inflicted upon Germany while supporting the efforts of the Allied armies in France.

EVADER

Captain JACK ILFREY, USAAF
79th Fighter Squadron, 20th Fighter Group
France, June 11–20, 1944

Jack Milton Ilfrey, a native of Houston, Texas, learned to fly with the Civilian Pilot Training program in 1939 while attending Texas A&M College. He entered the Air Corps in April 1941 and graduated from Luke Field, Arizona, five days after Pearl Harbor. Ilfrey was immediately assigned to the 94th Pursuit Squadron of the 1st Pursuit Group and learned to fly P-38 fighters while standing in defense of the California coast. In early July 1942, he was involved in the first mass flight of warplanes from the United States to England. Subsequently, he took part in the first all-American fighter sweep over northern France. In mid-November 1942, on his way from England to Tunisia to support the recent invasion of North Africa, Ilfrey ran low on fuel over the Atlantic Ocean and had to land in Portugal. Informed that he would be interned for the duration of the war, Lieutenant Ilfrey instead charmed his captors out of a tank of fuel and rejoined his squadron in the war zone.

Jack Ilfrey's first score was a shared credit on an Me-110 heavy fighter, which was downed over Tunisia on November 29, 1942. On the morning of December 2, 1942, Ilfrey shot down a pair of Me-109s over Gabès Airdrome, Tunisia. Next, he downed two FW-190s near Bizerte on December 26. On

March 3, 1943, 1st Lieutenant Jack Ilfrey became an ace when he shot down an Me-109 near El Aounia, Tunisia. After flying 208 combat hours in seventy-two missions, Ilfrey returned to the United States in April 1943 to instruct new P-38 and P-47 pilots.

Captain Ilfrey returned to Europe in April 1944 and assumed command of the 20th Fighter Group's 79th Fighter Squadron, an Eighth Air Force P-38 unit based at King's Cliffe, England. He bolstered his North Africa score by shooting down two Me-109s over Berlin on May 24, 1944. In that fight, one of the victims collided with Ilfrey's airplane and tore nearly five feet off the P-38's right wing.

All of us fighter pilots said it couldn't happen to us—"I'm too damn good to get shot down"—but deep down in our minds I think we all had a plan as to what we would do if it ever did happen.

It was ironic, the way I briefed my squadron just before takeoff late in the afternoon of June 11, 1944. I told the boys that in my opinion, if anyone was shot down in France from now on, the best thing to do would be to lay low and try to find a hiding place with some French family until the Allies moved into their section, or to possibly work up to the front lines.

Since the afternoon and evening of June 5, the 20th Fighter Group had been covering the invasion. At zero hour, 0756 hours on June 6, we had had a ringside command-performance view of the invasion. It was a sight I'll never forget. By June 11, Hitler's vaunted Atlantic Wall had been cracked wide open and a great Allied army was firmly established on the Normandy coast. The 20th Fighter Group was taken off patrol duty and assigned to dive-bomb and strafe targets behind the lines.

Our mission on June 11 was to dive-bomb the railroad bridge over the Loire River at La Possinere, not far from the city of Angers. Our P-38s were each loaded with two 1,000-pound bombs.

That day, I led sixteen ships of the 79th Fighter Squadron. We took off at 1848 hours and arrived in the target area at 2030 hours. We came in out of the west with the sun at our

215

backs and successfully dive-bombed the bridge. Our hits severed the tracks and inflicted serious damage on the bridge structure. Next, we were to strafe rail and motor traffic and any other targets of opportunity from the Loire Valley north into Normandy.

We had just reassembled at about 8,000 feet when I spied a locomotive with steam up in the village of Le Lion, just north of Angers. The Germans had become pretty wise to our attacks on the railroads and usually had several flak cars on the trains, including one right behind the engine. Therefore, in order to do a complete job of knocking out the locomotives, we planned coordinated attacks on them. The leader, as a rule, went after the engine while his wingman went after the guns on the flak car. The other planes in the squadron provided cover.

I dived down toward the engine. While I was taking aim, I caught a glimpse out of the corner of my eye at some tracer bullets coming up at me from the flak car behind the engine. Just after I opened fire on the locomotive, I saw the boiler explode. As I pulled up, my whole right engine burst into flame. Somebody yelled over the radio, "Bail out, Jack! You're on fire."

My cockpit immediately filled with smoke, which blinded and choked me. When I jettisoned my canopy, the smoke cleared. I could see that I wasn't very high above the ground. However, without any hesitation, I released my safety belt and went out over the left side, opening the parachute immediately. I had just looked up and yelled "That SOB works!" when I hit the corner of a farm house and bounced off into the yard.

So there I was. Within only one minute's time, I had experienced the sound of my P-38's guns, the roar of her engines, the smell of smoke, the touch of flames, and the rush of air as my body hurtled through space. Then I had felt the jolt of stopping in midair. Now I lay flat on the ground in enemy territory.

In a matter of seconds, I was up on my feet and determining that I was still in one piece. As I threw off my parachute harness and dinghy, I saw that the parachute canopy had fallen across the roof of the house. I didn't want it to be a beacon for the Germans, so I pulled it off and wadded it into a pile. Then I threw off my helmet, oxygen mask, goggles, Mae West, and heavy flying boots. While I was doing all this, a man with a pitchfork in his hand came out of the barn across the yard. Then three children appeared. They all stood there, just watching me. Without thinking, I asked, "Which way is north?" The man pointed. I grabbed my escape and first-aid kits, which were attached to the chute harness, and I tore off through the woods in the direction the man had pointed. By then, I could see the smoke from my crashed and burning P-38, and I could hear the ammunition cooking off. I wanted to make tracks out of the immediate vicinity, so I ran through trees and over, under, and through hedgerows until I was so exhausted I simply fell down in some tall grass. I had to urinate in the worst way, but I could not; the pucker factor was too high and I couldn't force it out.

I got out my rubberized waterproof map and determined my position to be about ten miles northwest of Angers. I was deep inside German territory. Thinking of what I had told my pilots only several hours earlier, I decided to get farther away from my airplane and try to find a place to hide. I dismissed entirely the idea of heading south and crossing the Pyrenees Mountains into Spain. This had been the accustomed route of escaping Allied airmen for several years before the invasion.

I took off my flying suit, insignia, and tie. That left me dressed in a gray sweater, a khaki shirt with open neck and no insignia, a pair of green olive-drab trousers, and GI shoes. I put all the various items from my escape and first-aid kits in my pockets and tried to relax on the grass. I had only a short wait until dusk, at which time I got out on a small country road and started walking north.

Within a few minutes, two teenage boys on bicycles approached me from the rear. One of them rode right up to me and asked in very broken English if I was the American *aviateur* who had jumped out of a Lightning a few hours earlier. I sensed that he was friendly, and I had nothing to lose, one way or another, because of the way I was dressed and the fact that I knew very little French. I told him I was the pilot. He told me that his name was Jean and his friend was Raymond. They were seventeen and nineteen years old, respectively.

Jean smiled and told me that he and Raymond had just ridden from the wreckage of my P-38, and that the Germans were in the neighborhood looking for me. He asked me to come with them to their village, where he would see about hiding me. I climbed on Jean's bicycle, but after a little while I let him ride while I pumped the pedals.

It was after dark when we got to the village of Andigne. Jean asked me to hide at the side of the road while he and Raymond went to see what might be arranged. I had already learned that Raymond's father ran a cafe and bar in the village and that Jean and his family lived next door to the cafe.

After a short wait, Jean and Raymond returned and led me to the cafe, which had living quarters upstairs. After I met Raymond's father and his sister, Odette, we all sat down over wine, bread, and a meal hastily prepared for me. Jean was the only one who spoke any English, but I could gather that the father seemed to be somewhat against my staying there because German soldiers came into the cafe from time to time. However, Odette pointed out that there were no Germans stationed in the area and that the chances of my being discovered were very remote.

Following a long discussion and much hesitation, the family agreed that I could stay until the village was liberated by the Allies from the north, an event we all knew would take place sooner or later, even though the father had heard the Germans say they were driving us back into the sea. With that, we all lifted our glasses and said "à votre santé." And then we all went to bed. I shared one with Raymond. It had been a hectic day for me, but by then I had the feeling that God was holding my hand.

When I went down to the kitchen the next morning, I was surprised to see that these people seemed to have plenty of chickens, eggs, milk, butter, and even some fresh fruit. We very seldom saw any of these items in England. However, they lacked such items as coffee, salt, and sugar. The kitchen, with its big table in the middle, served as the family living and dining area, and the rest of the downstairs was given over to the cafe. Just off the side of the kitchen was a cellar, which was well stocked with the wines they had made. There was no running water; all water had to be carried from the well in the village square, a half block away.

The whole family made every effort to please me, and they were eager to talk. The limited French I had picked up in North Africa seemed to be of no use to me. When Jean was there, we all were able to understand one another, and when he was away at school the English-French dictionary he had found was a great help in trying to talk with the girls. Besides Odette, there was another girl who came to help out in the cafe during the day. It didn't take much doing to pick up a little kitchen lingo. Whenever Odette wanted wood for the stove, she would just point to the stove. If she wanted the floor swept, she would point to the broom. Then, with the dictionary, we could make conversation out of one word or I would say one-word sentences.

My first fear of the Germans was partly overcome by watching them through the window when they passed on the road in front of the cafe. While I was never allowed into the cafe when customers were present, I once happened to be sweeping the floor when some young German soldiers came in for a drink of cool wine. I immediately started sweeping toward the back and right on into the kitchen. I prayed that the Germans hadn't noticed my casual but nonetheless hurried retreat.

The Jerries laughed a great deal and looked more like Boy Scouts than soldiers. Whenever they came in, I got a signal from Odette and dashed for the cellar. She said the enemy had never tried to take anything away from them and that they always paid for their drinks.

Odette kept me busy chopping wood, washing dishes, and sweeping floors. I even tried my hand at cooking, though more wine was served in the cafe than food. The electricity came on two or three times for five or ten minutes each day.

Whenever it did, I made a mad dash for the radio to tune in the BBC in the hope of catching the English-language news. At other times they would listen to the French-language news.

After supper, we gathered around the big table in the kitchen to drink wine and play records on an ancient Victrola. The well-used needle scratched out "Flatfoot Floogie," "Tuxedo Junction," and assorted French tunes. Scratches or no scratches, the music was good to hear. I'm sure we would have done a little dancing if there had been room in the kitchen.

These evening breaks brought a bombardment of questions about America. For example, when I told them that my father was a banker and that I had an automobile back home, they wanted to know if I was rich like the Americans they had seen in movies. I explained that I was not rich but that when I was commissioned a second lieutenant in 1941 my base pay had been $125.00 per month plus $75.00 for flight pay. By their standards, I guess I was rich. They didn't quite comprehend, either, that it had been very easy to trade in my 1937 LaSalle, which I had just then finished paying off, for a 1941 Mercury that carried a monthly payment of $27.50. No problem, I told them; the car dealers and finance companies were glad to see us.

Other villagers came into the cafe at night to discuss the war situation with the family. I was permitted to meet a few of the trustworthy villagers. After a few days, however, the family naturally became worried over the fact that word had spread around that I, an American *aviateur,* was being hidden by them. At the time, I did not realize the extent to which these wonderful people were putting themselves in jeopardy with their German overlords. In any event, I had been piecing together the news broadcasts that I was able to hear, and I had come to the conclusion that the Allies were bogged down on the Normandy front. It looked like they were going to stay put for a while. Also, the whole family was telling me what they were hearing on the French news. This, of course, was put out by the Germans, who were claiming to be driving the Allies back into the sea. In the end, I made up my mind to get up to Normandy before it became another Dunkirk.

I approached the family with my ideas. I asked if they could give me one of their bicycles and some French clothing so I could make the journey alone up to and possibly across the front lines. At first, my hosts balked. After talking things over thoroughly, it was decided that Jean could get me a French identity card from the town hall, as all Frenchmen had to be registered with the Germans. In my escape kit, I had several pictures of myself taken in civilian clothing. These would work fine on the identity card. Jean dubbed me Jacques Robert, *cultivateur* (farmer). My real age, height, and weight were given, and under Remarks he put that I had been injured in the bombings in Angers and was deaf.

Odette obligingly offered me her bicycle. After some discussion, my friends advised me to take the N162 main road north to Caen, which at the time was under siege by the British. I sat down alone and completely memorized my own set of maps and some French maps Jean had provided. I paid particular attention to learning the roads I was to take, the towns I was to pass through, and the distances interpolated into kilometers. Raymond's father and Jean and Raymond gave me many hints and pointers. By then, also, I was able to say many phrases in French—ask for food and water, get directions, greet people, and so forth.

I gave my hosts all the money in my escape kit, including American dollars, gold coins, British pounds, Belgian and French francs, German marks, Dutch guilders, and Spanish pesetas. They all laughed at my crisp, new-looking franc notes and explained that they had not seen any of those in years. In return, they provided me with a few worn franc notes and some bread coupons.

Odette composed a note in French that read something like:

To Whom It May Concern:
This boy, Jacques Robert, from Angers, is trying to get to Bayeux [which was in American hands] to see his

parents. He has been injured in a bombing raid. He is deaf and cannot speak. Please let him pass.

Dr. R. Armand.

We got up early the next morning. Before I left, Odette fixed me a good breakfast and prepared some chicken, bread and butter, and the inevitable bottle of wine. She put the food in a small canvas bag that I tied to the bicycle.

I was dressed in Raymond's black beret, pants, and coat; Odette's green shirt; and a pair of Jean's old shoes. I had nothing that would identify me as American or British. I didn't even have my dogtags, which meant that I'd have a hard time proving my identity to Allied soldiers—if I ever reached them. Jean also gave me a pocket knife and a few matches.

After much more embracing and kisses from the entire family, I departed at daybreak with many *bon voyages* echoing in my ears. As I pedaled away from the village in the cool crisp morning, it felt good to be out of doors again, and I fairly lapped up the fresh air. I longed for a cup of coffee and a cigarette. Somehow, I felt confident that all would end well.

After riding about five kilometers, I reached the main road, N162, which I was to take north. Up to this time, I had not seen anyone on the road. As I looked up and down the N162, I saw that three German trucks with soldiers were parked a short distance to the south. I was relieved I didn't have to go that way.

After riding up the road a few kilometers, I came upon a lone German truck parked beside the roadway. Literally shaking in my boots, I managed to pedal on. But just as I came alongside the truck, a German soldier jumped out and started yelling at me in German. I thought sure as hell that this was it. I was ready to surrender. But it didn't prove to be that serious. I had enough presence of mind to realize that the soldier wanted to know if I had seen the three trucks back down the road. I answered, *"Oui, Monsieur."* He got back into the truck and I continued on with renewed confidence. He was the first German I had ever seen at close range. He had spoken to me, and I hadn't died yet.

The French countryside looked very peaceful in the early morning. Some of the farms along the road were beginning to wake up. I passed through several small villages, but I didn't see much of anything along the road. Around mid-morning, I came to Chateau-Gontier, the first large town. I was impressed with the friendliness of the people who were walking or bicycling in the streets. Everyone had a *"Bonjour, Monsieur"* to say. I mostly just nodded back, hoping that the gesture was not too American. I noticed some damage along the railroad tracks, and I saw one shot-up boxcar. Passing through the town was uneventful, but I was glad to hit the countryside again.

At noon, I picked out a nice spot off the road and sat down to eat my chicken. As I was eating, several German trucks loaded with soldiers went by. The trucks were camouflaged with tree limbs and branches. After resting and drinking my wine, which did not quench my thirst, I started out again. I was going to have to find some water to drink very soon.

I spied a farmhouse off the road. A woman was working in the front yard. I rode up and asked in my best French for a drink of water. Evidently seeing that I was a traveler, she insisted on my having wine. I, however, insisted on water, so she pointed to a well and I went and got myself a drink. I hoped my typhoid shots would take care of me.

I saw many Germans and much equipment on and off the road during the afternoon. The Jerries didn't seem to bother the French people, and the French stayed away from the Germans. There were refugees on the road on bicycles and in carts. I looked just like one of them, even though most of them were going south and I was going north.

I was in fairly flat country and the going was easy. Even with the frequent rests, however, my first day on the road was getting rugged. I was making very good time down a small grade into the town of Laval when I suddenly noticed that the main road was going to pass through the outer perimeter of the local airdrome. Before I knew it, I rode right up to a sentry gate, and a German soldier stepped out to stop me. I decided it would look suspicious if I turned around, so, gathering all my wits, I rode straight up to the sentry and stopped. He spoke to me in French; I gathered that he wanted to know where I was going and had asked to see my identification.

I had to play my deaf act here because it would have been a dead giveaway if I had tried to speak French to him. I put over with hand motions that I was deaf and I showed him my identity card, which I hoped didn't look too new. He shook his head and said *"Nein,"* stepped into his booth, and punched a buzzer. I knew for sure the game was up.

A German officer appeared from a building next to the road and the two spoke in German as they came up to me. I handed the officer my note from the doctor. He read it and it seemed to satisfy him. He passed it back to me with a wave-on signal. However, the sentry was still holding my identity card. I politely reached out, took it out of his hand, and put both documents in my pocket. Though I felt faint, I was able to get back on my bicycle quickly and shove off.

I rode right through the airdrome and saw what was left of the installations. Most of the buildings and hangars had been knocked down. I took pride in the fact that I had dive-bombed this airdrome and contributed to some of the wreckage. I saw two wrecked P-38s and wondered what had happened to the pilots. There were also several of our external belly tanks laying around. In a camouflaged revetment under some trees, not over 100 feet off the road, I saw several Me-109s being warmed up, as if preparing for a flight. I pedaled slowly, looking around. In North Africa, over a year and a half earlier, I had flown an Me-109 that the Germans had left behind when we took over an airfield there. One of our crew-chief mechanics, who knew German, had carefully tuned it back to good flying condition. Over all the instruments and flying controls he had written on adhesive tape the English name of each. I took it up on a dare. When it had come time to land, I quite suddenly discovered that neither the sergeant nor I had ever mentioned or marked the flaps control. I had one hell of a time getting that little airplane back on the ground. It fleetingly occurred to me that maybe I could do it again. But these were delusions, and they left me as quickly as they had come up.

I pedaled on. I continued right through the base, went unmolested past the sentry box at the other end, and then rode on into Laval. It was in the city that I saw the first major damage inflicted by American bombers. The railroad station, rail yards, and surrounding blocks of houses were demolished. There were a lot of Germans in town, including women.

It was dark by the time I got through Laval. I knew the Germans had a curfew on French citizens from sunset to daybreak, and I was tired, hungry, and thirsty. So I started looking for a place to spend the night. I saw a barn way off by itself in the corner of a field, and I went over to it.

Inside the barn was a nice sandy dirt floor, which felt pretty good when I fell down on it. I ate the rest of my food and drank the little wine I had left, but I had to go without water. Sleep was not too far off, but I started to feel the chill. There was a two-wheel dray in the barn with a canvas top on it, so, with the little Boy Scout knife Jean had given me, I cut out the canvas top and covered up with it. "Poor Frenchman," I thought, but at least he had donated it to the Allied cause.

I slept soundly and awoke with the chickens. My legs felt stiff and sore, but otherwise I was greatly refreshed. When I pushed my bicycle out to the road, I discovered the front tire was flat. I sat down feeling disgusted and at a loss as to what to do. It wasn't long, however, before a priest came by on a bicycle. He stopped to ask if he could be of assistance. I felt safe telling him I was an American trying to make my way up through the lines. He was amazed at first, but then in good English he told me to follow him to his parish, which was about three miles up the road. He told me that he would fix my tire and give me something to eat. We both pushed our bicycles and talked all the way to his church.

A second priest at the church prepared a very good meal for me. After imbibing some tea and cognac, I felt reinvigorated. I had never been a Catholic, but these young fellows in that church, which was actually a seminary, treated me like royalty. I spent the rest of the day and night with them. Most of the seminarians spoke at least a little English, and they continually asked me all kinds of questions about the United States, or about how the war was really going. They couldn't get over the fact that I was a fighter ace.

The priests and seminarians had been hoarding things since the start of the war. For the occasion of my visit, they brought out a bottle of Early Times, a carton of Lucky Strikes, and even some good German chocolate. I can hazily remember them throwing me on a feather mattress, the likes of which I had never experienced in South Texas. The mattress folded up around me and I went off into blissful dreams, for once oblivious to the war.

Next morning, back to reality, hangover and all, the priests fed me a hearty breakfast and repaired my tire. By then, I was thinking that I might like to stay there in Utopia until the glorious Allies came through the area. But then a new priest came pedaling up the driveway. The others told me that he was very anti-American. Apparently, the Americans had bombed him out of his church and killed many of his parishioners and friends in Laval. The seminarians told me that I should get going right away. So, with my canvas bag filled once more with food—and water this time—I took off.

I pedaled on north for a while without much difficulty until I came to a barrier in the road. A German sentry asked for my identity card, looked me and my knapsack over thoroughly, and let me through. I had been told by the priests that I would probably run across these barriers and that they were nothing to be afraid of.

I reached the town of Mayenne in the early afternoon and pedaled through it without incident. I saw very little damage. The road followed a pretty little river and at a secluded spot off the road I decided to take a much-needed overall bath. I hadn't had one since before leaving England on my incomplete mission. I stripped and plunged into the cool water. It felt wonderful! While I was using some sand as a substitute for soap, I looked up and saw two French boys on the bank, staring at me. They appeared to be in their late teens or early twenties and one spoke to me, but I didn't understand what he was saying. When I started swimming toward them, the boy spoke again. When I didn't reply, he got angry and talked louder. Since I had no clothes on, I stayed down in the water, sweating out what was going to come next. Finally, I got the idea that they wanted to know what I was doing there. It came to the point where I had to talk or do something. So, with gestures and a few words in French I told them I was deaf. I climbed out and brushed the water off me. I was going to have to put my clothes on over my wet body.

The boy who had been doing all the talking tossed me a rag he had and gave me a friendly smile. I felt relieved, so I reached into my bag and pulled out the food and the few remaining cigarettes the priests had given me. I offered them to the boys. They both immediately took a cigarette and, while I was putting on my clothes, they tried to engage me in conversation through gestures. I was now convinced that they were good boys, so I told them in my best French that I was an American aviator on my way to rejoin the Allies. This brought on exclamations of surprise, and the one who had done all the previous talking burst out in almost perfect English, "Why didn't you tell us? You had us fooled. We thought you might just be up to no good and we were only interested in seeing that you didn't get too far on our property and steal something from us."

They invited me to their home. Upon our arrival there, they opened a bottle of Calvados. The two boys were brothers. The older one, who spoke fair English, had been to Canada and the United States before the war to visit relatives and friends. We seemed to have a lot in common and talked about everything. They thought my plan was a good one, but they wanted me to stay with them for a while. I gratefully accepted their offer of food and a bed for the night.

We arose early the next morning and, even though I had a Calvados headache, my confidence and morale were way up.

Then I bade farewell to my friends on the little farm by the river near Ambrieres.

Now I began to hit the hilly, rolling countryside of Normandy and, oh, how I did cuss those hills! If I pushed that bicycle up a hill once, I did it a thousand times, each time falling on it and coasting swiftly to the bottom of the next hill. Then I had to start over again. All of my previous thoughts of a bicycle trip through Europe were now leaving my head, but I was thankful that I did have my *bicyclette*.

All in all, I did pretty well that day. During the mid-morning, I sort of played tag with a convoy of six trucks full of Nazi youths, none of whom appeared to be over seventeen or eighteen years old. The trucks were moving slowly and stopped often. Once, after we had passed each other three or four times, a soldier in one of the trucks motioned for me to hang on if I wanted to. I was so tired that I did. The Germans said nothing to me, but they were all laughing and talking, just like any group of teenagers anywhere.

We had covered only a few miles when a flight of six P-38s appeared. Brother, did those Germans stop and get out of the truck in a hurry! I pedaled for all I was worth. The Lightnings spotted the trucks despite the fact that the vehicles were highly camouflaged with leaves and branches. As I watched, the fighters echeloned for attack.

I got up to the top of the next hill and watched the fighters strafe the hell out of the trucks. It was a very exhilarating experience for me and I felt like jumping up and down, clapping and screaming approval. The P-38s set all of the trucks on fire. It occurred to me then that I was out of a lift.

This part of France was beautiful. The road was still following a river, and there were only occasional Germans and equipment to mar the beauty of the scene. At one bend in the river, several German soldiers were bathing and shaving.

A little past the bathers, the expected finally happened. At all the places where I had stopped, everyone had said that one of my greatest dangers would be the Germans taking my bicycle away from me. As I neared Domfront, a lone German soldier walking in the opposite direction stopped me and demanded my bicycle. I put up a determined fight to keep it by telling him my mama and papa lived down the road quite a piece and I had to get there. But my getting home didn't make any difference to this Nazi. I was just about to get off the bicycle when a truck came down the road, going his way. I pointed to it, and he flagged it down and got in. I was saved again.

I went on through Domfront, which had been pretty badly damaged by Allied bombers. When I got on the other side of the town, a truckload of Germans stopped and asked me for directions to someplace I didn't know. I just pointed and they tore off. Lucky again.

Late in the afternoon, I was approaching the town of Flers, a beautiful place sitting upon a hill. Everything was pretty and green, and large open valleys were all around. I heard a large group of bombers in the distance and knew by the sound that they were B-17s. I sat down to rest and watch the show. I had not waited long before the bombers, escorted by P-38s—most likely some from my own 20th Fighter Group—flew right over Flers and bombed the railroad yards. It was a beautiful sight to me—but not to the French, I'm sure—to watch the B-17s drop their bombs. I was only several miles out of the city, sitting on a hill and looking down on the spectacle. As far away as I was, the ground trembled from the impact of the bombs.

After the planes left, the whole center of the town was a maze of dust, fire, and smoke, which rose several thousand feet into the air. There was no doubt that the bombers were supposed to have bombed only the railroad yards, but it was impossible to concentrate on so small a target from such a high altitude. Even though some of the bombs had hit the railroad yards, many had hit long or short and crashed into the buildings surrounding the yards, causing heavy destruction and fires. The streets were full of rubble, though lots of it was from previous bombings.

After pushing my bicycle over piles of rubble I was able to get back to the main road on the other side of Flers. It was time for me to start thinking again about looking for a place to stay. For several days now, I had been doing very well, and now I felt like an old hand at it. I could vaguely hear the guns on the front, and a new sort of feeling came over me. Was I really going to complete my mission at last? Even though I still had thirty miles or so left to go, hearing the guns made it seem closer.

I spotted two old ladies in a farmyard and went right up and asked for food and drink. When they hesitated, I pulled out a few of my French francs and offered to pay. I suddenly realized that in almost 200 miles of travel I had not spent a single franc. The old ladies still hesitated, so I pulled out a few bread ration coupons, and that turned the trick.

The ladies led me into the dirt-floor kitchen, in which chickens were roaming around at will, and cooked up some eggs, potatoes, and meat. I couldn't tell what kind of meat it was, but it was good. So was the wine they offered me. One of the old ladies indicated that I could sleep in the barn. I didn't know if I could trust them, but I was a light sleeper, so I figured I would hear if anything out of the ordinary took place. Hell, I slept like a log on the hay, and even the bugs in it didn't bother me until the first rooster crowed practically in my ear.

While I was washing my face and drinking some cool well water, one of the old gals came to the back door and said she had something for me to eat. It turned out to be more eggs and some sort of hot chocolate drink that was rather tasty. That did the trick, and all I had to pay was a well-worn franc note.

After breakfast, I departed the farm. My memory of the maps I had studied was beginning to fade somewhat, but I finally remembered that Conde was the largest town up from Flers. There were more refugees on the road, heading south, and German trucks and equipment were moving north. I didn't bother anyone and nobody bothered me. I reached Conde at around noon.

It took me a couple of hours to get through Conde. Or I should say "over" Conde, for most of this town was a big mass of rubble. The bombers had really done a job there. Instead of streets, there were just lanes through and between toppled buildings. Now and then there was a gaping hole where a bomb had spread the rubble. I wondered what had happened to all the people. No one was stirring; it was ghostly quiet. A few small fires were burning and smoke was coming from some of the rubble around me.

A river ran through the town. I saw dead cows and other livestock floating in the river, and a couple of bloated human bodies as well. For a moment I didn't know how I was going to get across because there were no bridges left standing. I finally found a damaged bridge whose under-structure still stretched across the river. I used this to inch my way over to the other side.

It was hard to decide which way to go, but my fighter-pilot training and combat flying had left me with a sixth sense of sorts as to direction. I instinctively knew which way to go to reach Caen. I had to carry my bicycle over long blocks of knocked-out buildings and strewn rubble, but I gradually worked out toward Conde's residential section, which was not so heavily damaged. The streets there were passable. I pedaled on into open country and was able to make good time.

There were many more Germans now, and a lot of military equipment. Communications men were busy stringing wires. I pedaled and pedaled, feeling somewhat oblivious to the war going on around me. In the late afternoon, as I approached Thury-Harcourt, I began to see large guns in position in the fields. All of them were expertly camouflaged.

At this point, I became undecided as to whether I should continue on to Caen. It was not very far off, but I didn't know who held it—British, Americans, or Germans. So I turned northwest toward Bayeux and decided to rely on my note from the doctor. I knew that earlier at least Bayeux had been in American hands.

In a roundabout way, and again relying on my instinct for direction, I pedaled into the village of Erecy. Dead cows and horses were lying around and I could hear the whiz and explosions of shells from Allied long-range guns. I still

231

didn't know whether I was in front of American or British troops. While I was resting at the well in the village square, drinking and filling my bottle with water, a young boy came up and asked me a question I didn't understand. He repeated the question and I caught something about my being a stranger and where was I going. I replied, "Bayeux." He started shaking his head no. I caught the words "Yanks" and "Tommys."

Erecy was still in German hands. Several Frenchmen were standing around looking unconcerned, and the kid seemed just as detached as the others, but I took a chance and told him I was hungry. He asked me to follow him to his house, which was on the outskirts of the village. His mother and sister made me welcome and the first thing they did was to show me American and British flags. I gathered from what I could make out from the conversation that they were preparing for the liberation by the Allies and were very much enthused. When I told them I was an American *aviateur* there was much embracing and kissing in the good old French manner. It developed that the mother had lived in Maryland, right out of Baltimore, for several years before the war. She spoke fairly good English.

The daughter brought out wine and, in addition to the usual eggs, she fixed cabbage, something that resembled sweet potatoes, and some goat meat. We had a liberation celebration that night, although we had to keep quiet as we didn't want to arouse the suspicions of the Germans. Friends came by, mostly young people around the age of the girl and myself, and it was interesting to talk with them, mostly through the mother. I learned how the Occupation had been, that everything had been in short supply, and what they thought of the Germans. I'm sure the mother didn't translate all the cuss words.

We could hear the whine of the shells before they hit. The noise didn't seem to bother these Frenchmen, but it sure bothered the hell out of me. One man reported that Caen had been under terrific siege and that there was very bad destruction there. But he also said the city might be in

British hands. He thought the Americans held Bayeux and that the only thing holding up the Allied advance were the Jerry big guns. Everyone seemed to think that if I just went up the road I would eventually make contact with the British or possibly even the Americans. The mother didn't translate what they thought my odds were of making it.

Around 10 P.M. they prepared to retire. The mother said I could sleep with the boy but that we should all keep our clothes and shoes on in case we had to make a hasty exit. Some sleep! About the time I'd doze off, the big guns would start firing and I'd keep listening for the one with my name on it. Daybreak came none too soon and I felt better only after I splashed cold water on my face. The mother made some hoarded coffee and liberally fortified mine with Calvados. That put a charge in my stomach and confidence in my mind.

The way out of the village was a narrow, winding road bordered by hedgerows and trees. It was filled with branches and leaves that the shells had knocked off the trees. Shells from both Allied and German guns were whizzing by over my head. So, this is no-man's land, I thought. It was a most uncomfortable feeling. The riding was hard. In fact, I was doing more pushing than riding.

Shortly before I reached Fontenay, I ran head-on into two young German soldiers who were carrying a wounded comrade. Their eyes lighted on my bicycle and I could see the "mama-papa" act wouldn't work. When they demanded the bike to put the wounded boy on, I got off and let them have it at once. Before letting me leave, one of them frisked me thoroughly and came out with the knife Jean had given me. He also put one hand inside my shirt, at the neck, and felt under my arms. If I had been wearing my dog tags he most certainly would have found them and my game would have been up. At *best*, I would have become a prisoner of war.

I walked on toward Fontenay. There were quite a few Germans on the roads and in the fields, all in camouflaged helmets. I noticed few vehicles and self-propelled guns, and

I realized that this must be part of a rear-guard action. Surely I couldn't be far from my objective. I walked on into the village, which seemed strangely quiet.

Some damage was evident, but it all appeared to be from small arms and field artillery shells instead of the bomb damage I had seen in other towns. German soldiers were milling around in the town square, working on various pieces of equipment. Others were catnapping. I saw two soldiers trying to get an American jeep started. A few Frenchmen were also milling around, but the Germans didn't pay any attention to them or to me. I did not hesitate; I kept walking north through the outskirts of the town and into open country.

I walked on a mile or so and came to a point where the trees stopped and the road ran through a clearing. As I was just about to step out into the clearing, I heard voices over to my left and saw some Germans in the tall grass right at the edge of the clearing. They were yelling at me and motioning for me to get down. I promptly fell to the ground. One of the soldiers crawled over my way and motioned for me to follow him back into the grass. I crawled a few yards and came up to a group of them lying around beside fighting holes. Several near me started asking questions in German, which, of course, I didn't understand. I couldn't pull my deaf act with the shells going overhead and hitting the ground every now and then. I was flinching, and they could see that I could hear.

One of the soldiers asked me in English if I spoke English, and I put on my dumbest I-don't-understand-a-word-you're-saying face. Thank God, no one spoke French to me. We lay there for a while, until one of the soldiers near me was hit in the leg and stomach with shrapnel. Other soldiers motioned to me, and I readily caught on that they wanted me to put the wounded soldier in a wheelbarrow that was in the ditch by the road and wheel him to a first-aid station I had seen back on the road just after leaving Fontenay. I dragged the wounded German through the grass, put him in the wheelbarrow, and started wheeling. The job was easy at first, but it soon proved to be hard labor. The wounded kid didn't seem to be over seventeen. He was in great pain and sobbed frequently. I felt sorry for him and looked to see if he had any medications on him to ease the pain—or cyanide, maybe, so I could completely get rid of him.

I struggled on with the wheelbarrow and was finally able to deposit the boy in front of the first-aid station. Some medical men came out and took him, and I turned to walk back into the village. When someone at the aid station yelled "Hey!" I froze in my tracks. I turned around and saw a medic motioning for me to come back. When I got up to him, he gave me the surprise of my life—two cigarettes and some kind of candy bar. I thanked him in my best French, bowed out, and took off walking toward the village square. I certainly didn't want to retrace my steps to the clearing with the German soldiers in it.

I was at a loss as to what to do next. I had that feeling—so near, yet so far. I was off my memorized track, but I knew that Bayeux could not be far. When I reached the square, I turned west and walked on out of town without incident. Not too far along, I saw two teenage boys standing by a gate leading up to a farm house. They had a horse and plow, so I figured they had been working in the field and were now just resting. They eyed me as I came up the road, and I eyed them back. As I came alongside, they gave me a friendly greeting, *"Bonjour, Monsieur."* I took a chance and said *"Allemands?"*—Germans? They pointed to the northeast. I said *"Américain?"* To this, they pointed northwest. Naturally, my accent put very curious expressions on their faces.

When I told them that I was an American *aviateur,* they gasped, but then they came on with broad grins. I tried to put over what I was trying to do, and they caught on. One got a stick and scraped a sketch on the dirt to show me where we were just outside of Fontenay. He drew a line to the west and said, "Tilly." And he showed me where, just before I would get there, a small dirt road branched north to where the British were entrenched—less than a mile up the road. I gave the boys a few francs and started off, following their directions. I wished I had had a few more slugs of Calvados.

The country was beginning to open up. There were not as many trees, and across open fields I could see farther into the distance. I saw several large gun emplacements, but very few soldiers. Several Spitfires came over low, probably looking for targets to strafe. I saw German fire hit one, and it went off smoking to the north.

At the intersection of the road where I was to turn were several knocked-out British tanks and trucks. Some had been knocked out by guns, but a few up the dirt road appeared to have been wrecked by mines. I turned to the north, as directed by the boys, and started along the narrow open road, watching carefully for mines. I have often thought how funny I must have looked—a poor, dumb French farmer out on this road, jumping over some places and sidestepping others—but I had to be careful where I placed each foot.

About a quarter-mile along the road, I approached an intersection of hedgerows. I heard a British voice exclaim, "What the bloody hell is a French civilian doing out there?" I looked up and saw good old British helmets.

As I hit the intersection, one of the Brits yelled at me in French. I yelled back, "Sorry, Tommy, I don't speak French." He looked surprised, took a tighter grip on his rifle, and said, "Don't pull that stuff around here." He motioned with his rifle for me to get over to him. I hurriedly explained that I was an American pilot who had been shot down and had been working my way out of enemy territory. His look was pure "Oh yeah." He didn't believe a word of it. I asked him to call his sergeant or whomever was in charge as I wanted to be taken back to the headquarters of this outfit.

A sergeant did appear. The Tommy gave him a brief explanation and he kept his rifle on me as we walked several hundred yards back to a tank. There, the sergeant ordered several soldiers to strip-search me while he climbed into the turret to use the radio.

It was a cold day in Normandy to be standing there without a stitch on. One of the soldiers threw me a greatcoat and another handed me a tin cup of delicious hot tea. I started to sweat when I realized that I might be in for a procto search. The sergeant got out of the tank and was briefed on my body search while I put my clothes back on. Then we got in a jeep and drove several miles to a large headquarters house.

I was taken into a large room to meet several serious-looking officers. One was a British colonel and another was an American major. They seemed quite upset that I didn't have identification except for my forged French identity card, but they agreed that the picture on it was of me. My being an evader seemed to present them with a new and difficult problem. The American major asked all sorts of questions in an attempt to establish me as an American. It turned out that he was both a fellow Texan and a fellow Aggie. After I answered a few questions that only a Texan and an Aggie could answer, the major burst out, "My God! He's got to be an American!" With that, the rest of the group burst out laughing and a bottle of scotch was produced. Over drinks, they all shook my hand, slapped me on the back, and repeated, "Good show. Good show."

Soon, the major drove me to a newly established P-47 field. Luck was with me again as I knew some of the pilots. After they tired themselves out laughing at my story and costume, they arranged a flight for me on a casualty-evacuation plane that was going back to England. We deposited the wounded at a base in England and the pilots were good enough to fly me back to King's Cliffe. I was a mild sensation when I walked into our operations office dressed as Jacques Robert.

Captain Jack Ilfrey resumed flight operations shortly after returning to England and, soon thereafter, the 20th Fighter Group transitioned to P-51 Mustang fighters. On November 20, 1944, Ilfrey's wingman made a forced landing in enemy-occupied Belgium. Ilfrey landed his P-51 in an open field, picked up the stranded pilot, and flew him to nearby Brussels.

In all, in his two combat tours, Jack Ilfrey flew 528 combat hours in 142 combat missions. Along the way, he destroyed

7½ German fighters and rescued a downed pilot. He left the service at the end of the war after serving briefly in a Stateside assignment.

JUMPED

1st Lieutenant DICK ASBURY, USAAF
382d Fighter Squadron, 363d Fighter Group
Falaise, France, July 18, 1944

Richard Woodward Asbury was born on September 24, 1920, at Prince Frederick, Maryland, and he was raised on a tobacco farm on the Patuxent River in Calvert County, Maryland. After completing high school in 1937, Asbury worked as a carpenter and civil servant until he enlisted in the Army Air Forces as an aviation cadet in April 1942. He was called to active duty that summer and he earned his wings at Marianna, Florida, on May 28, 1943. During his training as a fighter pilot, Asbury excelled in aerial gunnery and usually outscored his gunnery instructor. He trained as a P-39 pilot in California and Nevada and was subsequently assigned to the new 363d Fighter Group, which was being formed at Santa Rosa, California. Lieutenant Asbury left the United States with the 363d Fighter Group and arrived in England in early December 1943. At that time, the group was outfitted with the new P-51B Mustang.

The 363d Fighter Group, only the third of its kind to arrive in England, was based at Rivenhall, in Essex, as part of the Ninth Air Force, but it spent its first months in the war zone on loan to the Eighth Air Force for bomber-escort duty. Between missions over Europe, the group learned fighter-

*bomber tactics. As D-Day drew near, the group was trans-
ferred to the 100th Fighter Wing, a unit of the Ninth Air
Force's new XIX Tactical Air Command. It was then assigned
to conduct dive-bombing and fighter-sweep missions over
France. On the night of June 5–6, 1944, the group escorted
paratroop-laden transports over Normandy. On June 25, in a
running fight southeast of Le Havre, France, Lieutenant Dick
Asbury and another pilot from the 382d Fighter Squadron
teamed up to destroy an FW-190. Asbury also was given
credit that day for damaging an Me-109.*

*On July 4, 1944, the entire 363d Fighter Group moved to
the former Luftwaffe airdrome at Maupertus, France, on the
Cherbourg Peninsula. Even before the freshly captured
German base could be cleared of wrecked German aircraft
and the bodies of German servicemen, the 363d Fighter
Group began mounting close-support missions and fighter
sweeps from the grass runway.*

As I lifted off the runway at Maupertus at 0855 hours on
July 18, 1944, I was closing in on 200 hours of combat flying
time. It was my fifty-first combat mission. The bulk of my
previous missions, thirty-four, had been bomber-escort
missions on which our group and squadron leaders ruled
with an iron hand, demanding that we stay with the
bombers at all costs. I had seen enemy aircraft on numerous
occasions, but they could not be engaged because of our
orders to "stay with the bombers." In fact, prior to our move
to Maupertus, the 382d Fighter Squadron had had only five
confirmed kills to its credit.

July 18 was a rather dreary morning, with broken overcast
layered from 3,000 feet on up. However, there was a forecast
of better weather to the east, on our course.

Our mission comprised two four-plane flights led by 1st
Lieutenant Bob McGee, who had scored the squadron's first
confirmed victory on April 13. I was leading White Flight,
which was composed of the usual four ships—myself; my
wingman, Lieutenant Carleton Palmer; my element leader,
Lieutenant Bill Bullard; with his wingman, Lieutenant Ed

Pawlak. We flew in two loose fingertip formations, mine to the left of and on line with McGee's. Our mission was to conduct a fighter sweep in order to maintain control of the air and generally protect our ground forces in the area between Falaise and Argentan.

After takeoff, we set a southeasterly course and climbed up as the weather permitted. On the way up, we encountered a number of bogies to the north of us, but they turned out to be P-47s, probably on the way out to conduct a mission of their own. We soon lost sight of them.

Very soon after leveling off at 7,500 to 8,500 feet, the silence was broken by an excited voice—I have no idea whose—calling "Break!" At the same instant, I spotted perhaps twelve Me-109s close behind me, directly at my 6 o'clock. It seemed to me that the German fighters had dropped out of the clouds behind us and were on their attack run. My surmise was correct. They were closing on us rapidly with the excess speed they had built up in their descent. By the time I saw the squadron behind me, they already were firing at us. They were close enough for me to see puffs of smoke coming off their guns.

I broke to the left with my wingman, Carleton Palmer. At the same moment, Bill Bullard broke to the right with Ed Pawlak. Instantly, the battle became a melee; every friend and foe had enemy fighters on its tail. I started a tight circle to the left that soon went from level to half vertical. The 109 pilot on my tail was very good; he stayed with me through several circles, perhaps as many as four. As I went around, every time I crossed another 109 in range in front of me, I fired. I saw definite strikes on two of them, but I was unable to see the results because I had to keep circling. The guy on my tail was still there, trying to get into position to fire at me. I had to shake him. Finally, I decided to pull the circle as tight as I could; I was willing to spin out if I had to.

I pushed the throttle and prop pitch full forward, pulled the nose up quickly to bleed off a little speed, and simultaneously rolled to the left. I also lowered about twenty degrees of flaps. The use of the flaps decreased the airplane's stalling speed and thus allowed greater maneuverability at lower speeds. By increasing the lift over the wings in this manner, I was able to complete a much tighter turn where otherwise I might have spun out. Flaps could be used this way only momentarily, but I had become fairly proficient at this maneuver. I had a lot of confidence in the P-51. As long as I kept the air flowing over the wings, it would fly for me. *Queenie II* was a great airplane, and she didn't let me down.

By applying the stick and rudder, I pulled the airplane around so quickly that the 109 on my tail could not stay with me. In fact, I immediately wound up on its tail. As soon as the enemy pilot saw what was happening, he reversed his turn and split-essed—turned upside down and headed for the deck—as fast as he could. As the 109 dived away, I followed. I finally closed to within firing range on him at low altitude and pulled the trigger. Lo and behold, only one of my four .50-caliber machine guns would fire—the outboard gun in my right wing. All the others must have jammed when I was firing them in my tight turns above, because of the high G forces. It was a common problem in the P-51B.

I moved my gunsight to the 109's left wingtip and fired again. The recoil of the one gun kicked my airplane to the right slightly, but the motion allowed my bullets to go from wingtip to wingtip. After the first burst, the German pilot did nothing more to evade me. This leads me to conclude that I wounded him. I fired twice more, dragging the bullets from my one gun from the left wingtip to the right wingtip both times. During the last burst, the 109's engine erupted with black smoke and appeared to stop. By this time we were at low altitude, so the German pilot headed to a little field and crash landed into it. He plowed a furrow and stopped, then the whole airplane erupted in flames. I did not see the pilot get out of the airplane. After several passes over the spot, I turned west and climbed back toward the air battle.

More 109s had joined the fight by then. We later ascertained that we were engaged with fighters from *Jagdgeschweder* 3 and *Jagdgeschweder* 52. On the way back up, I encountered several more Me-109s. When I saw that a P-51 was mixing it up with them, I began chasing two of them, but I was unable to score again. The other P-51 pilot, Bob McGee, shot two of them down. One crashed and the pilot of the other bailed out at low altitude.

All of a sudden, it was over. The enemy disappeared—gone. I was wet with sweat but relieved. It seemed like I had been fighting all morning, but the battle had lasted only a short time, from 0915 until 0935. I returned to Maupertus with Bob McGee. We landed and taxied up to grinning ground crewmen, who could see that the protective tapes had been shot away from our gun barrels.

When Bob and I reported to the group intelligence officer for our debriefing, I was relieved to see that all our pilots were back on the ground except Bill Bullard, who we later learned had crash landed and been taken prisoner. Our eight P-51s definitely had destroyed ten Me-109s, plus another that could not be confirmed.

Following a complete combat tour with the 363d Fighter Group, Captain Dick Asbury took advantage of some deserved home leave, but he returned to Europe for the last phase of the war. On April 7, 1945, while flying with the 354th Fighter Group's 356th Fighter Squadron, Captain Asbury downed a long-nosed FW-190 over Bad Frankenhausen, Germany. Next, on April 14, Asbury shot down one Me-109 and one FW-190 in the vicinity of Gusten, Germany. He achieved ace status the next day, April 15, when he and another pilot from the 356th Fighter Squadron downed an He-111 medium bomber just to the east of Bayreuth.

Captain Dick Asbury left the service at the close of World War II, but he requested reinstatement in mid-1950 in order to take part in the Korean War. In Korea, he flew combat missions in P-51 Mustangs while serving as a tactical advisor with the Republic of Korea Air Force. In Vietnam, Lieutenant Colonel Dick Asbury again saw combat, this time as an air liaison officer with the Republic of Korea Capitol Division and as a senior forward air controller with the South Viet-

namese 22d Division. He also commanded Pleiku Air Base. Lieutenant Colonel Dick Asbury retired from the Air Force in 1972.

TWO MISSIONS, TWO FRIENDS

Flight Officer BRUCE CARR, USAAF
353d Fighter Squadron, 354th Fighter Group
Reims, France, August 9, 1944

Bruce Ward Carr was born on January 28, 1924, in Union Springs, New York. He enlisted in the U.S. Army Air Forces in Syracuse in August 1942 and was called to active duty on September 2. Already a commanding six feet, four inches tall, young Carr was appointed a cadet lieutenant when his class, 43-H, was assembled at Maxwell Field, Alabama. Before long, Carr tired of the make-work aspects of military discipline and was relieved of his leadership duties due to his "attitude." Offsetting Carr's outlook on military life, however, was the fact that he was an accomplished, natural pilot long before he reached the Air Forces. By sheer luck, Carr's instructor at Primary Flight School turned out to be the man who had taught him to fly at home. Thus, while Carr's classmates struggled merely to keep themselves aloft and alive, Carr surreptitiously spent his time at Primary polishing his advanced aerobatics skills. Then, thanks to a good word from his old instructor to his new one, also a civilian, Carr did the same through Basic flight training. And after only a few days at Advanced flight training, Carr and several other highly skilled cadets were assigned to an ad hoc group of five recently returned combat pilots to learn to fly P-40 fighters. After six weeks of daily combat-type flying, Carr was returned to his class in time to pin on his silver wings in September 1943. By then, young Carr had logged just over 243 hours of military flight time. His initial brush with authority, however, resulted in his being ranked a warrant flight officer rather than a commissioned second lieutenant.

Flight Officer Carr's first combat assignment was with the 363d Fighter Group, an inexperienced and scoreless P-51 unit he joined in England as a replacement in November 1943. Carr scored the 380th Fighter Squadron's first kill, an Me-109, during the mission to Berlin on March 8, 1944, but he had become rather vocal by then in expressing his feelings that the group was not being aggressively led. It was eventually agreed by all to part company, and Flight Officer Carr was reassigned to the 354th "Pioneer Mustang" Fighter Group, which by then had a sterling war record and numerous aces on its rolls. Carr was assigned to the 353d Fighter Squadron, where his exceptional skills as an aviator soon came to the notice of his superiors. Unfortunately, that translated into his invariably flying wing position on the squadron leader, and he thus had few opportunities to take on German aircraft. Carr's only score during his first months with the 354th was an Me-109 he probably downed during a fighter melee near Caen, France, on June 14, 1944.

Less than two weeks after the invasion of France, the 354th Fighter Group moved to A-2, a dirt fighter strip located near Omaha Beach. On an afternoon tactical mission from A-2 on June 17, Carr got back into the scoring column when he shared in the downing of an FW-190 near Vire, France. By and large, however, the 354th Fighter Group spent its time looking for targets on the ground.

After a few weeks in France, our squadron commander, Major Jack Bradley, by then a 14-kill ace, went home on a thirty-day leave, and Major Glenn Eagleston, a 13½-kill ace, became the squadron commander. Glenn led us for about ten days, and then he went home on leave, too. In his place, a newly promoted major, Don Beerbower, became commander of the 353d Fighter Squadron, and Major Wally Emmer became the operations officer. Don had scored 15½ kills by then, and Wally had 14.

On August 9, a bright sunny day, Don launched the squadron on a fighter sweep over France. We made a left turn after takeoff from A-2 and climbed to about 12,000 feet on a northeast heading. About forty-five minutes into the mission, we came to the town of Reims, France, which is about 80 miles east-northeast of Paris. Our maps had a circle at Reims, which indicated the location of an airfield—Empernay.

On this mission, I was flying a P-51B in the number-two position on Don Beerbower's right wing. Whenever I flew, I was on the squadron leader's wing. I guess it was because I could see better than anyone else in the squadron. I could also fly formation upside down in a dogfight.

When we got near Reims, Don told the Blue Flight leader to take over the squadron lead while Red Flight went down to check the airfield. He pushed up the power to about forty-five inches of mercury and 2,500 RPM.

We dove at the field, which was defined by a circular track about a mile in diameter, from north to south. When we leveled off a few feet above the grass, we were going 450 miles per hour or more. I was in tight, show formation as we went across the field. I had eyes only for Don's plane at that point.

Not a shot was fired at us during this pass. After crossing over the tops of the trees that impinged on the southwestern edge of the field, Don began a gentle left-climbing turn and called the squadron. He said, "There are airplanes in the woods on the west side of the field."

Don ordered the rest of the squadron to attack the field from north to south, but he said to Red Flight, "We will attack from east to west and take the flak." By then Red-3 and Red-4 had fallen back and out of my view, and I never did see them again on that mission.

When Don and I were about 180 degrees through our 270-degree turn, I looked up and could see the other three flights in line-abreast formation, diving at the field. Then, when we had completed our 270-degree turn, Don took us back to the deck.

I was flying in a close show formation with Don. That

means that my left wing overlapped his right wing. There was not more than three or four feet from my wingtip to his fuselage, and my left wing was *maybe* a foot lower than his right wing.

About a mile and a half before we reached the eastern edge of the field, we came upon a series of poles, with steel cables strung from pole to pole. The cables sagged so low that it was unsafe to try and go under, so we hopped over and then went back to the deck. About half a mile from the field, we came to another set of poles. Don was directly lined up with one of them, so he pulled up to clear the pole.

As Don passed over the pole, he was hit by two or maybe three 20mm cannon shells. I was close enough to Don's airplane to hear the shells strike it, and I could see what they did on impact. One or maybe two of the shells struck the underside of the engine, from just behind the prop back to the supercharger. The whole underside of the engine cowling was ripped away. One shell also hit the underside of the right wing, near the leading edge and inside of the inboard gun.

Don's aircraft burst into flames from the front of the engine to back beyond the trailing edge of the wing. I know the engine quit because I had to throttle back to idle power to keep from overrunning.

Don yanked the airplane up very hard and rolled left. At about forty-five degrees, he jettisoned his bubble canopy and rolled left inverted. I rolled with him. After a second or so, he stood up in the cockpit, but he could not get all the way out because the nose of the airplane had started to drop and gravity of the falling plane was holding him in the cockpit. He hunched down and tried to jump again, with the same result. On his third try, he came out of the cockpit and hit the horizontal tail. He ended up bent double over the tail, facing aft. It was obvious that he was stunned because it was at least a second or two before he pushed himself off the tail.

At this point, I became aware of the ground and realized I was about to crash upside down! As I was rolling upright, I applied full power and back pressure to the stall point. I came as close to the ground as I ever want to be without my wheels down. I nicked the trees on the pullout. I flew home alone and landed.

I don't remember how many others we lost on that mission. As soon as everyone who was coming back had returned, Major Wally Emmer called a meeting. He announced that he was the squadron commander and that we were going out again that afternoon. Wally was the leader and, as always, I was Red-2, the leader's right wingman. The mission was another fighter sweep over France.

We flew a little way into Germany, turned northwest for awhile, and set a course for A-2. On the way home, I could see Reims off in the distance to our left. Nobody said anything about it as we passed. We were on a course that was taking us about twenty miles north and west of Paris. We had been airborne about two and a half hours. No one had said anything on the radio. We had not received any flak, and we had not seen any targets of opportunity.

As we crossed the Seine River at about 12,000 feet, four rounds of 88mm flak were fired at us. One round hit Wally Emmer's brand-new D-model Mustang square in the fuselage tank, just behind the cockpit. His airplane exploded into a great fireball and the flaming debris flew in all directions. The right wingtip passed across my airplane, between the prop and my windshield.

I applied full power, lowered the nose, and set course for A-2. I had lost two great friends, two fine pilots, two great squadron commanders on two missions and had never fired my guns.

Don Beerbower was killed at Empernay, but Wally Emmer miraculously survived the complete mid-air demolition of his airplane and was taken prisoner. Unfortunately, Emmer died in German hands on February 15, 1945, from a disease listed as myocarditis. Bruce Carr, who did not learn until 1991 that Emmer was taken alive, surmises that the Germans made no attempt to save Emmer's life once he fell ill because Emmer was Jewish.

Bruce Carr was finally commissioned as a second lieuten-

ant around the beginning of September 1944, and his combat record thereafter was meteoric. He downed three FW-190s near Frankfurt on September 12, and attained ace status on October 29 when he shot down two Me-109s near Bockingen, Germany. Following a leave, 1st Lieutenant Carr was made a regular flight commander, and between March 9 and April 15, 1945, he was credited with destroying eight German fighters and one and a half German bombers. In addition, he claimed three Me-109s destroyed on March 16, 1945, but official credit was withheld due to a malfunctioning gun camera. In all, then, Captain Bruce Carr ended the war in Europe with fifteen confirmed kills, one probable, and three unconfirmed kills.

Carr remained in the service after the war. He overcame his initial maverick image and retired from the Air Force as a colonel in 1973.

CHAPTER 9

From its inception in November 1943, the Fifteenth Air Force had made a vital contribution to the Anglo-American Combined Bomber Offensive against Axis strategic targets and, especially, to Operation POINTBLANK——the defeat of the Luftwaffe. By damaging or destroying vital industrial targets far in the "rear" of the strategic battlefield in Germany, and by tying down or destroying hundreds of German and other Axis fighters, the Fifteenth was going a long way toward defeating the Luftwaffe in particular and the Axis in general.

Unlike the other American air forces in action against Germany and Japan, the Fifteenth was a blunt instrument. Its only job was to bomb strategic targets. In its final form, its strike force consisted of seven heavy-bomber wings and one fighter wing——no air commands, no air divisions, no middle-level headquarters at all. The job was to bomb targets in southern Europe, period. After Major General Jimmy Doolittle left on January 3, 1944, to assume command of the Eighth Air Force in England, the Fifteenth Air Force was turned over to Major General Nathan Twining, a forceful leader who had earned his battle experience during the darkest days of the war in the South Pacific, in support of American forces on Guadalcanal.

After a concerted campaign that gutted Axis air power in northern Italy at the start of 1944, the Fifteenth Air Force turned its attention against Germany and her allies and slave states within reach of its bases in southern Italy. As a partner in the February 1944 Big Week campaign of Operation ARGUMENT, the Fifteenth had dealt heavy blows to the German interceptor force simply by appearing over Austria and southern Germany at vital moments. The Fifteenth had administered powerful right crosses against the Luftwaffe while the larger Eighth had delivered the heart-stopping body blows from the left. The lack of sufficient long-range fighters had not deterred the Fifteenth's bomber wings. They had gone out against Steyr and Regensburg and Gotha with confidence, and they had suffered their heavy losses in silence because the Eighth had used the opportunity and the sacrifice to defeat the Luftwaffe interceptor force and thus claim a vital and lasting victory.

When the campaign against Axis transportation targets had been announced at the end of March, the Fifteenth had hoped to be unleashed to strike with all its weight at Axis petroleum targets in southern Europe. But the air chiefs had opted for an all-out pre-invasion air campaign against transportation targets, and that obviated the petroleum campaign favored at Fifteenth Air Force headquarters. Though forced to tow the line set at Bushy Park—Tooey Spaatz's USSAFE headquarters in England—Twining and his staff noticed a way to get at the petroleum, too.

The keys to Axis oil production and distribution both lay in Ploesti, the vast complex of oilfields and refineries in south-central Romania. Ploesti had been struck from the south—from as far away as North Africa—on and off since August 1, 1943. But the periodic raids had been inconclusive. Ploesti was huge, and incapacitating its many parts would require an ongoing bombing campaign of considerable magnitude and duration. The Fifteenth Air Force had the power to incapacitate Ploesti, but its many other commitments prevented it from concentrating or sustaining that power over a long enough period of time.

Denied permission to bomb Ploesti's oil-producing facilities into submission, Fifteenth Air Force headquarters rather cannily set forth a plan whereby its bomber wings would go after the complex of railway targets that carried Ploesti's petroleum products to the Axis military forces and industries.

The first Fifteenth Air Force mission against transportation targets in and around Ploesti took place on April 5, 1944. The heavies dropped 588 tons of bombs that day. The aiming point was the local rail nexus, but most of the bombs went astray. A great deal of subsidiary damage was inflicted on storage tanks, refinery buildings, and other production facilities that stood near the railroad line.

Fortunately, the Fifteenth Air Force planners had an important ally at the top of the chain of command. On April 14, the Combined Chiefs of Staff had relinquished to General Dwight Eisenhower the direct *operational* control of all the British and American strategic air forces in Europe. On April 17, Eisenhower directed that the strategic air forces give top priority to destroying the Axis petroleum industry and its resources. In his statement, Eisenhower made it clear that he was as interested in forcing the Luftwaffe and other Axis air forces to defend the oil as he was in bringing the Axis war machine to a standstill.

Unfortunately, the relatively small Fifteenth Air Force was charged with taking on a vast array of vital targets throughout southern Europe, so it was able to visit Ploesti only once in a while. The Eighth Air Force was scheduled to attack petroleum targets on April 21, but it was grounded by bad weather. However, the Fifteenth Air Force did hit Ploesti that day, and twenty-seven Axis fighters were downed over Romania. The Me-109 plant at Weiner Neustadt, Austria, was the Fifteenth Air Force target on April 23, and another twenty-seven Axis fighters were downed along the bomber route.

SHOT DOWN

Captain FRED TRAFTON, USAAF
308th Fighter Squadron, 31st Fighter Group
Lake Balaton, Hungary, April 23, 1944

Fred Osborn Trafton, Jr., was born in New Durham, New Hampshire, on August 5, 1918. He enlisted in the U.S. Army in June 1940 and served in a field artillery unit for about ten weeks before he was accepted for Army Air Corps flight training. A week before his graduation from Primary flight training at Randolph Field, Texas, Aviation Cadet Trafton signed up for the Royal Air Force under the Eagle Squadron program. He had completed Primary and about one-fourth of Basic flight training when, on December 8, 1941, he received his discharge from the Army Air Corps. Shortly, Trafton resumed flight training at a contract school in Lancaster, California, and he graduated as a pilot officer in the RAF on March 28, 1942. Ten days later, he boarded a ship in Canada and sailed to the United Kingdom, where he received advanced training. Pilot Officer Trafton flew RAF Spitfires operationally for several months before he transferred back to the U.S. Army Air Forces as a second lieutenant on October 28, 1942.

After ferrying a P-39 ground-support fighter from England to North Africa, Trafton was assigned to the 31st Fighter Group. Flying with the 308th Fighter Squadron, Trafton took part in fighter operations over Tunisia and against a number of Mediterranean islands that came under Allied air attack in the months leading up to the invasion of Sicily. On March 22, 1944, in one of the 31st Fighter Group's last Spitfire missions, Trafton severely damaged an Me-109 near Cassino, Italy. Then, while flying a new P-51B on April 18, 1944, Trafton downed an Me-109 and damaged another over Udine, in northern Italy. He was credited with his second confirmed Me-109 and one Me-109 probable over the Ploesti oilfields on April 21, 1944. By then, Captain Fred Trafton, who was a seasoned flight commander with 148 combat missions to his credit, was nearing the end of his combat tour.

Our mission on April 23, 1944, was to escort our B-24 bombers across Hungary to the Me-109 plant at Weiner Neustadt, Austria, and then escort them all the way back to Italy. We had been told that the Weiner Neustadt plant produced a large percentage of the Luftwaffe's Me-109s.

The 31st Fighter Group's forty-eight P-51B Mustangs were to have picked up the bombers over Lake Balaton, in southwest Hungary, but when we got to the lake there were no bombers in sight and no word about when they would arrive. We therefore had to mill around over the lake, waiting.

After a while, my element leader, Yellow-3, called in to say that he was having trouble with his oxygen. He was already descending by the time he called, and he had soon dropped all the way down to about 10,000 feet with his wingman. I decided to follow them down with my wingman to give them added protection for the trip home. When I got to them, however, Yellow-3 kept turning into me instead of with me. After a few of these maneuvers, I tried to get Yellow-3 to cut me off and join up behind me and my wingman, but he kept turning into me.

As I continued to try to get my second element to join up properly, I spied a large number of Me-109s, FW-190s, and Mc.202s—I estimated about 150 of them—about 2,000 to 3,000 feet higher up and to the west of me. They were in one large gaggle and heading north. I saw that there were three shiny, brand-new-looking Me-109s within easy reach. They were flying in trail formation right in front of me, so I decided to bounce them.

I made a firing pass at the three 109s, which immediately half-rolled and headed straight for the deck. It was a sucker maneuver, but this was my one hundred forty-ninth mission, so I didn't bite. As the three 109s dove away, however, I spied three Mc.202s. They were in line-astern formation

253

and right at my altitude, so I made a firing pass at them, too. I sprayed all three of them as I closed to within fifty to seventy-five yards of the left side of their formation. I saw many strikes along all the fuselages. I am positive that my API bullets killed or wounded the three pilots. All of the Mc.202s headed straight down. The leader definitely crashed into the deck, and I was given full credit for it. The last I saw of the second one, it was going straight down about 100 feet behind the leader, but it had not yet crashed. The third, which was about 500 feet higher than the second one, was also going straight down, but I lost sight of it behind my wing. I leveled out just then, but I didn't see the second or third Macchis hit the ground. In addition to the leader, which I saw crash, I later claimed the second Macchi as a kill, but I was never given credit for it or the third one. I found out much later that Captain Floyd Rodmyre, the squadron operations officer, had followed my flight down and had opened fire on an Me-109 that was coming down on me during my firing pass at the Macchis. I never saw that 109 or Rodmyre's P-51.

As I leveled out, I cleared my tail by skid-turning quickly to the right and then back to the left. I hoped I would be able to see where the Macchis had gone in, but I only saw my wingman's P-51. It was to my left, so I turned left and flew across its path, right in front of it. Next, I banked to my left and flew around until I was beside my wingman's P-51, heading in the opposite direction.

This was my wingman's first mission in a P-51. He had flown a large number of long-range missions in a U.S. Beaufighter group before volunteering for duty with the 31st, but this kind of action was new to him. I had personally trained him and had only just checked him out in the P-51. Anyway, I hoped he would realize that I wanted him to get on my wing.

Just as I was passing my wingman's P-51, I saw an explosive bullet detonate high up on its engine cowling, about four feet in front of the windscreen. My wingman immediately jettisoned his canopy and came out of the cockpit with his pilot chute streaming behind him. I cut left to get out of the way of the enemy fighter that had hit my wingman's airplane, and continued around in a fast 180 to try to locate my wingman and cover him as he descended in his chute. However, I could not see him or his airplane. It's possible that the hasty release of his chute while still inside the cockpit caused the lines from the pilot chute to get hung up in the cockpit or on the P-51's tail assembly. Whatever the reason, I didn't see the chute canopy.

What I did see was a large gaggle of Me-109s, FW-190s, and Mc.202s coming right at me from the west. I guess there were over fifty of them. Away to the west was another large gaggle of Jerries, but they were way high up and heading north. I guess there were as many as 150 to 200 of them.

I continued on a westerly course, right at the gaggle that was near me, head-on at the lead 109. It came straight at me, all guns blazing. I could see the faint smoke from its two wing-mounted machine guns and the 20mm cannon in the spinner. I waited until I was in range and then I fired my four .50-caliber machine guns at his nose. After I passed him, I kept snap-shooting at other 109s until I got all the way through the gaggle. I must have shot down the leader because another pilot confirmed a kill for me from this gaggle. He reported that the pilot of the leading 109 bailed out after I passed him. I was given credit for the 109 leader, but not for a second 109, which the same American pilot saw hit the ground a few moments after the first one.

As I flew out the rear of the enemy gaggle, I opened my throttle all the way and dove almost straight down. Lake Balaton was directly beneath me. When I finally leveled off, I think I was going about 600 miles per hour. I stayed nearly on the deck and took a direct course for home.

I thought I was in the clear as I throttled back to an economical cruising speed, but I was only about ten minutes along toward home when three Me-109s came up behind me. There was one on either side of me and one right behind. They might have trapped me then, but I broke up and to the left. I was able to get my sight on the left-hand 109 long enough to fire a short burst. I saw several strikes along

255

the entire length of the enemy fighter, then he rolled to the right and hit the ground. I am sure that I killed the pilot with my bullets. A few moments later, the other two 109s turned and departed, probably to return to their base for fuel. After they left, I throttled back to conserve my own fuel and hugged the deck to make myself harder to see.

Another eight or ten minutes later, I spied two more 109s following me. One was to the left of my course and level with me; the other was to the right of my course and level with me. I immediately broke to the left and pulled up because I had no room to go down, but the 109s quickly boxed me in. They continuously attacked me in turn—after each attack, each 109 would go around and do it again.

The attacks went on for a while. Fortunately, my being so low to the ground kept them from getting underneath me. Even though I had to scoot up with each evasive turn, they could only get to me from my level or above. Also, I kept turning to the left because I knew that the Me-109 had the advantage in turning to the right. They fired from as little as fifty feet off my tail, but neither of them hit me. I couldn't get a shot at either of them as they passed me unless one of them pulled to the right instead of the left after making his run.

The two 109s kept making passes at me. One of them eventually ran out of ammo, but he kept making passes at me anyway. The other must have been very low on ammo by then. Finally, I took a solid burst right into the left side of my cockpit canopy. When I looked, the entire instrument panel was gone, except for the engine instruments. One of the 20mm explosive cannon shells had hit about an inch behind the throttle; it left a hole eight to ten inches in diameter. And there was blood all over the cockpit— enough to paint a barn.

I thought, It's just like a Hollywood movie. Then I broke to the left and climbed around to attack the two 109s. However, I "redded out"—a red film clouded my vision— so I reached for the jettison cord on the right side of my canopy and gave it a hard tug. The canopy didn't pop off as it was supposed to, so I hit the canopy rails on both sides a couple of times with my elbows. As the canopy finally left the rails, I trimmed the Mustang's nose down, rolled it over on its back, pulled the pin on my safety harness, and went out head-first. I held my knees against my chest until the chute popped.

I had just enough time before I hit the ground to pull off my face mask and look down. Then I did as I had been taught in parachute training and rolled forward as I hit. I came down in about eighteen inches of ice-cold water. I immediately jettisoned my parachute, but I stayed low in the water because one of the 109s was circling overhead, probably radioing my position to people on the ground. My throat was so dry that I drank several deep swallows of the cold water. That refreshed me a little.

I tried to get out of the water, but it really felt good, so I didn't hurry. When I finally did get out of the water, I took a chance and crawled on all fours in the opposite direction to the 109. I had just reached the top of a little ten-foot-high knoll when my legs gave out and I collapsed. I was too exhausted to move.

After a few minutes, I saw about twenty-five people coming in my direction. They were deployed in a skirmish line. I stretched out as low as I could and watched as they came on. They were very close before I recognized the insignia on their headgear—the red Communist star. They were Yugoslav Partisan fighters. I called to them in some Croatian words I knew and they veered toward me. One of them retrieved my chute and they wrapped me in it.

As we worked away from where I had landed and my plane had crashed, the Partisans hid themselves and me in trees whenever an airplane passed by overhead. Later, they took me into a house. There, they gave me a shot of white lightning, but that made me heave. They also tore up some sheets and wrapped nearly my entire body, from head to foot.

Captain Fred Trafton remained with the Partisans for three months. After he recovered from dozens of shrapnel wounds, he joined the Partisan band and took part in many hair-

raising adventures in Yugoslavia. Trafton intended to stay with the Partisans through the rest of the war, but he was eventually evacuated to Italy with fourteen other British and American airmen who had been downed over Yugoslavia, Hungary, and Austria. Trafton asked to be returned to flight operations with the 31st Fighter Group, but because he had learned so much of Partisan activities and organizations during his long stay behind enemy lines, he was ordered to return to the United States to keep the information from possibly falling into enemy hands. His combat flying days over Europe were at a permanent end. At a boisterous farewell party on his last night in Italy, Trafton was stripped naked so his flying comrades could count the scars he had acquired in his last encounter with German fighters. The drunken airmen ran out of steam at ninety-five.

Captain Fred Trafton finished out World War II as an instructor and flight commander with the P-40 and P-51 operational training unit based at Perry Field, Florida. He remained in the service after the war. In fact, Trafton opted to remain in the Army after the Air Force became a separate service, even though it meant relinquishing his commission. Fred Trafton retired from the Army in 1968, immediately upon his return home from a twenty-one-month tour with the 1st Cavalry Division (Airmobile) in Vietnam.

Following a few days of undertaking minor raids over Yugoslavia and Italy, most of the Fifteenth Air Force went to Toulon, France, on April 29. Then there were a few more days of raids against scattered targets in northern Italy. But it was back to Ploesti on May 5, and again on May 18. In between, the Fifteenth Air Force heavy bombers struck throughout southern Europe and on up into Austria and even Bavaria, in southern Germany. But Ploesti bought it again on May 31, and then again on June 6.

Another Fifteenth Air Force mission on June 6, 1944, was as none other that had gone before. Four days earlier, on June 2, 130 heavy bombers and 70 P-51s had left their bases in southern Italy to bomb the railway yards at Debrecen, Hungary. Instead of turning back to Italy, however, the heavies and their escorts kept going until they reached three American-run airbases in the Crimea. Dubbed Operation FRANTIC, this was the Fifteenth Air Force's first "shuttle" raid. On June 6, 102 of the heavies and 42 of the P-51s took off from their Crimean bases to bomb and strafe the airfield at Galati, Romania.

LUCK IS WHERE YOU FIND IT

2d Lieutenant BARRIE DAVIS, USAAF
317th Fighter Squadron, 325th Fighter Group
Galati, Romania, June 6, 1944

Barrie Spilman Davis, of Zebulon, North Carolina, was attending Wake Forest College when the Japanese attacked Pearl Harbor. After learning that his brother, a career soldier, had been killed in action in the Philippines, Davis dropped out of school and devoted his energies to enlisting as an Army aviation cadet. He completed the paperwork on June 1, 1942, and was sworn in five days later, but there were then too many cadets for the available training slots, so it was not until August 1943 that Lieutenant Davis finally completed training and was awarded his silver wings at Dothan, Alabama. After training as a P-47 pilot, Davis sailed for the war zone on Christmas Eve, 1943. Upon reaching North Africa, Davis was shanghaied for several months into the Mediterranean Air Transport Command, to ferry new fighters to the front in Italy. Finally, following advanced fighter training in Tunisia, Lieutenant Davis was assigned in April 1944 as a replacement pilot to the 325th Fighter Group, which was then flying P-47s from Lesina, Italy. He flew twenty scoreless missions with the 317th Fighter Squadron before the entire group transitioned into new P-51Bs.

* * *

Others have decorations they have earned. I have one which should have been awarded for raw luck.

On June 6, 1944, Allied forces crossed the English Channel to land on the European coast. That same day, the 325th Fighter Group was escorting American bombers from a base in Russia to a target deep inside Romania. Our mission began at the Russian airfield at Mirgorod, but for me it ended somewhere else.

The morning was comfortably cool. When we arrived at the field from our accommodations, dew covered the grass, enough to soak our shoes as we walked from the operations building to our airplanes. When we got airborne, we had no problems with visibility; there were only a few clouds. Flying in line-abreast formation, we could see for a hundred miles. This made navigation easy for our squadron leaders and spelled trouble for any Germans who might fly into our part of the sky.

I was element leader—number 3 man—in a flight of four. Before we reached the target area, one member of our flight dropped out and returned to Mirgorod. That left three of us, which was viewed pleasurably by the flight leader, who then had two friendlies to guard his rear in case of a fight.

As we approached the target—Galati, Romania—bandits attacked the bomber formations, and we went after them. During the ensuring confusion, the third member of our flight disappeared. Since our fuel supply was dwindling, my flight leader turned back toward Russia, and I took a position on his right flank. We had been taught that when flying in pairs the safest formation is side by side, with each pilot searching the sky in the direction of the other. This permits a pilot to watch half the sky and keep his partner in sight at all times. That's what I was doing, and that's the last thing I recall until I came to and found myself being whipped by a freezing wind.

My airplane was flying, but its canopy was gone and the right wingtip was a mangled mess. My shoes, which had gotten quite wet during my early-morning walk through dew, were no longer wet. They were quite literally frozen! There were holes in each leg of my pants. And my head hurt.

For all my aches and pains and the damage I could see on my airplane, the P-51 was flying well. I shivered in the frigid wind and thanked my lucky stars that the vista was so clear. It was a simple matter to locate my position on my map by viewing landmarks on the ground. I set a direct compass course for Mirgorod and continued flying. The field and a number of circling planes came into view at the proper time, and I lined up with a runway.

Strangely, the tail of my plane wouldn't come down for the usual three-point landing! Strangely, too, after landing I received wondering stares as I taxied across the field. When I killed the engine, an enlisted man asked: "You ran into trouble, sir?"

"A bit," I responded casually. Then I turned to see what had captured his attention. The elevators of my plane were nearly gone, presumably shot away by the same German who had butchered my wingtip. The rudder was also shattered. Bullet holes were strewn across the tail section. And all four blades on the propeller had been hit with cannon shells. When the maintenance people checked the P-51 more thoroughly, they found a hole in the rear of the eighty-five-gallon fuel tank installed behind the seat. When they removed the top of the fuel tank they found an unexploded 20mm cannon shell inside.

My flight leader, who had landed ahead of me, related how, about twenty miles northeast of Galati, he had observed a third plane approaching us as we flew line abreast toward Mirgorod. He was satisfied that it was the third member of our flight rejoining our formation—until the stranger pulled directly astern of me and began firing. P-51s did not treat other P-51s in such a vulgar manner! As the flight leader called on me to break, he whipped his plane into a tight turn toward the Messerschmitt. But the advice came a bit too late for me. The Me-109's first round had shattered my canopy and knocked me out.

It was too late for the German, too. My flight leader made short work of him, shooting him from the sky in a short, sweet fight.

The worst was yet to come. It was not too bad having the

flight surgeon pick shell fragments and Plexiglas from my scalp and legs. I could walk fairly well, even though my legs were wrapped mummylike with long strips of gauze. What upset me were the orders I received directing me to fly back to Italy the following day as a waist gunner in a B-17. The thought turned my backbone to jelly. To me, the vaunted B-17 Flying Fortress appeared to be a sitting target. I was scared!

That afternoon, a Soviet Air Force C-47 dropped down at Mirgorod and I climbed aboard, joining a mixed group of Russians for the flight to the big bomber base at Poltava. Across from me sat a lady with a chicken under her arm. A middle-aged man with an attache case sat further back. The pilot, copilot, and several passengers were in uniform. Toward the front, a .30-caliber machine gun was mounted in a Plexiglas bubble in the top of the plane, a Russian innovation I had never seen before in a C-47.

Fifteen minutes after takeoff, the left engine developed a roughness that none of the other passengers seemed to notice. My concern, however, was obvious. We landed at a small emergency strip only ten minutes later, and the pilot and copilot ordered some ground crewmen to bring out a wooden stand. Then, working together, they removed the cowl on one of the engines and went to work. "Lord help me," I thought, because I knew that if American pilots pulled a wrench on an engine it probably would never run again.

Fifteen minutes later, we were back in the air. Both engines purred agreeably, and the rest of the flight to Poltava was uneventful. An American sergeant met me as I climbed from the C-47 and showed me to a tent. "You can sleep here," he said, pointing to an empty cot. "Chow is in thirty minutes. We'll get you up at five in the morning." This was not exactly red-carpet treatment, but I was more concerned about my next day's assignment than about any lack of hospitality.

At 2200 hours, I finally dropped off to sleep, but someone soon roused me. "Lieutenant, we got a call that you gotta fly a plane back to Italy."

"A helluva joke," I complained. "I can't fly a B-17."

"Oh no, sir," came the response, "somebody over at the fighters is sick and you gotta fly his plane back."

I scrambled up, searching for my shoes in the darkness. "We had to get your papers approved all the way from Moscow," said the young lieutenant. "We've got a truck to take you back to Mirgorod. You ought to get there before briefing."

The truck driver, a young American enlisted man, looked none too happy about having to make a drive across seventy-five miles of strange Russian territory. We talked very little as we drove through the night. At all railroad crossings and in some villages our 2¼-ton truck was stopped by Russian soldiers who read our papers and waved us on. When we finally arrived at the fighter base, I gave profuse thanks to the driver and climbed from the cab with a grin of relief on my face. The driver grunted in response, shifted gears, and disappeared in the darkness.

It was a happy ending; I returned to Italy in a Mustang. The sick pilot recovered in a couple of days and was flown home via Cairo. A week later, I was given a brand new P-51 to replace the damaged airplane I had had to leave in Russia.

Four weeks later, Major General Nathan Twining, the commanding general of the Fifteenth Air Force, came to the 325th Fighter Group's base at Lesina to pass out medals. As he pinned a Purple Heart on my blouse, he asked: "What did you do to get this, Lieutenant?"

"Sir," I replied, "I had my head up my ass . . . and it was full of luck!"

Lieutenant Barrie Davis's luck held out through the remainder of the summer. His first air-to-air victim, an FW-190, was downed near Bucharest on June 28, 1944. He downed five additional German fighters—another FW-190 and four Me-109s—in July and August 1944 over Hungary and Poland.

Captain Barrie Davis, then only twenty years old, returned to the United States in November 1944. His first assignment was at Las Vegas, Nevada, flying target aircraft for fighter-pilot trainees. The Bell RP-63 Kingcobra airplane type Davis flew at Las Vegas was a larger and more powerful P-39 variant that was specially built to be fired on—and hit—by frangible ceramic bullets. Finally, following a brief tour as a P-47 instructor, Davis was released from the service in October 1945. He subsequently served for many years in the North Carolina Army National Guard, in which he eventually served both as a divisional artillery-group commander and as a helicopter pilot rated as a Master Army Aviator. Davis retired from the Guard in 1978 with the rank of colonel.

Although General Eisenhower himself had made Axis petroleum sources a prime strategic target, the Fifteenth Air Force simply had not been able to muster the strength to flatten Ploesti by means of a concerted, sustained heavy-bomber offensive. The handful of attacks between early April and D-Day had caused major damage to the storage and refining capacities at Ploesti, but the target-assessment experts thought it was not enough. Ploesti was still a major supplier of Axis petroleum needs. As often happens in war when simple, straightforward solutions do not seem to be working, someone dreamed up a complex plan that was supposed to take care of Ploesti by stealth and bravery rather than by directness and bravery.

ACE IN A DAY

**2d Lieutenant STUB HATCH, USAAF
71st Fighter Squadron, 1st Fighter Group
Ploesti, Romania, June 10, 1944**

Herbert Brooks Hatch, Jr., was born in St. Paul, Minnesota, on May 23, 1918, and raised in several western cities before his parents sent him to Kemper Military School, in Boonville,

Missouri, and the Cranbrook School, in Bloomfield Hills, Michigan. He entered Stanford University in 1935, but was injured playing polo in 1938. Rather than return to school after recuperating, Hatch decided to marry his fiancee and go to work at his father's Chevrolet dealership in Stockton, California.

When the war broke out, Hatch, who had been flying since 1932, immediately enlisted in the Army Air Corps as an aviation cadet. A glut of qualified enlistees prevented him from being called to active duty until September 1942, and then a series of bizarre delays prevented him from earning his wings anywhere within the expected time frame. At Pre-Flight, just before taking his motor-skills test, he broke two fingers on his right hand while playing "touch" football. This set him back several classes, until the fingers healed. Then, on his first day of Primary flight training at Visalia, California, Hatch was diagnosed as having an inguinal hernia. The corrective surgery set him back several more classes, and he contracted a blood disorder near the end of his stay in the hospital, thus losing an additional two weeks. Finally, just before leaving home again, the twenty-four-year-old cadet contracted chicken pox from his two-year-old son. When he finally returned to Visalia to start Primary flight training again, Cadet Hatch had been on the base rolls longer than most of the permanent personnel.

After completing Primary at Visalia and Basic flight training at Lancaster, California, Hatch was shipped to Williams Field in Chandler, Arizona, and there he finally earned his wings and commission on December 5, 1943. Lieutenant Hatch was sent to a replacement training unit at Santa Maria, California, and then on to Foggia, Italy, where he joined the 1st Fighter Group. When Stub Hatch finally arrived in Italy, he was twenty-six years old, the oldest operational fighter pilot in the 1st Fighter Group. In fact, he was about four years older than his squadron commander.

By June 10, 1944, 2d Lieutenant Stub Hatch had been overseas for about three months, had flown twenty-six combat missions, and had been to Ploesti three times. His only official credit thus far was a half share in an Me-109 probable that he had encountered during a fight near Campina, Romania, on May 6, 1944.

Ploesti was the oil-refining complex in Romania that furnished the Axis, and Germany in particular, with the vast bulk of its oil and fuel products. It was one of the most important targets that the Fifteenth Air Force had during 1944, and our bombers had been working on Ploesti for a considerable period of time. The first try had been made on August 1, 1943. The actual bombing campaign against Ploesti from bases in Italy got underway on April 5, 1944. By then, Ploesti was well within the range of our fighter escorts.

Despite the virtually full attention of the Fifteenth Air Force over a period of a month, there was one particular part of the Ploesti complex that had received very little serious damage. That was the Romano-Americano Oil Refinery. It was at the Romano-Americano cracking towers that they produced high-octane gasoline. For whatever reason, that refinery seemed to lead a charmed life, so some bright guy up at Fifteenth Air Force Headquarters decided that, since the heavies couldn't do it from 20,000 to 25,000 feet, he was going to send in the P-38s from 10,000 feet and let them dive-bomb the place. That was the whole idea behind the June 10, 1944, mission.

We were briefed that morning very early. We got up at about 0400, had some breakfast, and went down to group headquarters for the briefing. When we walked in and sat down, it was apparent that something unusual was in the air because the group commander, the group intelligence officer, and all the other brass in the group were at the briefing. When they went to the map and drew the line to Ploesti, all of us kind of went "Uh oh." And then, when they told us what the mission was, there was absolute silence in the briefing area—and utter disbelief on the part of all of us who they were going to send over 600 miles to surprise the Germans at Ploesti.

In the course of the briefing, it came out that the P-38s from the 82d Fighter Group were going to be doing the bombing. The 1st Fighter Group had been selected for fighter escort. I cannot adequately describe the sense of relief that went through that gathering of fighter pilots when we found out we weren't going to be the ones carrying a 1,000-pound bomb on one side of the airplane and a belly tank on the other—or the ones to try and dive into that unbelievable flak.

I was quite elated for an additional reason. For the first time, I was boosted up to the post of element leader. Until then, I had been flying only wing and number four positions. As a matter of fact, I had flown about six missions as Green-4, which, owing to its exposed position at the very rear of the squadron, we called Purple Heart Corner. On this particular mission, I was boosted up to being Cragmore Green-3, the element leader of the fourth flight. Cragmore was the 71st Fighter Squadron's call sign. At that time, I was flying a P-38J-15.

The weather was CAVU; there wasn't a cloud in the sky anywhere. Takeoff, which began at 0505, was perfectly normal. Each squadron in our group launched sixteen ships and three spares. There was no problem except in Cragmore Green Flight. The last to take off, we were coated with all the dust from everyone else's takeoff while we stood on the dirt strip waiting our turn. After the entire squadron formed up, we had no problems joining up with the 94th and 27th Fighter squadrons before heading out over the Adriatic.

The 1st Fighter Group rendezvoused with the bomb-laden 82d Fighter Group on schedule. The orders for the mission were to go all the way in on the deck. And I mean *on the deck!* As soon as we had hopped over the Yugoslav mountains, the group leader dropped down to where we were flying at only 50 to 100 feet off the ground. Just short of the point of no return, we had one abort from the squadron, so one of my tentmates, who was flying a spare, filled in. That was about the thirteenth or fourteenth abort by that one particular pilot, and all of us had the same reaction when we saw him turn back. I don't need to mention what that reaction was.

Anyone who has flown formation at low level knows the difficulty in keeping a squadron of sixteen aircraft together —let alone three squadrons. It's pretty tough to keep any type of formation on the deck for over 2½ hours. Two groups amounting to ninety-six aircraft were almost impossible to keep together and, in fact, the 82d Fighter Group did go more or less its own way after we crossed the mountains. Nevertheless, we hit our IP right on time. It was a small lake south of Bucharest. We then executed our formation turn to the north, as we had been instructed.

At that point, we were supposed to have dropped our belly tanks and climbed to altitude in order to escort the 82d Fighter Group over the target. As we completed our turn, however, we flew right over an enemy airfield. And in the airfield pattern were four or five Do-217 twin-engine transport planes. No fighter pilot can turn down a target like that. Our squadron leader, 1st Lieutenant John Shepherd, turned in and went after them, and three of our four flights followed him. Only our Cragmore Blue Flight could not complete so sharp a turn from its position in the formation, so it was out of the fray.

I followed my flight leader sharply around ninety degrees to the left, to a north heading. The transports didn't last long. I only wasted some ammunition by firing at one of them at the tail end of the little fight.

At this point, we were no more than maybe 250 to 300 feet off the ground. At the end of the little shoot-down over the enemy airfield, as we pulled up slightly off the airfield to turn back north again, somebody hollered, "Cragmore, break left for Chrissake." I instinctively looked off to my left—and there was a whole flock of what appeared to be FW-190s headed in from 2 o'clock high to my position. (I learned many years later that they were, in fact, Romanian Air Force IAR-80 fighters, a hitherto unknown type designed and manufactured by Industries Aeronautiques Roumaines. In flight, the IAR-80 bore an uncanny resemblance to the

German FW-190. I also have learned since that no FW-190 units were based anywhere near Ploesti at the time of this mission.)

Our entire squadron broke to the left. As I continued around in my sharp left turn, a lone IAR-80 came out of nowhere and pulled right across in front of me. He was so close—fifty to seventy-five yards away—that all I could see in my ring sight was the belly of his fuselage and the wing roots. I opened fire with all four of my .50-caliber machine guns and the 20mm cannon, and I just damn near blew him in half. I blew a two-foot hole in his fuselage directly beneath the cockpit. That saved my neck because, when I rolled out to shoot at that particular IAR-80, I looked out to my right—and here comes the first big bunch of IAR-80s from my 2 o'clock.

There were four IAR-80s in the lead. I did the only thing I could do. I turned sharply to my right, pulled up, and opened fire again. The leader was 150 to 250 yards away and nearly head-on and slightly to my left. I set the lead IAR-80 on fire with a burst that went through the engine, the left side of the cockpit, and the left wing root. The Romanian rolled to his right and passed me on my left. I didn't see him crash, but my gun-camera film showed the fire, and my wingman, 2d Lieutenant Joe Morrison, confirmed that he crashed. Unfortunately, the other three IAR-80s in that flight went right over my head and down on the tails of the Green Flight leader and his wingman. Both P-38s were shot down.

As I continued to turn on around to my right, my wingman stayed with me. I saw another IAR-80 right up behind one of my tentmates, 2d Lieutenant Joe Jackson, who was Cragmore White-4. I closed in on the IAR-80 from about his 5 o'clock and tried to shoot his canopy off from less than 100 yards. But I was too late to save Joe. By then, the IAR-80 had set Jackson's plane on fire. The P-38 rolled over and went in, and Joe was killed. I did get my burst into the IAR-80's cockpit area, however, and he followed Joe right into the ground.

I was still turning to the right, going quite slowly by then because I had my combat flaps down. I turned maybe another 90 degrees to my right and then saw one of our 38s coming head-on at me with an IAR-80 on his ass. I pulled up a little—we were still at no more than 300 feet—and the P-38 passed over me by another fifty to seventy-five feet. I pulled my nose up and opened fire on the IAR-80 head-on from a distance of 150 to 200 yards. He kept coming at me head-on and I thought to myself, I can hold as long as you can, you son of a bitch. And then I shot the bottom half of his engine off. He nosed down, still shooting at me, and I had to dump the stick hard to miss him. He was burning when he went over me—not more than three feet—and part of his right wing caught my airplane and knocked about three inches off the top of the left rudder.

As this IAR-80 went over my head, I saw three more making a pass at me from my left. I turned so fast that I lost Joe Morrison, my wingman. I missed my shot that time, but when these three IAR-80s had gone over me—they went after Morrison—I saw two more diving at another one of our 38s. I snap-shot at the leader from about a 100-degree deflection. I hit his left wing and shredded the aileron, and he fell off on his wing and went in. He was so low that there was no chance for him to recover. I kept on going around to my left and shot at the second one, which was going away from me on my left. I hit him, but I'm not sure if he went in. I know that I knocked a bunch of pieces off his cowling and fuselage, but I did not have time to see what happened to him.

I looked up at 2 o'clock—and here comes another IAR-80, right at me and shooting for all he's worth. It was too late for me to turn. I just shut my eyes and involuntarily hunched down in the cockpit. I thought I had bought the farm right there. But he missed me. God knows how! I was a sitting duck for sure. But he never even hit my ship.

I think the reason he missed me was that I was going to slow that he overestimated my speed and was overleading me. I started to turn his way and, when he went behind me, I continued on around. There was another one out there, so I closed in on him. I took aim and fired, but my guns went off only about ten times and quit. All the ammo was gone. I damaged him a bit, but he flew away.

I cannot adequately emphasize what a melee it was. There were *at least* twenty-four P-38s in that little area, all of them at low altitudes. Somewhere between twenty-five and thirty IAR-80s were also in there. None of us, Romanians or Americans, was at more than 200 to 300 feet, and some of us were quite a bit lower. The topography was a kind of little hollow with some hills on each side of it. It was by far the wildest melee I saw in the sixty-odd combat missions I flew.

There were aircraft going in, both P-38s and IAR-80s, all over the place. I could hear the open radio net carrying the sound of gunfire. I heard one guy who had been wounded pretty badly scream until he went in. It was a wild, wild few minutes.

And a few minutes is all it was. According to the mission report that resulted from our debriefing, the whole fight took place somewhere in a period of only three to six minutes. I had no inkling as to the elapsed time while it was going on. I was too damned busy trying to stay alive.

Up to my last burst, things had been going too hard and too fast for me to begin to get scared. But when I woke up to the fact that I was out of ammunition, 600 miles into enemy territory, and all alone, I broke out of the area, jumped over the hills, and went looking for some company.

In only a few minutes, I found one of the other planes in my squadron that was headed in my general direction. I called the pilot, 1st Lieutenant Carl Hoenshell, on the radio and we joined up. About that time, I heard Joe Morrison, my wingman, start hollering for some help. He said that he was on a single engine and pretty badly shot up—and would someone please come and help him. So Hoenshell and I turned back to look for Joe. We finally picked him up down at about 200 feet. After we got him headed in our direction, we started to climb out of there to the west.

Joe's airplane looked like a lace doily. The two IAR-80s

that had gone right over the top of me had then gone right down on Joe's tail. Joe's P-38 was flying, but just barely. And Hoenshell and I were both out of ammunition.

The three of us just tried to make ourselves as small as possible and headed west. We hadn't gone more than another four or five minutes before another P-38 joined up with us. This chap, 2d Lieutenant John Allen, was from the 94th Fighter Squadron. We were happy to see him and hoped that he had some ammunition. When we called to ask, however, we found that his radio was out and we couldn't talk to him.

We hadn't gone more than twenty or twenty-five miles west and were just starting to get a little altitude when we ran into a bunch of flak. Unfortunately, Joe Morrison became separated from the rest of us because he could not maneuver as quickly to get out of the flak. We had to turn around and go back to get him.

We nursed Joe along for a long, long time. Finally we got out of Romania into Yugoslavia and climbed to about 12,000 feet. We were essing back and forth over Joe because, on his one engine, he couldn't fly as fast as we could. As I was turning from one of the esses, I spotted six Me-109s at about 8 o'clock. I hollered to Hoenshell, "Bogies! High at eight o'clock." He saw them, too, and cautioned, "Hold it, hold it. Joe, hit the deck." Joe didn't lose any time. He stuck his P-38's nose down and headed for the deck.

Carl, Allen, and I held the turn as best we could, and when the 109s broke formation and came at us from 6 o'clock, we turned up into them, hoping to scare them off by looking like we were ready for a fight. Well, they didn't scare worth a damn. When Hoenshell, who was leading, hollered on the radio, "Hit the deck, Hatch!" I didn't waste any time doing just that. I rolled my airplane over on its back and split-essed out of there.

One 109 was chasing me and a couple of the others were going after Hoenshell, but I don't know where the other 109s went. There was an undercast beneath us and I didn't have the faintest idea where the hell the mountains were—

Yugoslavia is full of mountains—but there was no choice at that point. An armed Me-109 was chasing me and I had nothing left to fight with, so I went through that undercast so fast I didn't even see it. I was hitting close to 600 miles per hour when I came through the bottom into a valley between two high ridges. The Lord was sure with me that day!

I kept going. When I was sure I had lost the 109, I pulled back up over the overcast and started looking around for Hoenshell, Allen, or Joe Morrison. Anybody. I heard Joe hollering for help, but my fuel level was getting down to the point where I couldn't afford to turn around and go back. I continued on toward Foggia.

As I flew across the Adriatic, I was one wrung-out boy. I was wet with sweat. I was tired. I had gone past the point of being scared. I was just all shook up. The business of enjoying that kind of combat might be true for some people, but for this boy—well, I was just damn glad to be out of there and headed for home.

When I landed back at our home base, Foggia-3, I was the first member of our squadron to return from the mission. It was noon, and my elapsed time on the mission was six hours and fifty-five minutes. I don't think I had enough gas to make it around the circuit if I hadn't been able to land on the first approach. There was quite a welcoming committee at the revetment when I parked the aircraft. Shortly after I landed, Cragmore Blue Flight came in—all four of them. They hadn't been in the fight at all. We had lost them in the turn to go after the Do-217s over the enemy air base, but I never learned where they went from there. Next in was our squadron commander, Lieutenant John Shepherd, and his wingman, who was my tent mate. They landed long after any of us would have run out of fuel. It turned out that they had returned by way of a little island off the coast of Yugoslavia that was being held by a bunch of British commandos. There was an emergency field there for airplanes that ran out of gas. Shepherd and his wingman had to land there and refuel before they could continue on to Foggia.

Much later that evening, long after debriefing and after the seven survivors of the mission had all imbibed a little of that so-called medicinal alcohol that the flight surgeon was kind enough to put out, who should come wandering into our officers' club but Joe Morrison, my wingman. He had gotten that lace doily of his across the Adriatic, but he had had to dump it on the beach at Bari, Italy. He'd hitched a ride on an Army truck and walked back into the squadron that evening. To say I was glad to see him is an understatement.

The 71st Fighter Squadron sent sixteen pilots out on that mission, and we got eight back—all four from Cragmore Blue Flight, John Shepherd and his wingman from Cragmore Red Flight, and myself and Joe Morrison from Cragmore Green Flight. Of the other eight, I believe three were later found to be prisoners of war. They came back after the Russians had taken over the Ploesti and Bucharest areas. One of the returnees was Carl Hoenshell, who had to crash-land his P-38 in Bulgaria after it was shot up by the Me-109s we encountered on the way home. Hoenshell was credited with an IAR-80 and two Do-217s. The pilot from the 94th Fighter Squadron, 2d Lieutenant John Allen, was also shot down and taken prisoner. He was credited with a Fiat CR.42 ground-support biplane fighter.

Altogether, we sent out ninety-six P-38s from the 1st and 82d Fighter groups on June 10, 1944, and we lost twenty-four of them. That was the highest loss ratio for any mission flown by P-38s—or any other fighter type, I guess—in Europe during the war. I don't think enough damage was done to the Romano-Americano Oil Refinery to have warranted that kind of a loss. I never did find out whether the dive-bombing mission was successful or not. I do know that the 82d lost a bunch of planes in the flak.

After all the smoke and dust had settled, I was credited with five confirmed victories, two probables, and one damaged. It has been my opinion—and I guess all fighter pilots feel the same way—that those two probables were pretty sick puppies. I have a hunch that neither one of them ever flew again, but I can't prove it. I didn't see them crash, and it turned out that my gun-camera film broke after the third kill. Other members of the 71st Fighter Squadron were credited with destroying nine other German transports or Romanian fighters.

We had another mission the next day. I flew it, but the 71st Fighter Squadron had an awful time getting enough ships in the air that day because we didn't have very many left.

From April 5 through August 19, 1944, there were 5,479 heavy-bomber sorties against Ploesti. The heavy-bomber groups lost 223 planes in that period, 4.1 percent.

Stub Hatch encountered enemy airplanes on only two more missions, and he was given credit for damaging both of them. He returned home in October 1944 after flying over sixty combat missions. Following a tedious War Bond tour, he was ordered to an administrative, nonflying job at Kingman, Arizona, and there became so frustrated that he volunteered for duty as a target pilot in the Army Air Forces's new frangible-bullets program. In his new capacity, Hatch flew modified armor-plated RP-63 Kingcobra fighters, which student bomber-crew gunners fired at with ceramic bullets. Following a brief tour near Oklahoma City, Captain Stub Hatch left the service on July 24, 1945, and purchased his own Chevrolet dealership in northern California.

As in the case of the British and American air forces in northern Europe, by early July 1944, the Fifteenth Air Force was ranging far and wide across the length and breadth of its area of responsibility, attacking whatever it was directed to attack, whenever it chose, and wherever it needed to go. In so doing, it cumulatively destroyed its share of the Axis industrial base and what remained of the Axis air forces. The schedule was grueling—there were missions every day—and, over time, the young pilots on the winning side started to wear out, though the supply of replacements never abated.

275

LAST CHANCE

1st Lieutenant DICK LAMPE, USAAF
2d Fighter Squadron, 52d Fighter Group
Budapest, Hungary, July 2, 1944

When Richard Charles Lampe was a small boy growing up near Globe, Arizona, he cleaned up early every morning for the mechanics at the small local airport, and in return the pilots took him aloft for a swing around the field on Saturday mornings. Over the years, and despite an extremely impoverished upbringing, Lampe managed to pay his way for flights with the barnstormers who visited Globe and other nearby towns now and then during the Depression years. Lampe graduated from high school in 1937, at the age of seventeen, and while working locally, he qualified for a scholarship for the Civilian Pilot Training program. He earned a private pilot's license early in 1941 and was well on his way toward earning a commercial license when, in the summer of 1941, Army Air Corps recruiters arrived in Globe looking for high-school graduates who wanted to learn to fly military airplanes. After passing the Army's written and physical tests and being sworn in as a private in November 1941, Dick Lampe was ordered to remain at home (on full pay—$21 per month) until a slot opened up for him at an Air Corps training base.

Lampe spent only two weeks getting checked in and inoculated at Pre-Flight and then, because of his previous flying experience, he went straight to Primary flight training at Ryan Field in Tucson, Arizona. Cadet Lampe took Basic flight training in Pecos, Texas, and Advanced at Luke Field in Phoenix. He pinned on his silver wings and gold second lieutenant's bars on February 6, 1943, four days before his twenty-third birthday.

After transitioning into P-39s, Lampe was transferred to a replacement depot in Casablanca. In early June 1943, he was assigned to the 52d Fighter Group, which was flying Spitfires out of Palermo, Sicily. Lampe flew dive-bombing and tactical bomber-escort missions in Spits out of Sicily and Corsica for nearly a year without ever getting a shot at an enemy airplane.

In April 1944, the 52d Fighter Group left Corsica and transitioned into P-51Bs. In late May, we started flying out of Magma Airdrome, which was a few miles south of Termini, on the east coast of Italy. Our primary mission was to escort B-17s and B-24s against industrial targets in southern Europe, including southern Germany. I damaged an Me-109 on May 24, 1944, the first day the 2d Fighter Squadron got into a fight while flying our new P-51Bs. On June 11, about 250 miles short of our target—Constantsa, Romania, a port on the Black Sea—we were jumped by about thirty FW-190s and Me-109s, and I shot down one of the FW-190s in a real old-fashioned, hoedown dogfight. I shot down an Me-109 on June 16, another FW-190 on June 23, and another Me-109 on June 26.

Our preparations for our morning mission on July 2, 1944, were normal for that period of the war. We were awakened well before dawn, got dressed, and went over to the mess hall to eat. Then we were driven over to the flight line and briefed in the group operations hut. That day, we were told we were going to be the withdrawal escort for B-24s that were bombing industrial targets in Budapest. They gave us our heading-out course, altitude, time of intercept, and the altitude the bombers were supposed to be at. We were to take the bombers over the target, stay with them as long as we could, and come home. As usual, they gave us an emergency heading home. If we got into combat and got confused, we could fly on our emergency heading for about 90 minutes and then call in to get a radar course to Magma.

Our take-off time was around 0800. The weather was CAVU; I don't think there was a cloud in the sky, and the sun was very bright.

We picked up the bombers right on time at about 1000, just before they began their bomb run. The 2d Fighter

Squadron got in position between the sun and the bombers, and we were flying parallel with the bombers. My flight was high cover that day. We were up-sun and quite high—somewhere around 29,000 feet, about 3,000 feet above the bombers. Fortunately, the P-51s handled real well at that altitude.

We still had our wing tanks on when we got over the bombers, and we were using fuel from them. We had our throttles cut way back to save fuel, and we were flying very slowly because we were trying to stay in position right over the bombers, to protect them.

As we neared the target, I saw a flight of what looked like nine aircraft in a box formation heading in towards the bombers. There were four of these aircraft flying in line-astern formation on one side of the box, and four others in line-astern on the other side. One airplane was out front, like he was the leader. At that point, these aircraft were probably two to three miles away from the bombers and closing in on them. I called my boys and told them to drop their belly tanks and follow me because we were going down to get the enemy—who were maybe Germans, but might have been Hungarians flying German airplanes. I also called up another flight and told it to cover us.

I dropped my external tanks, switched over to my internal tanks, turned on my gunsight, switched off my gun safeties, and peeled off and headed down. From our position, we only had to spiral down to intercept the Germans. That would keep us in the sun.

We'd made only about one spiral down—we were still nearly 2,500 feet over the bombers—when my wingman called me to say that his windshield was icing up. About that time, the element leader called and said the same thing. And then the element wingman said *his* windshield was iced up. They'd all forgotten to turn their defrosters on. I told all three of them to go on instruments, turn on their defrosters, pick up the emergency heading, and go home. I also told them that if their windshields cleared and they hadn't gotten too far away, then they could come on back if they wanted to.

I was still in a perfect position, sitting up above that flight of enemy fighters, spiraling down on them from inside the sun. I had nothing to do but take another look and decide what I wanted to do. I said to myself, "Well, we talked about it and heard if you got the leader of the bunch, why, the rest of them will break up and run away." A lot of the enemy pilots at that time were new recruits who didn't know how to fight. We'd even heard that a lot of them didn't have parachutes because there weren't enough to go around. So shooting down the leader was the best thing to do because he was probably the only one who knew what he was doing.

All I had to do was stick the nose of that old 51 down and head for the leader. Catch him on the way down. So I said out loud, "Hey, here we go."

I was still about 1,500 feet above the enemy fighters when I rolled over and pulled almost straight down on the leader. I wasn't even using a lot of power; I didn't need it. I was going fast enough out of my dive.

I went down a little underneath them and pulled up underneath the leader, right under the bottom of him. I lined my sight pipper up right behind the tail of the leader's Me-109 and got everything set. When I started getting in range, about 250 yards, I pulled my nose up to where he was under it, and I cut loose with my guns. I got him dead center. I could just see his cockpit and that I was getting strikes in his tail. I pulled the nose on up. I couldn't see what I was hitting anymore, but I kept on firing. I knew I was getting real close, so I rolled the 51 a little to the left to get the left wing down so I could see what I was doing.

I followed through with a diving left turn and went underneath the 109. He just practically blew up right in the sky. Pieces of him went everyplace. As I was going around, I saw the corpse of the pilot in the air and saw the aircraft spinning in. I got a good picture of that on my gun-camera film, too.

I went right on by the wreckage and pulled back. Then I put my nose down and made another diving left turn away from the bombers. I made a complete 360-degree turn and lost altitude to about 16,000 feet. While I was doing that, I saw one of our 51s below me, tailing a 109 by himself. There were a lot of enemy fighters around and I didn't want to leave him there without anyone helping him. So I went down to cover him. I cut my power back and dropped ten degrees of flap to slow down. I got in beside the 51, practically in formation with him and the 109. The 51 was messing around and messing around with that 109— shooting at him, but not getting him.

We got down around 10,000 feet and the 51 still hadn't shot the 109 down, so I got his number and called him on the radio. I said, "Move off. I'm going to take this guy outta here." He moved right out.

I slipped in behind the 109 and dropped down below him, to where he couldn't see me. I was directly behind him and going about the same speed. I put on a little power and pulled right up to him, right underneath him. I put my nose underneath his belly and got my gunsight and everything set. When my sight showed me I was in range and my pipper was directly underneath the 109's prop, I cut loose with the four .50-calibers loaded with API.

I blew him up. I blew him out of the sky. The API blew out the whole bottom of the 109. I fired another short burst and the canopy came off. I don't know if the pilot got out, but the 109 disintegrated.

I led the other 51 back up toward the bombers, but when I looked around for more enemy fighters, they were all gone and the B-24s were turned around for home. I called the other 51 and said, "Let's get the hell out of here and go home, too." When we got home, the other 51 pilot told me his gunsight had gone out and he was aiming his airplane at the 109, trying to shoot him down. That's the reason he wasn't doing any good. I gave him half the second 109. I didn't know whether he hit the 109 or not, but I shared it with him. I had 5½ victories.

As it turned out, the pressures of a full year of flying combat missions had left the 52d Fighter Group's newest ace with a nervous stomach—a common malady among fighter pilots despite their tender years. Vomiting attacks Lampe thought he had been experiencing in secret had been noticed and reported by concerned comrades. The morning after Lampe achieved ace status, he was pulled from a mission and ordered to see the group flight surgeon for a physical. The doctor decided that Lampe had seen enough combat, but the group commander granted Lampe's wish to fly one more mission. First Lieutenant Dick Lampe led the 2d Fighter Squadron to Romania on July 4 and departed from Magma on July 7 to return to the United States.

A SWARM OF ANGRY BEES

Captain GEORGE LOVING, USAAF
309th Fighter Squadron, 31st Fighter Group
Rosiori de Vede, Romania, July 31, 1944

When the United States entered World War II, George Gilmer Loving, Jr., of Lynchburg, Virginia, was a freshman at Lynchburg College, pursuing a course of study aimed at qualifying him for the U.S. Army Air Corps Aviation Cadet Program. In January 1942, when the aviation program's entry requirements were lowered to include high school graduates at least eighteen years old, Loving applied. He was accepted in March 1942 and earned his wings at Marianna, Florida, in March 1943. After Loving completed advanced fighter training in North Africa in October 1943, he joined the 31st Fighter Group in Naples, Italy.

During the 31st Fighter Group's tour with the Twelfth Air Force in Italy, Lieutenant Loving flew 101 Spitfire sorties in support of the U.S. Fifth Army during the assault on the

*Gustav Line and the landings at Anzio. On April 18, 1944,
shortly after the group's transition to Mustangs and transfer
to the Fifteenth Air Force, 1st Lieutenant George Loving shot
down his first enemy fighter, an Me-109, near Cervignano,
Italy. He next destroyed an Me-210 over Austria on June 26,
1942. On July 25, 1944, during the 31st Fighter Group's
Operation* FRANTIC *shuttle mission to Russia, Captain Loving
destroyed a Ju-52 transport over Poland.*

On July 31, 1944, the 31st Fighter Group, to which I was
assigned, was tasked to provide high cover during penetration, target operations, and withdrawal for B-24s of the
Fifteenth Air Force's 304th and 49th Heavy Bombardment
wings. The bombers were to attack oil stores and the
Prahova Oil Refinery at Bucharest, Romania. In total, over
360 heavy bombers were involved in the mission, together
with ninety-six escorting fighters from the 31st and 325th
Fighter groups.

The group leader's aircraft rolled down the San Severo
runway at 0905 hours, and fifty P-51s followed. I was
leading the eight Mustangs in Yellow Section, flying, as I did
during my entire tour, in a P-51B, serial number 42-106583,
with the letters WZ-D on the fuselage.

The group's three spares, which had been launched in case
anyone aborted, turned back at the Adriatic midpoint while
the remainder of the formation—three squadrons of sixteen
aircraft each—continued on course to rendezvous with the
rear elements of the 304th Bomb Wing. We met the B-24s at
1100 hours over Rosiori de Vede, Romania, which was
about 60 miles southwest of Bucharest and 410 miles from
San Severo. The bombers were at 25,000 feet. As planned,
my squadron, the 309th, moved ahead to position itself on
the right flank of the lead bomber group. Our battle formation was a "fingertip" formation. The lateral distance
between aircraft was such that all four pilots could concentrate on searching the skies while still maintaining the
formation.

My senses were fully alert as we were now entering an area
that had been the scene of many past battles. Suddenly, the

radio came alive with a terse report: "Bogies. Eleven o'clock slightly high at five miles." There were specks and vapor trails in the distance. In all likelihood, these were enemy fighters, probably FW-190s or Me-109s. Our squadron leader, Lieutenant Colonel Victor Warford, responded with a curt acknowledgment and an order to jettison external fuel tanks. Immediately, Colonel Warford began to climb. Only our squadron moved toward the bogies; the other two squadrons of the 31st Fighter Group remained far to the rear, with the bombers.

A few minutes earlier, as we had approached the bomber stream and raced forward to reach our assigned position, our flight formation had closed up a bit. Upon hearing the report of "bogies," I fishtailed my aircraft as a signal for my section to open up the formation. After my section had moved into battle formation, I released my external tanks, armed my four .50-caliber machine guns, and slid the throttle forward. Altitude and airspeed were the key factors at this point—keep the airspeed up and gain altitude.

As I passed upward through 27,000 feet, I watched intently as the two formations of fighters moved closer together. When we were within about a mile of the other formation, I could see that an air battle was just beginning. There were about forty Me-109s and FW-190s flying in a clockwise Lufbery circle. They were being bounced from a thousand feet above them by another P-51 formation, a squadron from the 325th Fighter Group. Already, it was a whirling mass of confusion, like a swarm of angry bees.

I was astonished to see that the Germans were employing a Lufbery circle, which was a World War I defensive formation. It was the last thing I expected to encounter, but there they were, just waiting for us to have a go at them. And go we did. Air battles had a way of ending as suddenly as they began, so I knew we'd have to act fast to be in on the action.

I turned my section directly toward the swirling mass of fighters and maneuvered into a loose counterclockwise circle about 1,500 feet directly above the circling German fighters. We were thus circling headon to the 109s and FWs. It was a wild scene. There were forty German fighters and thirty-six P-51s in the fray, all in a very small piece of the sky. Four black bursts of heavy flak exploded in the center of the Lufbery circle, and fighters were going in every direction.

My next thought was, How are we going to break up the German's Lufbery so we can get in some serious licks? I wasn't about to slide down into the Lufbery and risk getting nailed from behind, and I wanted something better than a hit-and-run high-angle deflection shot at one of the circling fighters.

Our overhead position put the enemy fighters in a highly vulnerable position. Every few moments one, two, or as many as four German fighters would dive from the relative safety of the Lufbery in an attempt to escape what would eventually come—certain destruction because of our superior position.

The most promising strategy, I thought, would be to latch onto a group of fleeing fighters, hopefully without having an FW or a 109 fall in behind me. Moments later, the opportunity came when a flight of four Me-109s exited the Lufbery in wingovers that carried them directly away from me, initially into a near-vertical dive and then in a forty-five-degree descent. I reacted instantly. I pushed my airplane's nose down sharply and shoved the engine controls to the firewall. Simultaneously, I depressed the mike button and called out, "Hobnail Yellow Flight, taking the four at twelve o'clock."

The steep descent carried us rapidly down to 20,000 feet before they saw us. We were in hot pursuit, closing steadily. I knew the instant they spotted us; the two rear Me-109s broke sharply to the right and the two lead aircraft continued down. I hung on tight to the rear pair and left the leading pair to my element leader and his wingman. I held my position as the maneuvering pair pulled up into a tight chandelle, continued around in a steep 180-degree turn, and then sliced down into a sharp descending turn. The G forces were heavy, well within my greyout range. Though I was hunched down with my chest and belly muscles tightened to counter the G forces, I nevertheless concentrated intently on my quarry, watching their every move so as not to lose my advantageous position.

As the Me-109 pilots continued their desperate maneuvers, I edged closer. Finally, at seventy-five yards, I began firing short bursts at the rear aircraft. I had about a 10-degree deflection shot. My ammo load was 1,260 rounds of .50-caliber, with tracers in every fifth ammo link. My aim was dead on; I observed concentrated strikes along the wing root and in the cockpit area. Suddenly, my target slowed and I had to chop back on the throttle and slip up and to the side to avoid a collision. The Me-109's canopy came flying off and the pilot bailed out. We were at 15,000 feet.

Moments later, I observed another Me-109 several thousand feet below me and about 30 degrees to my right. He was closing on a single P-51. The pilot of the lone P-51 was my wingman, who had become separated from me during the violent maneuvering. I glanced behind me to the left and right to clear my tail and then executed a sharp wingover, pushed the throttle full forward, and dived straight toward the Messerschmitt. It was descending on a straight course, and my approach to it was from the rear.

The Me-109 pilot was too busy concentrating on the lone Mustang to notice me. I closed to about 100 yards before firing a long burst. I observed strikes on the left side of the Me-109 and along the left wing root. The Me-109's landing gear suddenly dropped down and the aircraft nosed over and crashed in flames. It was my fifth victory, a great thrill. My wingman rejoined me. He sounded a bit shaken, but he said his airplane was intact.

The action had been brief and chaotic. It had been a real workout, but it was over. Moments earlier there had been airplanes careening all over the sky. Now the sky seemed empty except for a few descending parachutes. On the ground, there was a lot of burning wreckage.

I had a good feeling when we were back over the Adriatic, headed for home base. There I could remove my oxygen

mask, suck in some fresh air, and relax. We landed back at
San Severo at 1405 hours, following a five-hour mission,
which was about par for the course.

In total, the 31st Fighter Group destroyed eleven Me-109s
and one FW-190 that day, and we damaged two others. We
lost one aircraft whose pilot was listed as missing in action.
The 309th Fighter Squadron war diary for July 31, 1944,
summed up my feelings very well: "Morale couldn't be
better tonight as the squadron sits around the club drinking
beer in celebration of today's victories."

*Following his ascension to acedom on July 31, 1944, Captain
George Loving flew nine more combat missions, bringing his
World War II total to 101 Spitfire missions and 50 Mustang
missions. Loving returned to the United States in September
1944 and spent the rest of the war instructing new fighter
pilots at the P-47 school at Millville, New Jersey. He remained in the Air Force and flew 111 missions in Korea. He
retired from the Air Force as a lieutenant general.*

BLACK FLIGHT*

1st Lieutenant BOB GOEBEL, USAAF
308th Fighter Squadron, 31st Fighter Group
Ploesti, Romania, August 18, 1944

*Robert John Goebel, a native of Racine, Wisconsin, enlisted
in the Aviation Cadet program on April 4, 1942, as a*

---

*Robert J. Goebel, *Mustang Ace: Memoirs of a P-51 Fighter Pilot*
(Pacifica, California: Pacifica Press, 1992). Revised and quoted
with permission.

high-school graduate with no college credits. He was commissioned on May 23, 1943, at twenty years of age, and he served in the Panama Canal Zone from June to December 1943. Second Lieutenant Goebel arrived in North Africa in February 1944, checked out in Spitfire V fighters, and joined the crack, veteran 31st Fighter Group in April 1944, just as it was transitioning from Spitfires to Mustangs and moving from the Twelfth Air Force to the Fifteenth Air Force.

Goebel's first aerial victory was against an Me-109 over Wallersdorf, Austria, on May 29, 1944. Thereafter, in little more than two months, he methodically shot down four more Me-109s and one Me-110, and scored one Me-109 probable.

When the 308th Fighter Squadron's commander left for the States in late July, he was succeeded by Captain Leland "Tommy" Molland. Tommy was one of the few remaining pilots from the early Spitfire days and was, by any scale of reckoning, a fighter pilot's fighter pilot. He had three victories in Spits, and was one of the few old-timers who took the change of aircraft and type of mission in stride, continuing his outstanding combat record in the Mustang. Tommy looked the fighter-pilot type; he was handsome, of average height but lean, and he moved easily, with a certain grace that marked him as an athlete. He was not given to idle chatter, generally remaining quiet unless he had something to say, and never using two words when one would do. But he could fly that machine; he really was a great pilot and a courageous and resourceful leader in the air to boot.

I developed an intense loyalty to Tommy as a military superior, and a great fondness for him as a friend. I like to think that he reciprocated. When Tommy made squadron commander, I was button-holed by the adjutant, who said he thought it would be a good idea henceforth to address Tommy as "Captain Molland," at least in front of the rest of the officers. I instantly concurred. I remember the first time I spoke to him in that fashion in the Operations Quonset hut before a mission. He looked at me squarely with those bright blue eyes and a half smile at the corner of his lips, and I knew he understood.

One evening in late July or early August, 1944, Tommy came over to my quarters and we talked flying, as usual. I could tell he had something on his mind, but with Tommy you had to be patient, sure that whatever it was, it would come out in time.

Even though enemy fighters were getting scarcer, it was Tommy's opinion that this was apparent rather than real, and that it resulted from a change in tactics—not from attrition of the German fighter forces. Looking at the air battle from the Luftwaffe point of view, their pilots were not doing well against the Mustang and, any way you sliced it, knocking down heavy bombers had to have a higher priority than fighter-on-fighter engagements. We agreed that the best tactic for German fighters would be for them to get off the ground at the approach of the bomber stream, avoid the covering fighter escort, and watch for bare bomber groups or stragglers to pick off.

We concluded that our best chance to meet enemy fighters was to loiter in the target area after most of the attacking force had left for home. The logical thing for us to do was to pull back the power as much as possible, thereby saving fuel and increasing our time over the target vicinity.

Another way to extend the time aloft was to cheat a little on the fuselage tank. During the design of the early prototype P-51, an internal eighty-five-gallon fuel tank was installed aft of the cockpit to supplement the ninety-two gallons in each wing. With a full fuselage tank, the aircraft flew all right in normal attitudes, but, in a high-G turn, the aft center of gravity caused a stick reversal. The plane tended to wrap the turn tighter without any back pressure on the stick and to generally behave like a pregnant sow. The standard procedure was to burn the fuselage tank down to fifty gallons immediately after takeoff, even before going on external tanks, so that if the tanks had to be jettisoned unexpectedly, you were already in a condition from which you could fight.

Leaving fifty gallons in the fuselage tank involved some risk, but I didn't give it a second thought; I was getting pretty cocky, assuming that attitude of invincibility so common in fighter pilots. I had gained tremendous confidence in the Mustang and in my ability to fight with it. Experience had gradually cooled my hyperexcitement, and I found that I could now keep a detached calm in a fight in spite of all the screaming on the radio and the physical and mental exertion. My senses had been honed to a razor-sharp edge, and my reflexes were lightning quick. At least that was how I felt, and it was a good feeling.

I got my sixth Me-109 on August 3. It was on a return trip to Friedrichshafen and wasn't much of a fight. I let fly from very close range and scored such a concentration of hits that most of his tail disintegrated.

Tommy came over one evening right after that with great news. He had gotten permission to put up four extra aircraft—he called it Black Flight—whose sole responsibility would be to flog around the sky looking for enemy aircraft. He intended to lead Black Flight, and he offered me the opportunity to fly his element lead, a proposition that I eagerly accepted. The plan was to join on the squadron after takeoff, but, once in the target area, we would range far out to either side of the bomber stream, free-lancing. It was an ideal setup for testing our ideas.

Our chance came on another scheduled attack on Ploesti on August 18. Tommy assigned one of the other senior pilots to lead the squadron, and he and I, with our wingmen, tagged along as a fifth flight, using the call sign Border Black Flight. By then we were flying P-51Ds, which were armed with six machine guns.

As we neared the oil fields, I called out some tiny dark specks just above the horizon away to the east. And off we went. However, I failed to keep them in sight, so after stooging around out there for a few minutes, Tommy turned back toward Ploesti. I was stacked down on his left. We hadn't been straight and level for thirty seconds when I happened to look back and upward—and my blood froze. There were 109s up there, a whole lot of them, and they were close. I could see the leader's spiral-painted spinner turning, creating that peculiar optical illusion. I was dumbfounded. I couldn't believe that they had gotten that close undetected, and I sure as hell didn't understand why they hadn't bounced us—unless they were as surprised as we were.

"Border Black Leader, break left," I called.

Instantly, Tommy was in a vertical turn to the left, and I broke to the right, underneath him. I saw about half of them turn away from us, and the rest followed Tommy and his wingman. As I got partway around, I caught sight of them again. I could see that they hadn't closed on Tommy, and they didn't seem to be turning hard. I whipped up into a wingover and came barreling down in the opposite direction, picking out the nearest one. I waited until I couldn't miss, and then I cut loose with all six .50s. I poured a steady hail into him at very close range. The pilot left the 109 immediately. As soon as he and his jettisoned canopy were clear of his aircraft and out of my vision, I forgot about him and got back to business.

Pulling up slightly, I made a quick check around me and spotted another one low and ahead on the left. I was still at max throttle and had come down below 10,000 feet, so I was really moving. I closed on him very fast, almost on the deck, and I got strikes all over him with the first burst. I held the trigger down for another second when, suddenly, the cockpit canopy whipped off and he came hurtling out. I let up as quickly as I could, but some of the rounds were still on their way as he separated from his machine. Turning tightly so as to keep him in sight, I watched him tumble end over end, waiting for his chute to blossom. It never opened. He hit in a ploughed field not far from where a Romanian farmer was working with his horse. I had never seen the actual death of one of my adversaries before. It was rather unnerving. Although it had not been deliberate, I must have hit him as he came out. I wondered if I could have been a split second faster in releasing the trigger. No time to worry about that now, however, unless I wanted to join him.

When I looked around, I was alone in the sky. I had no idea where my wingman was and only a vague idea where I was. Somewhere east of the target area, no doubt, and I would have to recross it alone on my way home, a prospect with which I was not enthralled. As I reduced the throttle and prop settings and checked my fuel, I tried raising Tommy on the radio, but without success. Ruefully, I recalled how I had hoped to remain in the target area until everyone had left. Well, I was getting my wish, but it looked a little different from where I was sitting at that moment. I had seen enough 109s for today, thank you. There was no on-board round counter, but I estimated that I had a couple of seconds of firing time left, and that I had enough fuel to make it back. Briefly, I considered staying down on the deck, but I decided that any advantage in being able to escape detection was outweighed by the disadvantage, possibly fatal, of not being able to dive away if attacked and cornered. I set power for a climb back up to altitude and began making sharp turns every ten seconds or so to clear my tail as I climbed.

BANG! The aircraft shuddered. I broke right by reflex as I went to full power. Then I sneaked a peek back. Sure enough, there were two 109s coming hard with black smoke pouring out of their exhaust stacks from the water injection. I continued my max-rate turn, and then we went through some violent gyrations, but they didn't seem to press the attack. I suspected that they were low on fuel. They broke off the engagement, probably assuming that I would be more than a little relieved and willing to do the same.

Logic was all on their side; I should have jumped at the opportunity to break off a fight 600 miles from home, low on fuel and ammo, on the deck, and outnumbered. No chance! My adrenalin was really flowing now, and I was determined to have a go at them. I latched on and closed steadily even though they were leading me away to the northeast. They were flying line abreast about 300 yards apart. I began to move in on the one on the left, but, as I approached firing range, he started a turn away from the other. That didn't appeal to me since it would have put his friend in behind me. I rolled out, and they did, too, putting everyone back in his original position.

North was the wrong way for me; I couldn't afford the gas, so I was going to have to do something soon. I moved in again on the left one, but this time his buddy turned too quickly and steeply, and he passed over me at a ninety-degree angle. No way could he reverse his turn in time to get a shot at me, so I forgot about him and pressed in boldly. As I began banging away, almost immediately I saw tracers. This meant that I was almost out of ammo. The armorers put in a tracer every so often in the last fifty rounds as a warning. It was too late to play timid now. I kept at him. I was down to two guns firing when he hit on a slight rise in the middle of a wheat field.

I could see no sign of his buddy, thank God, for I was in serious trouble now with no ammunition, marginal fuel, and an engine that was running but not very well from having been tortured beyond its design limits. I left the throttle at take-off power and again started to climb. Twice in the space of fifteen minutes, enemy aircraft had materialized as if by magic in spite of my best efforts to see them first. That had never happened to me before, even once, and it really shook me.

The engine smoothed out and ran surprisingly well, and I was soon at 20,000 feet homeward-bound. Great black clouds of smoke rose from the oil refineries and, higher up, close to my level, a lighter cloud of dark dissipating flak bursts was still hovering over the target. I didn't spend much time sight-seeing; my head was really on a swivel now, as if my life depended on it.

I transmitted in the blind and succeeded in raising 1st Lieutenant Jim Brooks, of the 307th Fighter Squadron. He said that he had already departed the target area with his flight but would turn back to try to find me. Even though the link via the ether waves was a tenuous thread indeed, it was enough to make me feel that I was not alone. My spirits rose a little. Jim tried, but I must have been too far out—a tiny little airplane in a great big sky. Finally, when his flight declared minimum fuel, he had to start for home.

That flight back was the longest of my life. My flight suit was soaked with sweat, the parachute harness and lap belt felt tight, and the rubber oxygen mask made my face itch continuously. The high tension of combat had given way to nervous anxiety and a slight touch of nausea. With nothing better to do, I found myself checking the fuel tanks every minute or two even though the needles couldn't possibly have moved, and I knew it. It was going to be close. I had everything pulled back as far as I dared in order to conserve fuel as I droned across Yugoslavia and the Adriatic Sea.

When I caught sight of the strip at San Severo, I was running on fumes. I made a straight-in approach and drove it down on the wheels, the worst landing I ever made. Langlois and Carpenter, my armorer and crew chief, were still waiting at the end of the runway with one other ground crew. When I turned to clear the runway, and they could see my markings, they were visibly relieved. Langlois raised his arms above his head with clenched fists. When they both got up on the wing for the ride into the parking area, we left the other crew, now disappointed, still standing there searching the eastern sky for one more Mustang. They looked disheartened and I felt sorry for them, for I knew their vigil was in vain. As I taxied, I glanced over at my passengers and held up three fingers, which set them to laughing and slapping each other on the back.

After I shut down, we scrutinized every inch of that machine from nose to tail, but we could find no damage of any kind, not even a scratch. Two exhaust stacks were gone, but that was from running at too high a power setting for too long. The crew chief, Carpenter, first gave voice to a suspicion that had been lurking in the back of my mind. "Do you suppose," he asked, "that you weren't hit at all, but that the engine just detonated?"

I wasn't sure. How could I be? But I was sure of one thing: If it was a detonation, the timing was perfect. Two or three seconds later and it would have been "lights out" for me.

The rest of Black Flight was already down. Tommy Molland had gotten one, but in the process he had lost contact with me and the other enemy aircraft. My wingman got lost on the first break, but he managed to join up and come home with Tommy. No one had witnessed my last two claims, but, luckily, my film of all three encounters was some of the best that had ever been shot in the 31st Fighter Group. On the last one, the 109 could be seen clearly as it hit the ground.

When all of the day's film was shown the next evening before the feature, mine caused a bit of a stir. The audience applauded and commented loudly and appreciatively. Mechanics, armorers, and even the clerks were connected to the aerial battlefield only through their work on the aircraft and guns, and they participated in the fighting only vicariously, through the gun-camera films. Small wonder they were appreciative.

A month later, I completed my tour and was ordered back to the States. It was a bittersweet time for me. I was happy to be going, but I was painfully aware of separating from the people to whom I was indescribably bonded. Tommy Molland waited until last to say goodbye. As he shook my hand, he looked me squarely in the face with those bright blue eyes and said, "I wish we had flown more Black Flights together." I didn't trust myself to speak, so I said nothing. I wish I had, for I never saw Tommy again. He was killed in the back seat of a T-33 jet trainer in Korea a few years later. What a waste.

By the time Captain Bob Goebel left Italy, he had flown a total of sixty-one long-range combat missions, including an Operation FRANTIC *shuttle run to Russia. He was credited with eleven confirmed victories—ten Me-109s and one Me-110—and one probable, an Me-109. He attended college on the GI Bill, and earned a B.S. in Physics in 1948. Major Goebel commanded a squadron of the Wisconsin Air National Guard until he returned to active duty in 1950. He retired from the Air Force as a lieutenant colonel in 1966 following many years of service with the Manned Space Program.*

Two days after Lieutenant Bob Goebel's Black Flight mission over Ploesti, the Red Army attacked directly into Romania. On August 23, King Michael of Romania unconditionally surrendered his nation to the Soviet Union and, on August 25, Romania actually declared war on Germany. Finally, on August 30, following a lightning drive across the former Axis partner, Red Army units occupied the Ploesti oilfields and the ruins of the once-great refinery complex.

On September 1, 1944, the German Army began withdrawing from Greece and the Ionian and Aegean islands. The Fifteenth Air Force was called to immediate action against the German lines of withdrawal from Greece, especially along the rail lines through Yugoslavia. A two-week bombing campaign conducted as an addition to the Fifteenth Air Force's numerous preplanned missions prevented many thousands of German soldiers and their weapons and supplies from being used on any of the active fronts in the east, west, and south.

On September 5, 1944, the Soviet Union declared war on Bulgaria and, on September 7, Bulgaria declared war on Germany. This defection, along with Romania's and the German withdrawal from Greece, left the Fifteenth Air Force with a much shorter strategic target list and thus allowed a heavier concentration of missions against industrial targets in southern Germany, Austria, and Czechoslovakia, the most industrialized of the Axis partners.

THE BOUNCE

Major GEORGE BUCK, USAAF
309th Fighter Squadron, 31st Fighter Group
Czechoslovakia, October 16, 1944

George Thad Buck, Jr., a native of Tchula, Mississippi, graduated from West Point with the Class of 1942 and went straight to Primary Flight School. He earned his wings at Craig Field, Alabama, in December 1942. After graduating from a P-40 replacement training unit in Virginia in April

1943, Lieutenant Buck expected to be assigned to a fighter squadron overseas, but he was retained as a P-40 instructor. He later transitioned to P-47s and, late in the summer of 1943, was transferred to a P-47 replacement training unit in Norfolk, Virginia, as a gunnery instructor.

In April 1944, Captain Buck's repeated request for assignment to one of the war zones was finally granted. He soon shipped overseas as head of a detachment of forty replacement pilots. But while at sea, aboard a slow ship bound for an unknown destination somewhere across the Atlantic, Captain Buck learned that his orders had been lost. The ship wound up in North Africa, but because Buck and his contingent of fighter pilots had no orders, there was no way for them to surmount the Army Air Forces' bureaucracy and win an assignment to an operational combat unit. After facing weeks of endless frustrations—including advice from superiors to take it easy and spend the rest of the war safely in the rear areas—Buck was aided by the commander of the Mediterranean Air Transport Command in Tunis in the form of a C-47 flight bound for Italy. Once there, he more or less assigned himself and a half-dozen of his charges to the renowned 31st Fighter Group.

Initially assigned to the 307th Fighter Squadron, Captain Buck downed an FW-190 on July 18, 1944, over Memmingen, Germany. He next downed an Me-109 on July 21, and another Me-109 on August 7. Once Buck had served his apprenticeship in the crack Mustang group, his seniority and ample experience as a flight and gunnery instructor earned him slots as a flight leader and mission commander. He was promoted to the rank of major in early October 1944, and, shortly thereafter, he was named to replace the commanding officer of the 309th Fighter Squadron, who had been shot down over southern Europe a few days earlier.

On October 16, 1944, the 31st Fighter Group was assigned to escort-withdrawal cover for three groups of B-17s coming off an industrial target at Brux, Czechoslovakia. The 307th took off first because it was supposed to pick up the first group of B-17s coming off the target, and the 308th left about five minutes later so it could pick up the second group of bombers coming off the target. Finally, the 309th was to pick up the last group of B-17s.

It was a pretty day when we took off at about 1000. Of course, the area was always beautiful when the weather was good. But about seventy-five miles north of the Alps, the weather started getting a little bit messy. A headwind slowed us down, and the 307th was still about fifty miles from the target when it picked up its bomber group and started home. Five or ten minutes later, the 308th picked up its B-17s and also started home. After they left, I kept flying toward the target.

We were at 28,000 feet, and an undercast of clouds had developed about 3,000 feet below us. I couldn't see through the clouds, but the B-17s had to be somewhere below, so I kept flying until I figured I was over the target area. I knew I was in the right place because, until we hit the undercast, we had hit every one of our checkpoints just right—right on time.

We were still above the undercast when we reached the target area. I circled around a few times, looking for some clear spots so I could get down below the clouds and find the bombers. But it was just solid as the devil. I couldn't find any holes, but I could see the black smoke from whatever the bombers had hit on the ground. I figured the B-17s were on their way back home by then—considering the spacing of the first two groups—so I turned my squadron around and started back, too. We were still at 28,000 feet, and I knew that the B-17s would be at about 22,000.

Well, about three minutes southeast of Brux, the undercast began to break up a little bit. All of a sudden, when I could see that it was getting clearer in the distance, I spotted a hell of a batch of Me-109s. It looked like about three groups of them, at least. Each group was flying about a half-mile behind the one in front of it, and the Me-109s were all lined up in rows. They were flying right down the contrails of the B-17s I was supposed to be escorting!

I was about two miles behind the last row of 109s, and we had about a 5,000-foot bounce on them. Even though we were badly outnumbered, I told my Yellow Flight leader to continue on at 28,000 feet and cover the rest of the squadron while we went down and tried to break up the German formation. Considering the odds, I told him to keep his radio open as we might need some help.

I thought we could catch the Germans by surprise and just break them up good—make them forget about the B-17s, make them start milling around or maybe chase us. I told the rest of the squadron, "Look, we're badly outnumbered, but I think we can get a few of these guys. Everybody come up in line abreast—elements in line abreast." That way, every flight leader and element leader could fire without interfering with somebody else. I went on: "We have to drop our noses about twenty degrees. Just follow me. We're going to pick up a hell of a lot of speed and hit that last row of Me-109s—the last row of the last group. Pick off as many as you can, but don't tarry too long and just watch me. We're going to go through them and lose about five thousand or six thousand more feet. We'll pick up a lot more speed, so get out of there and head straight home."

I dropped the nose and we started down.

What I had not included in my calculation was that when we started diving at twenty degrees—thinking that's what it would take to hit the tail-end of them—we were going to pick up a *godawful* amount of speed. My P-51 started going a little bit too fast for me, getting a bit of a shiver to it. It didn't feel safe going into that twenty-degree dive that fast. I got worried about the airplane breaking apart, so I had to shallow out my dive a little bit. As a result, we hit this big bunch of 109s right in the middle of their formation.

Well, we caught them by surprise, all right. When they saw they were being attacked, they all pickled their wing tanks. But by that time we had an advantage on them. I shot one down right away. I just came straight in behind him and opened fire from about 200 yards. I fired all my guns for two or three seconds. He took no evasive action. He hadn't even had time to drop his wing tanks, and aviation gasoline covered my plane.

I watched the 109 fall away as I started pulling back up to

the right to get another shot at the German formation. I lost a lot of speed doing that, and the German formation was breaking up all around me—up and down and all around, like a bunch of geese.

There was a new lieutenant flying my right wing. As I looked around for another victim, he kept me informed, kind of like a play-by-play football announcer does during the game. He'd say, "One at one o'clock high. He's not going to bother us. There's one about three o'clock, about level. You gotta look at him, he might. And there's one right directly behind us, but he's going the other way." He kept me informed, so I had a good mental picture of exactly what our situation was.

I saw another 109 ahead of me and off to my right as it started turning slightly to the right. I turned right, too. I thought I could get directly behind him, but he kept turning, which meant I couldn't open fire. You can't shoot another airplane from straight back while it's turning because your bullets will fly straight ahead and miss the target. I had to take a deflection shot or he'd get away clean. I took a 10- to 15-degree deflection shot and pulled a couple hundred yards of lead on him. I hit him from the engine on back, and he went down trailing a lot of blue smoke and white smoke. The blue was from his oil and the white was his coolant. I didn't see the pilot bail out, so I figured he was dead.

I pulled up to the left and, about that time, my wingman told me there was another one at about 11 o'clock and going slightly away. The German didn't seem to be taking any evasive action, either. I was almost directly behind him at 150 yards, but I drifted a little to his left and put the sight on his wing root and cockpit area. I fired several bursts for a total of six or seven seconds, and I saw strikes all over the left side of his airplane. I knocked him right down.

About that time, I saw another one at about 11 o'clock. He was coming from below me and going straight ahead. I guess he didn't see my wingman and me, or maybe he thought we were 109s, too. When he got out a bit in front of me, he had a little speed advantage on me, but I dropped down and got right directly behind him. But before I could pull the damned trigger, I got into his prop wash and that just tripped me over on my back. I righted myself—that didn't take long—and I got my sights back on him. But when I pulled the trigger, one gun went *pop*, and that was it. I knew I'd fired a lot of ammo, but I didn't think I was all out! But I was burned out of ammunition.

I told the rest of the squadron what I was doing and told them not to tarry too long or run out of ammunition like I had because they might pick up some other Germans on the way home. I hit the deck with my wingman, and we headed away out of the fight. When I got what I thought was out of their range—six or seven miles to the south—I started circling to wait for the others. When I looked back, there was still a big gang of 109s, and about six or eight of my guys were back there hitting them, shooting them. I realized that the Germans had run low on experienced pilots. The guys we fought that day were obviously amateurs. I think they all panicked. Anyhow, in my opinion, they didn't take the right action.

The fight slowly ended. As my wingman and I milled around, I called my boys to join up. Except for Yellow Flight, which never got into the fight and was long gone by then, we finally got grouped together and went on home.

Altogether, seven members of the 309th Fighter Squadron were credited with ten confirmed kills for that mission. Our Intelligence later estimated that we had attacked 112 Me-109s.

The first thing I did when I got back to San Severo was look up the guy who had been leading Yellow Flight. I never heard from him or saw him after we started diving on the Germans. He swore he'd never seen a German airplane in the air that day. I didn't say anything at that time, but I saw the group commander the next day and told him about it; we decided that the guy would be better off flying transport aircraft down in North Africa. We got him transferred right out of the group.

The Me-109s George Buck encountered on October 16, 1944, were the last enemy aircraft he ever saw in the air. He completed his fifty-mission combat tour in December, and was preparing to return to the United States, when the commanding general of Fifteenth Air Force's 306th Fighter Wing ordered him to become his assistant operations officer. Buck flew four more combat missions while serving in this staff post, and he was still in Italy when the war ended. He retired from the Air Force as a colonel in 1970.

From mid-October 1944 until nearly the end of the war in Europe, Army Air Forces fighters based in Italy continued to range against targets throughout the shrinking Third Reich. Until the very end, the pilots of the Twelfth Air Force and Fifteenth Air Force had German airplanes to engage and shoot down, and new aces continued to emerge from these fights.

The very last German airplane to fall to an American fighter—a Twelfth Air Force P-47 Thunderbolt—was an Me-109 downed over northern Italy. It was the only aerial victory ever scored by 2d Lieutenant Roland Lee of the 57th Fighter Group's 66th Fighter Squadron. Fittingly, the very *first* confirmed Army Air Forces aerial victory in what would become the Mediterranean Theater of Operations had also been an Me-109 downed by a 57th Fighter Group pilot. The earliest victory, an Me-109 shot down over Egypt on October 9, 1942, was the only confirmed victory ever awarded to 1st Lieutenant William Mount, a P-40 pilot flying with the 57th Fighter Group's 64th Fighter Squadron. In between Lieutenant Mount's and Lieutenant Lee's victories, American fighter pilots based in North Africa, Mediterranean islands, and Italy, and ranging over North Africa, the Mediterranean, and southern Europe—even as far away as Russia and Poland—were credited with destroying 3,764 Axis warplanes —German, Romanian, Italian, Hungarian, and even Vichy French.

CHAPTER 10

The Luftwaffe fighter force had been in decline since Operation ARGUMENT, the decisive battles over Germany in February and March 1944. Strangely, though the Eighth and Fifteenth Air Forces had been trying to bomb the German aircraft industry to dust for two years, there seemed to be more German fighters aloft than ever. Perhaps there were; German single-engine fighter production had been *increasing* straight through 1944. There were *more* German fighters, but the pilots manning them were raw, and the performance of the two main types—Me-109s and FW-190s—had not been climbing appreciably, if at all. While the Germans waited for miracle weapons and the numbers of fighters rose, their ill-trained young men continued to die at the controls of their obsolescent first-line fighters. In the meantime, American fighter pilots got better and better at what they did, and they had technologies at their disposal that made killing less sportsmanlike and more businesslike by the day.

But it still took good men to brave the maelstrom. Dying was as easy for the presumptive victors as it was for the nearly vanquished.

TWO AGAINST TWO HUNDRED

1st Lieutenant RUDY YORK, USAAF
370th Fighter Squadron, 359th Fighter Group
Hanover, Germany, November 27, 1944

Robert Miles York was born in Portland, Maine, on September 11, 1921, and raised in the coastal village of Old Orchard Beach. He earned his private pilot's license in May 1942, graduated from Portland Junior College in June, passed his Air Forces exams, and entered the service in September with Class 43-E. York earned his wings and commission at Spence Field, Georgia, on May 28, 1943, attended gunnery school in Texas in July, and reported back to Spence Field as an advanced flying instructor. He was finally sent to England as a replacement pilot in July 1944, and he immediately joined the 359th Fighter Group's 370th Fighter Squadron, an Eighth Air Force Mustang unit. Lieutenant Rudy York's first aerial victory was an Me-109 downed on August 9, 1944, near Günzburg, Germany. By late November 1944, 1st Lieutenant Rudy York was the 370th Fighter Squadron's operations officer, responsible for training and pilot mission assignments.

On November 26, 1944, the group operations officer called me and related that there would be a briefing the next morning at 0830, at Group Headquarters. All flying personnel were to be there along with any other personnel who should be briefed. Group also wanted a list of all planes and pilots that would be assigned to this bomber-escort mission. And Group also informed me that the 370th Fighter Squadron would serve as the lead squadron.

I proceeded to contact the squadron maintenance officer so that I could have the number of airplanes available for combat flying duty by the next morning as well as their identification numbers and alphabetical designations. I placed calls to the operations officers of the 368th and 369th

Fighter squadrons and alerted them as to the scheduled briefing plans, plus the fact that the 370th was to be the host command for this bomber-escort mission. This meant that the 370th was to form and take off first, the 369th was to form and take off next, and the 368th was to form and take off last. The 370th Fighter Squadron, by taking off first, was to be the lead squadron. The 369th Fighter Squadron would be top cover, and the 368th Fighter Squadron would be the low squadron. I advised the other two squadron operations officers to check on how many pilots and planes they could muster and make a report to Group Headquarters for this mission. For combat missions, each squadron would attempt to provide all combat-ready airplanes in numbers of twelve to twenty-four. Each squadron had twenty-four planes assigned, but, due to losses, damage, inspections, or missing parts, only sixteen or less were usually available for flying duty for each combat mission.

In checking my list of flying officers for the 370th, I saw that Captain Ray Wetmore was next in line to command the 370th as its controlling flying officer. He was so notified, as were other flying officers of the 370th Fighter Squadron. Ray Wetmore was to end the war as one of the leading aces of the European Theater, with 21¼ aerial victories. He had begun his second tour with the 370th Fighter Squadron earlier in November 1944, and he had 11¼ German fighters to his credit before the November 27 mission.

At 0800 the following day, November 27, it was time to get organized and be trucked down to Group Headquarters for the briefing. Upon arrival, the group plans and training people proceeded to hand out strip maps of our mission over to Germany. These included compass headings, times, and the secondary target in case the bombers could not organize for the proposed mission or if the weather changed. The weather forecast was for a low overcast between 400 and 800 feet, and rain or drizzle up to 20,000 feet. The time was checked and watches were set. We took our maps and formed outside, where our ministers, priests, and rabbis offered a prayer for our safe return. We then boarded our trucks for the trip back to our squadron headquarters.

When we arrived at the squadron headquarters, we each checked our flying gear, including pressure suit, boots, gloves, helmet, pants, jacket, Mae West, and map. At about 0930, I grabbed a truck for transportation to my plane. I checked with my crew chief, cussed out the dropping ceiling—it was down to 500 or 600 feet—and waited for an abort signal from Captain Wetmore that didn't come. I cussed out the ceiling one more time, started my airplane's engine, and moved out on Wetmore's wing as he passed by.

Underway, I picked up the remainder of our flight, Lieutenant Jimmy Shoffitt and his wingman, Lieutenant Robert McInnes. As Captain Wetmore proceeded to the take-off runway, the remaining flights of the 370th Fighter Squadron formed and the pilots organized into their proper positions, followed by the pilots of the 368th and 369th squadrons. All the pilots expected a red light from the control tower because it was now raining and the overcast looked like it was at only 300 feet. However, the control tower flashed a green light at Captain Wetmore, so we gave our planes throttle and took off.

Ray Wetmore and I climbed in formation up to approximately 20,000 feet, where the sun was shining. When I looked around, not an airplane was in sight except our flight of four. Wetmore led us in a huge 360-degree circle while he attempted to contact the remainder of the group by radio, but to no avail. Nevertheless, he decided to complete the mission as scheduled, even though he had only one flight of four planes. We flew a compass heading that would take us to the English Channel by The Wash. We then adopted a heading across The Wash, across the North Sea to Holland, and then we took a heading to Berlin.

As we were flying on into the vicinity of Hanover, Germany, the weather began to clear and the overcast of clouds dropped from 20,000 feet to 4,000 to 5,000 feet. It was clear and sunny above that height. In the distance, in front of us, we noticed contrails, which appear when hot engine exhausts are expelled into cold air at altitude. Flying closer, we could see two groups with about 100 planes in each group. The upper gaggle was composed entirely of FW-190s, and the lower gaggle was composed of Me-109s. Our altitude at that time was 28,000 feet, and we were approximately between the two enemy gaggles.

We stood off from the enemy gaggles and flew on various compass headings while Wetmore contacted Ground Control by radio to give notification of where we were and what we were observing. This way, all friendly planes in the area could be sent to our assistance.

Inevitably, our four airplanes were spotted, and a group of FW-190s was sent toward our flight, apparently to determine whether we were friendly or enemy aircraft. We were visible because we were drawing contrails, but it's hard to determine what an airplane is if it is drawing a contrail. Captain Wetmore came over the radio and asked us what we wanted to do. It was unanimous—check our guns and gunsights and proceed.

I moved the safety switch to the On position for gun control and turned on power for the K-14 computing gunsight. I then fired a short burst to test the P-51D's six .50-caliber machine guns. Lieutenant McInnes's guns would not fire, so Captain Wetmore ordered Lieutenant Shoffitt to escort him to our home base at East Wretham. This left only Captain Wetmore and myself to do battle with all of the enemy airplanes.

As Shoffitt and McInnes departed, Captain Wetmore dived so as to approach the lower group, the Me-109s, which were at about 20,000 feet. It was after noon, and the sun was on my right. I was flying on the right wing of Captain Wetmore as he approached the Me-109s.

Wetmore started to fire as he got in range, and so did I. My K-14 gunsight was working perfectly. I selected a 109 that happened to be in front of me, and opened fire when I was about 2,000 feet away from him. He was flying straight and level, and I was in a slight dive. I was closing too fast, so I cut back on my throttle, but I kept the 109's cockpit in the center of my gunsight and the tips of its wings within the outer circle of the sight reticle. I kept the 109 in the sight from about 15 degrees to 0 degrees deflection and fired short bursts as I closed on it. I saw flashes from strikes all over the canopy and wings. The 109 started to smoke, then it flamed and headed down. I also saw the 109 that Captain Wetmore had fired on start to smoke and go into a spin.

As I cleared the first 109, I found another Me-109 in my sight. There were so many German airplanes in the sky, in this small area, that I did not have to maneuver at all to locate my next target. I believe that these Germans were in communication with one another, but there were so many and they were so confused that they were just creating more problems for each other.

I came up behind the second 109, centered it in my K-14 sight, and fired a long burst, four to six seconds. I saw strikes all over this plane. It started to tumble, and smoke was pouring out and pieces were falling off.

There were enemy aircraft all around me, wherever I looked. I could not see Captain Wetmore's airplane anywhere.

Directly in front of me, at about 800 yards, was another Me-109. It was in a slight dive, and I am sure the pilot could not see me. I turned and proceeded to cut him off. When he was in range, as determined by my K-14 gunsight, I gave him a long burst. The K-14 gunsight was zeroed in perfectly. I saw strikes on the canopy and in the wing roots. And as I went past, the 109 snap-rolled and exploded.

I spotted another Me-109 slightly above me and between 2 and 3 o'clock with reference to my position. This German pilot saw me at the same time I saw him, and he started to turn to cut me off and put me in his sights. However, I turned into him first and cut him off. When this 109 was ninety degrees to my course and 500 yards in front of me, my K-14 told me that it was a reasonable target. Even though the nose of my aircraft blocked the 109 from my direct view, I continued to match its projected line of flight with the K-14 and I opened fire with all six of my guns. I dropped the nose of my airplane to see if my bullets were finding their target and I observed strikes on the 109's fuselage, wings, and cockpit area.

Suddenly I saw tracers going past my wing! I looked back and saw that I had an Me-109 on my tail. I immediately pulled back on the stick and throttle, kicked the left rudder hard, and put my plane into a quarter snap roll and a diving turn to the left. I almost collided with the airplane I had just fired on, and I observed the pilot bailing out of it. I went past him in a high-speed diving spiral so that the enemy on my tail couldn't draw the correct deflection in order to shoot me down. I remained in the power dive, turning all the time, trying to reach the cloud layer below without allowing the German pilot an opportunity to draw a lead on my airplane.

I was having a problem breathing, so, while still in my high-speed diving turn, I put the oxygen selector from Automatic to 100 percent straight oxygen. After a few deep breaths to normalize my breathing and keep me from blacking out, I moved the control lever back to the Automatic oxygen setting. I advanced the throttle a bit to speed up my continuing diving spiral. As I hit the clouds, I quickly checked my rear and sides. The enemy plane had disappeared. There were no enemy planes around anywhere.

Taking a heading back to the English Channel, I flew along in the cloud layer with just my canopy showing, forever checking my surrounding area for unidentified planes. Every so often, I put out a radio call for Captain Wetmore, but there was no reply.

When I arrived in England, I landed at the first airfield I happened to come across. It was British. They gave me a few gallons of gas so I could make it back to East Wretham.

I was overdue at East Wretham, but my crew chiefs, along with the squadron intelligence officer, were still waiting for me. When I made my report, I claimed four Me-109s, but I was given credit for three destroyed and one probable, and I was recommended for a Silver Star. When Ray Wetmore made it back to home base, he claimed three Me-109s destroyed, for which he was given credit.

* * *

Lieutenant Rudy York's fifth and final confirmed victory was an FW-190 that he downed near Lüneburg, Germany, on New Year's Day, 1945. Captain York completed a seventy-mission tour with the 370th Fighter Squadron in February 1945. He was one of the first pilots released from the service at the end of the war. York attended law school on the GI Bill and joined the Army Reserve in 1955, eventually rising to the rank of lieutenant colonel and serving as the commander of a Reserve medical battalion.

MORE THAN ENOUGH TO GO AROUND

Major BUNNY COMSTOCK, USAAF
63d Fighter Squadron, 56th Fighter Group
Koblenz, Germany, December 23, 1944

Harold Elwood Comstock, of Fresno, California, started flying in 1935, at the age of fifteen, and he attended Fresno State College for two years for the sole purpose of qualifying for the Army Air Corps flight program. At the time Comstock's plan was put in motion, in 1939, the Air Corps was training pilots but not retaining all of them on active duty. Comstock's real intention was to earn his Air Corps wings and then take a flying job he already had been offered by the president of Trans-World Airlines. He took the Army Air Corps physical in June 1941, but he heard nothing back for several months, so he applied to the Navy flight program. Comstock was called up by the Army on October 1, 1941, and he reported for Pre-Flight training with Class 42-F at Kelly Field, Texas, on October 8. In the first batch of letters to reach him at Kelly was an order to report for Navy flight training. Cadet Comstock attended Primary at Sikeston, Missouri;

309

Basic at Randolph Field, Texas; and he earned his wings at Victoria, Texas, on July 3, 1942. Along with many other members of his class, 2d Lieutenant Comstock was assigned directly to the 56th Fighter Group, a new unit that was attempting to simultaneously train for combat and flight-test the new P-47B Thunderbolt at several bases in Connecticut and Mitchell Field, New York. Inadvertently, in October 1942, while diving from an estimated 50,000 feet in order to test the P-47's newly strengthened antenna assembly, Comstock might have become the first American pilot to exceed the speed of sound and survive. (Comstock himself never made the claim, but Republic Aviation, the manufacturer of the P-47, did.)

It was during the 56th Fighter Group's first weeks in England, in December 1942, that Lieutenant Hal Comstock was given his nickname. For reasons still known only to herself, Comstock's girlfriend (now his wife), Barbara, addressed all the letters she wrote to her man at the front to "Lieutenant Bunnynose Comstock." Of course, word of this appellation spread rapidly through the 56th Fighter Group, and Comstock has been known evermore as "Bunny."

First Lieutenant Hal Comstock's first victory was an Me-109 which, moments before Comstock shot off its wing, had shot down and killed another lieutenant in the 63d Fighter Squadron. That was on August 17, 1943, near Ans, Belgium. On October 4, 1943, Comstock downed an Me-110 over Bruhl, Holland. And he shot down another Me-110 over the Dutch coast on November 26, 1943, following a wild duel with the heavy fighter's rear gunner.

Though he tangled with and at least damaged seven other German fighters through the first months of 1944, Comstock had not scored another confirmed victory before he was sent home on a thirty-day leave at the end of May 1944. In late August 1944, Captain Comstock was made the 63d Fighter Squadron's operations officer, but he was all too soon given command of the squadron when his predecessor died as a result of flying into high-tension wires during an on-the-deck *strafing run. Bunny Comstock was promoted to the rank of major on September 17, 1944.*

On December 23, 1944, we were out just looking for a fight. Colonel Dave Schilling, who was then the group commander, was leading the mission, which consisted of three full squadrons of sixteen Jugs per squadron. Dave was leading the 62d Fighter Squadron, Captain Joe Perry was leading the 61st, and I was leading the 63d. I was low on the left, Dave was higher in the middle, and Joe was highest on the right. We were covering probably five or six miles along our frontage.

The 56th Fighter Group was still based in England, so we followed the old direct route across the North Sea into Germany. We flew this mission at around 30,000 feet, and we were definitely looking for airplanes, not ground targets. By that stage of the war, we usually flew under the guidance of radar controllers based on the Continent, so finding enemy airplanes wasn't just a matter of luck. The radar control system was two or three months old, and we had come to rely on it. We trusted the controllers.

At about 1130, two or three German fighters passed us, but the radar people did not call them out to us. We could see them, and Dave wanted to go after them. He pointed them out to the radar controller, but the controller said to let them go, that he had a *really* good target up ahead of us. Dave was not happy about leaving a sure thing. He told the radar operator, "You better be right," but he agreed to follow instructions.

The controller said the target was dead ahead. And right after that, one of my troops called out, "I got 'em! They're about ten o'clock to us and low." I could see between seventy-five and a hundred German airplanes out there, so I called Dave Schilling and said, "We're going down after them."

Schilling called back and said, "No, they're right ahead of *me; I'm* going after them!" I thought, You son of a bitch; you're trying to steal them from me! But then Joe Perry called and said, "They're in front of me."

Well, they were *definitely* in front of me; I could see that for myself. So I started down, thinking, Screw David; they're mine. But I didn't care to argue. I just nosed my whole squadron over and went after them. Well, it turned out that there were *three* huge groups of German fighters, and each one of them happened to be in front of one of our squadrons. We were all looking at different groups of Germans!

The Germans in front of me were in a huge gaggle that was circling to the left. They were flying ragged formations of FW-190s and Me-109s at all different heights, just swarming around. I guess they were waiting for their leaders to lead them against something. This particular swarm was made up mostly of FWs, and it looked like it was climbing.

They were probably between 22,000 and 25,000 feet when we saw them. I was at around 30,000 feet when I started down, and I led my squadron right down into the middle of them. I don't think they saw us coming.

The first one I picked out was an FW-190. He was slightly to my left—at around 11 o'clock—and not quite inside the swarm with the other German fighters. He was half-assed straightened out—in a slight right bank, actually. I was turning slightly left, so I ended up heading right directly at him. We met head-on. I had been flying in combat for two years by then, and I guess I had become a little foolish, or fatalistic. I was determined to make this guy break before I pulled away.

I'm sure I opened fire way out of range—a good 500 yards—but the closing rate was tremendous. My K-14 gunsight was still locked; it was not computing. I was shooting with my eye—by instinct—through what amounted to an old ring-and-bead sight. I hit him in the engine. I was maybe 100 yards from him when his prop stopped. I figured, Oh, hell, he's all through. I stopped firing and pulled up a little to clear the FW. It was covered with black oil, and gray smoke was pouring out of it, but there was no fire. There was no point in following it down; I had hit it good and hard, and it was on the way down.

As I came off the FW, I turned slightly to my right, to the northwest. I could see another FW up above me, about 1,500 feet higher than I was. We were both going in the same direction. He was going straight away from me. I had full power going, so I was able to pull up underneath him.

I looked around for my wingman, but he was long gone. He was a new lieutenant who had just transferred to us from the Royal Canadian Air Force. This was his first combat mission. I hadn't seen him since the initial dive, but I wasn't too worried about him. I hadn't heard any call from him, so I figured he was okay and had gone off to find his own German fighters to shoot down. There were more than enough in that maelstrom for everyone.

I drew a little lead on the German from straight back and below his tail; I put maybe half the sight ring on him and opened fire from about 250 yards. It was a really neat shot; probably the best shot I ever had. I hit him right in the cockpit from the belly up. I could see twelve or fifteen API and a few tracer rounds go into him. The tracer meant that I was almost out of ammunition.

The German airplane just relaxed. The nose dropped and the FW started down. It was obviously out of control. There's no question in my mind that I had killed the pilot.

I immediately turned to my right and saw another FW. He was flying north, straight and level. I dropped down a little bit and closed in on him. I turned on my K-14 this time and put the diamonds on his wings and the pipper right on him. It was the first time I'd ever used the K-14, and I was thinking, This is going to be duck soup. I squeezed the trigger—and I got one round out; one *pop*.

I heard myself say, "Oh shit," and I immediately peeled off to my left. I might have put that one round into the FW, because he turned sharply to the left, too. He was on me!

I firewalled the throttle, clear to the water injection, and started a max climb. Very shortly, I saw four airplanes way up above me—maybe 10,000 feet over my head. They looked like Jugs to me from that distance; they definitely had radial engines. I called them on the radio: "Four

313

Thunderbolts circling, I got this guy on my ass! Please come down here." But then I got close enough to see that they were on the wrong side; they were FWs.

The FW on my tail was *right* behind me. He was keeping up. But we were both very close to a stall, so he couldn't fire. This had happened to me once before, and I had learned that if I could keep my speed at around 155 miles per hour he wouldn't dare fire because that would have meant putting on about 400 horsepower in the wrong direction.

The four FWs ahead of me were going around to the right. I just pulled my Jug up and ruddered it over in pretty much of a stall. The airplane cartwheeled over. As I went down right past the FW that was chasing me, the other four FWs followed. All six of us were heading straight out for the deck.

I pulled up at treetop height, right in the middle of a column of German horse-drawn artillery. Just then, Dave Schilling called and told me to take over the group. I answered, "Sorry, I'm heading out. I've got five of 'em right behind me." But by then I had really outrun the FWs. My engine had been customized by the group's Republic Aviation tech rep, up to a highly illegal seventy-two inches of manifold pressure. There was no way those FWs could have caught me in that full-speed dive. I was just hauling ass.

I flew straight home and put in claims for my fourth and fifth kills, which were both confirmed by my gun-camera film.

Shortly after I landed, I received a call from the flight surgeon. He had my wingman in his office, and there was a problem. I assured him that there was indeed a problem because the lieutenant had left me as we were diving into the swarming German fighters. But the doctor told me that the kid had made it all the way through the Royal Canadian Air Force flying school with double vision. He had been able to fake his way through school, but his first look at nearly a hundred enemy fighters that day had just scared the hell out of him. He had taken off for home without saying anything. We grounded him, of course.

What was even more amazing to me was when the armament officer came into my office to tell me I had been firing only one bank of machine guns that day. My armorer had loaded the gun bays on both sides, but he had only locked and loaded the four guns on the left side. I had been so intent on my targets while firing the guns that I had not even noticed that the uneven recoil had been kicking my airplane around. I just hadn't noticed. Fortunately for my armorer, I wasn't the kind who raised hell. I just let him know he'd let me down.

By the end of 1944, Major Bunny Comstock had been flying combat missions for nearly two years. He flew several more operational missions after achieving ace status on December 23, and then he briefly ran the 56th Fighter Group's replacement training unit. He took a short leave at home and then trained with a unit that had been ordered to the Pacific to take part in the invasion of Japan. The squadron's train was just leaving for its West Coast port of embarkation when news arrived that the atomic bomb had been dropped on Hiroshima.

Bunny Comstock remained in the service after the war. In the early 1960s, as commander of a jet tactical-fighter squadron, he flew fighter-bombers armed with atomic bombs out of Far East bases, in the direction of the Soviet Union. His next combat was in Vietnam, where he flew 135 missions in F-100s. And he later served as an airborne battle commander over northern Laos. Colonel Bunny Comstock retired in 1971 after thirty years on active duty.

The pressure on the German industrial base never let up; the strategic bombing raids never stopped. When there were no longer enough industrial targets for the burgeoning Eighth Air Force bomber force, the B-17s and B-24s out of England simply laid waste to what remained of Germany's principal cities. As long as the heavies appeared over Germany, the Luftwaffe interceptors rose to challenge them. The fighting and dying in the skies over Germany never abated until the bitter end.

LONG ODDS

Major GORDON GRAHAM, USAAF
354th Fighter Squadron, 355th Fighter Group
Trier, Germany, December 25, 1944

*Gordon Marion Graham was born in Ouray, Colorado, on
February 16, 1918, and raised in Taft, California. He began
flying in 1935 and, after he graduated from Taft Junior
College in 1937, he enlisted in the Navy flight program.
Graham completed the Navy's elimination course, but he was
not yet twenty years old and therefore could not legally be
inducted into the Navy. After completing his junior year of
college at Berkeley, Graham took the Army Air Corps physical. He passed it, but he was not called up. Finally, in 1940,
after earning a degree in petroleum engineering and his
commercial pilot's license, he was accepted into the Air Corps
flight program and ordered to active duty in December.*

*After earning his wings and a commission on August 15,
1941, at Craig Field, Alabama, 2d Lieutenant Graham was
assigned as an instructor, and he served in that capacity, in
one form or another and at a succession of training bases,
until he was finally ordered to the European Theater
in mid-1944. After serving a brief flying apprenticeship,
Major Graham was given command of the 355th Fighter
Group's 354th Fighter Squadron, a well-blooded VIII
Fighter Command P-51 unit with over a year's success in
combat.*

On Christmas Day 1944, I was leading Falcon Squadron, the
355th Fighter Group's 354th Fighter Squadron. "Falcon"
was our permanent callsign. Our primary mission that day
was to escort the 2d Bomber Division on the last leg to
targets around Hamburg and on the first leg of their
withdrawal.

There were three heavy-bomber divisions in Eighth Air
Force in England; two of them were equipped with B-17s

and one, the 2d, was equipped with B-24s. Most of the fighter groups in VIII Fighter Command were equipped with P-51s, but there were still several P-47 groups and at least one P-38 group in the Eighth Air Force in late 1944. Most of VIII Fighter Command's work was escorting the B-24s and B-17s, but we also did some ground-support work, primarily strafing transportation targets and airfields. In fact, the 355th Fighter Group had the highest destruction total of aircraft on the ground.

Leading up to December 25, 1944, the Eighth Air Force had been flying virtually around the clock. The Battle of the Bulge had begun about ten days earlier, and everything the U.S. Army Air Forces could put in the sky was flying. In all that time, the 355th Fighter Group had not been back to our home base in England—because of weather. Then, on December 24, the group had been split up to undertake several missions. In the course of completing our assignments, the five four-plane flights in my 354th Fighter Squadron had landed at three different fields in England. I wound up at the 357th Fighter Group's base, at Leiston, with two flights. Then, when it came time to launch for the Christmas Day bomber-escort mission, two of my flights didn't get airborne at all because of the weather over their base, and one flight that had landed at another base joined up with one of the other squadrons in our group. As a result, I was leading only two of the 354th Fighter Squadron flights when we joined up with the B-24s and the other two squadrons of the 355th Fighter Group, the 357th and 358th. In fact, one of the P-51s in the flight accompanying my flight had aborted shortly after we left Leiston. There were seven of us.

When we took off from Leiston late in the morning, the weather over England and northern France was terrible, but it cleared up as we progressed toward the target. Over Germany, there was a thin—4/10—cirrus layer at about 29,000 to 30,000 feet, but no cloud cover below us. It was hazy, and the visibility was five to six miles—typical weather over the Continent in the winter.

The bombers were at about 24,000 feet. My two flights were at 27,000 feet. The seven of us were the only P-51s flying close escort on the B-24s. We were right abeam of the last box of bombers, on the left (north) side.

About twelve minutes before target time, the ground-control radar station known as Nuthouse called in a bunch of bandits twenty miles northeast of our bomber force. As I crossed over the bombers to get between the reported position of the bandits and the B-24s, I saw what appeared to be a gaggle of German fighters forming up in the area indicated by Nuthouse. However, at the time, the gaggle was too far away for me to leave the bomber force and investigate. I had to stay with the bombers.

Once we reached Hamburg, our bombers released their loads over several targets that were several miles apart. This meant that the bomber groups were scattered somewhat in the target area. As I orbited during the bombing, Nuthouse gave us another position report to the effect that the enemy fighter gaggle was approaching from the east. While we were orbiting, the leader of the three-ship flight, 1st Lieutenant Chuck Hauver, spotted a gaggle of bogies far below us, and he led his two wingmen down to bounce them.

About five minutes after turning on the withdrawal course, I directly observed a gaggle of at least fifty FW-190s approaching from 5 o'clock and level to a box of withdrawing bombers. They were about 4 o'clock to me and 3,000 feet below me. My flight of four P-51s was still flying at 27,000 feet, and the bombers were still at 24,000 feet.

Chuck Hauver's three-ship flight had not yet rejoined my four-ship flight. At the moment I saw the loose swarm of fifty FW-190s, Chuck's flight was climbing back up toward my flight, but it was only around 15,000 feet. (His bogies had turned out to be RAF Typhoon fighterbombers.) Even though there were only four of us between the German fighters and the bombers, I called a bounce. I dropped my tanks and went after the German gaggle, balls out.

Immediately after I called the bounce, my element leader reported that there were fifteen to twenty-five Me-109s about 3,000 feet above us; they were flying high cover for the main gaggle. As these Me-109s dived in to cut off Chuck Hauver's P-51s, my second element turned to engage them.

Now there was nothing between the bombers and the gaggle of fifty FW-190s except my wingman and me. At least, I *thought* there was my wingman and me. I didn't know it yet, but I was all alone. My wingman had not followed me.

I continued straight on into the enemy gaggle. I hoped to at least break up the big attack while it was about 800 to 1,000 yards behind the bombers. As I was closing, the entire German fighter gaggle fired simultaneously at the bomber force—from well out of range. I don't know if they fired from out of range because they saw me coming at them or if they just didn't know any better. I'm sure they didn't hit any of the bombers.

I closed rapidly toward the middle of the gaggle and opened fire. They had all begun to split-ess just before I hit them. As I went through, they all fired another long burst toward the bombers—also from well out of range—and then their gaggle broke up.

I closed fast on the nearest of the turning FW-190s. I was dead astern of it when I fired a long burst from about 250 yards. This was a perfect example of the simple, straightforward high-side gunnery pass I had taught to hundreds of trainees during my three years' service as an instructor back in the States. As I closed on the FW-190 at about 75 to 100 miles per hour faster than it was going, I observed many strikes around the wings. Pieces were flying off. As I pulled up in a left chandelle to go over the 190, the pilot either jettisoned his canopy or it was knocked off. The pilot was climbing out of the ship as I shot by. I claimed this FW-190 as destroyed.

From the top of my chandelle, I dove right back into the German gaggle. I closed rapidly on another FW-190 that was directly ahead of me, and I gave it a long burst from dead astern, beginning at 350 yards. Before this 190 fell off into a slow spiral to the left, I observed strikes on the wing root and fuselage, and around the cockpit.

By this time, I was through the main gaggle, which had

spread out in all directions. I saw a chute open, and I believe it was the pilot of the first ship I had fired on. The second ship was still in a slow, lazy spiral to the left. It was either out of control or the pilot was dead. I could not wait or follow it down until it crashed, so I claimed this FW-190 as probably destroyed.

As I looked back to cover my tail, I routinely pulled up and went to the right. As it turned out, three Me-109s from the high-cover gaggle were firing at me, but they were at least 800 yards back and their fire was breaking about 150 yards off my right wing. I called my wingman—to warn him—but he replied that he wasn't with me.

The Germans firing from behind me posed no threat yet, so I picked out the nearest German fighter and decided to go after it. This Me-109 was about 1,000 feet below me, in a diving right turn. I dove on him. He executed two or three aileron rolls—full-stick high-speed turns using a little rudder. I rolled with the German, but his evasive maneuver had the desired effect; I was unable to get in position to shoot. Before I could get my sight on him, he dove out and continued into a diving right turn. I fired a long burst at him from well out of range—a farewell gesture—and then I dove straight down to evade the other Me-109s.

The Me-109s behind me were still firing at me intermittently from out of range. I saw their tracers tumble by every time I looked around. By the time I gave up my own chase, about a dozen of them had queued up on either side of me, apparently waiting their turn to fire. All of them were out of range, I believe, and their fire never came very close to me, but I was outnumbered and it paid to be prudent.

I dove straight down. When I pulled out at 5,000 feet, I was pulling seven Gs. My G-suit connection blew apart. I ran through two flights of another Mustang group whose pilots apparently thought I was leading a bounce on them. They all dropped tanks and turned into me. When the P-51s did that, I turned into the German ships that were pursuing me. The P-51s then went after the Germans. I climbed back to 15,000 feet and headed home.

I wished to hell I'd had a wingman during my attack on

the enemy fighter gaggle! I had really expected a much better performance from him. He had been a crew chief in the squadron and had gone back to the States to go through pilot training. When he'd earned his wings, he'd gotten himself reassigned to the 354th Fighter Squadron. By Christmas Day, he had flown approximately one-third of his missions, and he had done well enough. However, there was something nagging at him. While he had been in the States, going to flying school, he had married. And just after his return to Europe, his wife had had a baby. The baby was very much on his mind; he had talked to me about it. I had asked him then how he felt about continuing to fly. He said it didn't bother him a bit. Later, after he had been promoted to first lieutenant, he came and talked to me one more time. By then, he was very apprehensive; he felt he couldn't continue to fly combat missions. The reason I had put him on my wing that Christmas Day—even though he had already flown element lead for some time—was to watch his performance firsthand. When I began the first bounce, he had turned and gone the other way.

After I got home, he came to my room and asked to talk to me. He broke down and became very emotional. When he told me he couldn't fly anymore, I told him what would probably happen—and it did. He was reduced in rank to private and reassigned to the Infantry. That was the last I ever heard of him. It was very tragic. He was a likable young man; everyone thought the world of him. But he couldn't forget his wife and baby, and what we were doing just then left no room for thinking about wives and babies.

Major Gordon Graham downed a pair of FW-190s near Hamburg on December 31, 1944, and he achieved ace status on January 14, 1945, when he accounted for another pair of FW-190s near Meppen, Germany. His last confirmed victories were two Me-109s that he destroyed over a German airdrome on April 8, 1945.

Gordon Graham ended the war as a twenty-seven-year-old lieutenant colonel in command of a fighter group based in England. He left the service in early 1946, but returned after only four months. Major General Gordon Graham served as deputy commander of the Seventh Air Force in Vietnam from mid-1967 to mid-1968. Then, in successive tours with the rank of lieutenant general, he served as commander of the U.S.-based Ninth Air Force; deputy commander of the U.S. Tactical Air Command; commander of the Fifth Air Force and United States Forces in Japan; and commander of the North Atlantic Treaty Organization's Sixth Allied Tactical Air Force, with headquarters in Turkey. By the time Lieutenant General Gordon Graham retired from active duty on July 1, 1973, he had amassed over 9,000 pilot hours in seventy-eight aircraft types, including seventy-three combat missions in Europe and 146 combat missions in Southeast Asia.

CHAPTER 11

The end game in northern Europe was pathetic. The German Army and Luftwaffe fought on, and tens of thousands of Germans died. The leading cause of death during the final months of the war against Germany was the Battle of the Bulge. In December 1944, thanks to a full-court press by both sides, particularly after the appalling weather over Belgium broke near the end of the month, Eighth and Ninth Air Force fighter pilots were officially credited with destroying an unbelievable 836 German airplanes of all types. The best single-day score was 135 German airplanes on December 23, the very day the weather broke. On the first day of 1945 alone, sixty-six German fighters and three German bombers were confirmed destroyed over eastern Belgium and western Germany by Eighth and Ninth Air Force fighters. The total number of victory credits awarded to Eighth and Ninth Air Force fighters in January 1945 was 301, of which a staggering 174 were awarded for combat on just one day, January 14. This, in some of the worst flying weather in recorded history! In February 1945, Eighth and Ninth Air Force fighters bagged—that's a good description—199 German airplanes of all types. And they bagged an even 400 in March 1945, more by steady attrition than because of any one big air battle.

Air combat over Europe was still a deadly game, to be sure. During the final months of the war in Europe, bad luck and operational accidents claimed the lives of many American pilots, including a few high-scoring aces. But many a fighter pilot saw the period as the last opportunity to become an ace or, in the case of aces, to set scoring records.

There was also a new spice being used in the old air-combat recipe. German jet fighters and bombers began appearing over Europe in late 1944, and they were damn hard to knock down. American-made jets were at least a year away from becoming operational, so the only means at hand for downing a German jet—other than getting it to fly into the ground, which happened on occasion—was to outthink the pilot or simply get lucky.

THE ARADO

Captain DON BRYAN, USAAF
328th Fighter Squadron, 352d Fighter Group
Remagen, Germany, March 14, 1945

Donald Septimus Bryan, a native of Paicines, California, began his flight training on January 6, 1942, at Moffett Field, California, and earned his wings at Luke Field, Arizona, on July 26, 1942. After flying P-40s and P-39s with two fighter groups, Lieutenant Bryan was transferred in March 1943 to the 352d Fighter Group's 328th Fighter Squadron, a newly commissioned P-47 unit. The 352d Fighter Group was shipped to England in the summer of 1943 and stationed at Bodney.

While serving as a flight leader in the 328th Fighter Squadron, Bryan shared his first victory, an FW-190 downed near Namur, Belgium, on January 29, 1944. Thereafter, he downed an FW-190 alone near Emmen, Holland, on January 30, 1944; shared an Me-110 with two other pilots over Holland on February 20; was credited with an Me-109 near

*Dummer Lake, Germany, on February 24; and destroyed
another Me-109 over Belgium on March 15.*

*In early April 1944, the 352d Fighter Group turned in its
P-47s for new P-51Bs. When Captain Don Bryan flew his first
mission in a P-51B, he had only an hour's checkout time in
the type. His next victory was a half credit for an FW-190,
which he helped to down over Holland on April 10. This credit
made Captain Don Bryan an ace with 5⅓ victories.*

*Bryan completed his first combat tour in May 1944 and
was married during a long leave in the United States. He
returned to the 328th Fighter Squadron as operations officer
in early August 1944 and scored his next victories—two
Me-109s destroyed and one Me-109 damaged—while flying
a P-51D near Frankfurt, Germany, on September 27. Captain
Bryan's best day of the war was November 2, 1944, when he
destroyed five Me-109s and damaged two others over
Merseburg, Germany, on a bomber-escort mission to Leipzig.
Next, on December 23, while flying from Bodney to the 352d
Fighter Group's new forward base in Belgium, Bryan shot
down an FW-190 near Liege, Belgium.*

I saw my first jets in the air—several lone Me-163 Komets
and Me-262s—late in 1944, but I was never in position to
attack. I also saw a strange-looking jet over Belgium in early
December 1944. This twin-engine airplane came in from
about our 10 o'clock position and passed about 500 feet
directly above me. He flew right over the top of my flight. I
looked right at him, but I thought he was one of our A-26s.
When I called it in to the flight as a "Big Friend," I heard my
number four man yell something, but I couldn't understand
the call. When we landed, my number four man told me the
"A-26" had had German crosses on its wings. We went to
Group Intelligence to look at drawings of German airplanes,
and we came to the conclusion that we had seen an Arado
Ar-234 twin-engine jet bomber. To the best of my knowledge, it was the first time any Allied pilot had ever seen one
in the air.

Perhaps a week or two later, I encountered a second

Arado bomber over Belgium. He crossed beneath our flight path, from left to right. This time, I proceeded to make an attack on him. I approached him the same way I had approached dozens of other German airplanes during the past year, straight in from his rear. However, by the time I got behind him, that Arado was almost out of sight. I didn't even bother to fire.

The third time I saw an Arado jet bomber was a few days later, on December 21, 1944. As had happened the last time, this one crossed beneath us from left to right. This time, I was smart enough to jump in way early. I commenced my attack much sooner than I would have against a conventional airplane. When I squared away behind him, I was only about 1,000 yards away. He was pulling away from me, but I put a little Kentucky windage into my sight picture and opened fire at him. I saw one strike, on a wing, but that didn't even show up on my film.

I saw my fourth Arado on March 14, 1945. I was leading the entire squadron that day. We were operating out of our base at Chièvres, Belgium, escorting Ninth Air Force A-26 and B-26 medium bombers against tactical targets in Germany. We picked up the friendly bombers east of the Rhine River.

The weather was beautiful, almost CAVU. The bombers were at low altitude, 12,000 to 15,000 feet, and we were just above them. We did not get too much flak over the target. After the bombers dropped their bombs, we escorted them back. With our wing tanks, we had more than enough fuel to make the round trip.

By then, the Luftwaffe was about used up. We were not encountering many German aircraft. We ran into a single once in awhile, but about the only thing that was getting to our bombers by then was the Messerschmitt jet fighter, the Me-262. These were not at all frightening to us as long as we could see them. I did not encounter any of the jet fighters, but I had heard from other P-51 pilots that we could outturn the Me-262 very easily. If they turned or tried to stay with us, our fighters invariably shot them down because the jet fighters lost power very quickly at lower airspeeds.

As we were coming back toward the Rhine River from the east on March 14, I saw an Arado crossing directly in front of us, north to south, from my right to my left. He seemed to be flying toward the newly completed engineer bridges around Remagen. A group of P-47s was over the bridges, providing aerial cover, but I decided to try to get him. I broke away from the bombers and started chasing him. By then, however, I was way back of him; it seemed like a million miles.

As I turned to my left (south) to follow, the Arado turned to his right (west) and crossed the Rhine from due east to due west. When he made the turn, I saw my chance and tried to cut him off by turning obliquely to my right (southwest) inside his turn. I did cut him off, but he outran me again and crossed the river. Then he made a second right turn, due north, and followed the course of the river directly toward a floating engineer bridge that ran north-to-south across a jog in the Rhine. There was no possibility I was going to be able to catch up with him. Instead of trying to follow him, I turned to the northeast so I could head him off as he came off his run on the bridge, which he was now committed to attacking. I figured the SOB had to go home sooner or later. This turn placed the Arado several miles behind me to my left but traveling more or less in the same direction—my northeast to his north.

Sure enough, he made a diving south-to-north attack along the roadbed of the floating pontoon bridge. As far as I could see, he didn't drop any bombs. At any rate, I didn't see any explosions. When he pulled up, he turned to his right (east).

As he pulled up and began his withdrawal, he was several miles to my left. If he stayed on course, he would have to cross my line of flight. I knew I was in position to cut him off. He was coming out underneath me. Instead of waiting until he got in front of me, I dove down then and commenced my attack. I wanted to be right on top of him as he flew by me.

I rolled to the right, almost over onto my back, and started my dive. I was trying to keep him in sight. As he flew past, I don't think he was more than 100 yards from me. I then rolled fully to the left. He was flying flat and I was in a full ninety-degree bank at the time I hit him. He was directly in front of me, at 100 yards, and I was closing.

There was no need to lead him. It was just point and pop. All the Gs were off; I was in a neutral position when I opened fire. Fortunately, I did some good shooting for once in my life. I saw strikes on both of his engines. I knew he was not getting away from me. I then rolled into a normal position and fell in right behind him, at his 6 o'clock position. His engines were dead. He was slowing and I was throttling back. I had all the time in the world to poke at him with my guns.

I glanced back and saw that my entire squadron was right behind me. Behind it was the rest of the 352d Fighter Group. And behind our group, I could see a great many P-47s. I was number one, right behind the Arado, and I was damned if I was going to let anybody else get in on him. I wanted to be damn sure no one got in there and made any claims.

I just stayed there, right behind the Arado, squirting bullets at him now and again. I was chopping him up real good. There was no prop wash or jet wash to rack me around, and I was doing some real good shooting.

He finally rolled to the right and flew directly in. I followed him down until he hit the ground. I pulled a little less than eight Gs to keep from hitting the ground myself.

Between his first kill, on January 9, 1944, and his last—the Arado—on March 14, 1945, Don Bryan's score rose to 13⅓ confirmed victories.

SLOW JET

Captain JACK WARNER, USAAF
356th Fighter Squadron, 354th Fighter Group
Karlsbad, Germany, April 17, 1945

Jack Alfred Warner was born in Cut Bank, Montana, on May 24, 1919. He was working as a clerk in the town post office when his father-in-law organized a flying club and talked young Warner into joining. Warner soloed in the club's Piper Cub on September 20, 1940.

Jack Warner enlisted in the Army Air Corps in April 1942 and was called to active duty as an aviation cadet in November. He earned his wings on June 30, 1943, at Craig Field, Alabama, and was assigned to a replacement training unit in Tallahassee, Florida. Lieutenant Warner joined the 363d Fighter Group, a Ninth Air Force P-51 unit, in England in February 1944 and flew sixty-nine combat missions—199.55 combat hours —before he was sent home for a thirty-day leave. Up to that time, Warner had never even seen a German airplane.

While Warner was on leave, the 363d Fighter Group was disbanded and turned into a photo-reconnaissance unit. As a result of the 363d's demise, Jack Warner and many of his comrades were reassigned to the Ninth Air Force's 354th Fighter Group. Before Warner could join the 354th, however, he was selected to serve as a forward air controller with the 11th Armored Division, and he did so through the Battle of the Bulge. He finally flew his first mission with the 354th Fighter Group on November 17, 1944, and he shot down a pair of long-nosed FW-190s while guarding a bridge near Hanau, Germany, on March 23, 1945. On April 11, near Halle, Germany, newly promoted Captain Jack Warner downed two Me-109s and damaged a third.

* * *

The 354th Fighter Group arrived at Y-64, in Mainz, Germany, on March 17, 1945. It was rather a novelty to be flying out of an ex-Jerry base in the Fatherland and even to live in former Luftwaffe barracks. Our morale was very high. While we were at Mainz, it seemed as if everybody scrounged a motor bike or bicycle. I managed to scrounge a Mercedes-Benz, which I painted olive drab. I even painted registration numbers on it.

From the start of our tour at Y-64, our Mustangs flew two- or three-hour armed reconnaissance missions every day. It was becoming pretty apparent by around the middle of April 1945 that the Germans were on their last legs. In fact, as it turned out, it was on April 11 that I saw my last large formation of German aircraft. In that fight, I was credited with two Me-109s destroyed and one damaged. After that, we did not see much activity in the air during our armed recon missions.

I did not feel any fear in going on these missions. As the squadron assistant operations officer, I regularly scheduled myself as leader of a flight or of our entire squadron.

On April 17, 1945, I scheduled myself to lead a two-flight armed recon mission in and around the Karlsbad area, roughly between 100 and 200 miles from Y-64. We did not have any specific target. By the latter part of April, the only type of missions our group was flying were patrols to certain areas of Germany.

Our standing mission was to search along the roads, railroads, canals, or any other place in our patrol sector where we thought we might encounter movement of military traffic. On these missions, all the planes in a flight flew just about abreast of the leader. In this way, everyone could watch the rear of everyone else in the flight—just in case the enemy jumped us. We usually patrolled our sectors at 10,000 feet, which was too high for the German light antiaircraft fire and too low for their heavy antiaircraft fire.

The weather on April 17 was ideal, with a few patches of clouds, and the visibility was very good. There did not seem to be anything moving; there was nothing to fire on. After cruising the area for awhile, I told the leader of the other flight to patrol on his own as we had not been able to observe any hostile action; separated, we could cover a larger area without endangering the pilots in our patrol.

At 1345, while my flight continued to cruise at 10,000 feet, I noticed an unidentified aircraft below us at about 1,500 feet. He was going about 180 degrees to my line of flight and did not appear to be traveling very fast. I was unable to identify the type of aircraft.

I called the others in my flight and told them I was going down to investigate an unidentified plane and that they should all follow me. I rolled over and dove straight down on the plane, which was flying away from me. I gradually decreased the angle of my dive so as to intercept him. As my airspeed approached 400-plus miles per hour, I was able to get very close to the bogey. I was approaching straight up its tail, and I got close enough to see the German markings on the side of the plane. I realized only then that it was an Me-262.

I had not recognized the bogey as an Me-262 because I had only seen the type a very few times—and then only at a distance. The German jets usually dived through our formations to try to make us drop our bombs and wing tanks or just generally disrupt our mission. Most of the time, they were gone before we knew it. Whenever we saw them coming, we immediately went into a tight turn to make ourselves a more difficult target. As a result, we got just a fleeting glimpse of them as they sped away.

I figure it was pure luck that I ever noticed this Me-262. By this time, I was no longer thinking of becoming an ace because I was convinced the war would end before I had any more chances. My only thought was that I had a wife and daughter I was anxious to go home to. However, when I saw that Me-262, I figured it was the icing on the cake. I always thought that to be able to shoot down an enemy aircraft, you had to be lucky, and be in the right place at the right time.

My airplane had just had a new K-14 computer gunsight installed. The sight was set prior to any combat by manually moving two lighted dots or pips that were projected on the windscreen to the wingspan of the enemy aircraft. By using a handle similar to the throttle of a motorcycle, these pips could be moved horizontally out and back from the bull's-eye pip in the center, which was placed right on the target and was where all the guns would converge. When the target's wingspan was covered by the two outside pips, you knew that you were within range of hitting the target. There were marks on the sight for the wingspans of several common German aircraft, but there were none for the 262.

This was the one and only time that I had anything to do with this type of gunsight, so I was not familiar with its operation. As I did not know the wingspan of the 262, I set the sight for the smallest German fighter I knew about, the Me-109. Then, as I got within very close range, I fired a burst into the right engine and moved the bull's-eye pipper over to the left engine.

I could see hits on the plane but there was no fire, nor any pieces or debris flying from the Me-262. Suddenly, much to my surprise, the German jet began flying lower and slower. This forced me to gain altitude and then dive so I could continue to fire on it.

The German pilot flew over a small town. My first thought was that he was dragging me over the town to have someone on the ground shoot me down, but I did not receive any hostile fire.

The Me-262 continued to lose altitude and airspeed until I had to drop my wheels and lower my flaps in order to stay behind him. By then, the other pilots in my flight had left me because, as they told me later, they were afraid they would stall out and crash. I continued to fire rounds at the jet, but it was by then so low and flying so slow that I had to gain altitude continuously and then dive to fire down at it. I tried to stay about 100 yards behind the jet, but I would have crashed or probably hit some object if I had stayed at its altitude or gone lower.

Finally, the Me-262 flew through the top of a grove of trees and crashed into the side of a hill. I am sure the pilot did not survive the crash. I immediately pulled up my wheels and flaps and staggered over the hill to rejoin my flight, and we then returned to base.

Captain Jack Warner never saw another German airplane in the skies over Germany.

The Luftwaffe never gave up. Its defense of Germany was unrelenting until the bitter end. In April 1945, the last full month of the war in Europe, 471 German airplanes were downed over the shrinking Reich by Eighth and Ninth Air Force fighters. But the end was near. The announcement on May 1 that Hitler had died the day before by his own hand took the wind out of every German sail, save those of the most ardent Nazis. Nevertheless, two German fighters were downed over Germany on May 1; there were three kills on May 2; one kill on May 3; five on May 4; one on May 7; and nine on May 8, 1945, the last day of the war in Europe.

The very last German airplane to be downed by an American fighter in World War II was a Siebel Si-204 twin-engine staff plane that was downed at 2005 hours on May 8, 1945. Perhaps it was attempting to carry a high Nazi official to sanctuary in South America. In any case, the lucky pilot of the American fighter, a P-38L, was 2d Lieutenant Kenneth Swift of the 429th Fighter Squadron, an element of the Ninth Air Force's 474th Fighter Group. The Siebel was Lieutenant Swift's only combat victory in the war, but it was the 7,504th victory credit awarded to a U.S. Army Air Forces pilot in the European Theater of Operations. The very first had been for an FW-200 Condor four-engine reconnaissance bomber that two pilots—2d Lieutenant Elza Shahan of the 27th Fighter Squadron and 2d Lieutenant Joseph Shaffer of the 33d Fighter Squadron—downed near Iceland on August 14, 1942.

Altogether, in the air war against Germany and her partners, U.S. Army Air Forces fighter pilots were officially credited with 11,268 aerial victories.

EPILOGUE

KRIEGESGEFANGENER

Captain WAYNE LOWRY, USAAF
317th Fighter Squadron, 325th Fighter Group
Stalag Luft 1, Germany, October 1944–May 1945

Wayne Lowry was born on January 24, 1921, in Mason City, Nebraska. In March 1940, during his freshman year at the University of Nebraska, Lowry enlisted in the National Guard, and he was called to active duty in December 1940. Following a full year of Guard service, Lowry qualified for flight training, and he earned his wings and a commission at Kelly Field, Texas, on October 4, 1942. Lieutenant Lowry was sent to dive-bomber school, but he finally transitioned into P-47s at Tallahassee, Florida, in early September 1943, and he shipped out to Europe with fifty other Thunderbolt pilots on October 1, 1943. After nearly a month at sea, the replacement pilots landed at Casablanca, Morocco, and, from there, were routinely dispatched as needed to all the fighter units in the Mediterranean Theater. Lieutenant Lowry ended up at Mateur, Tunisia, where he was assigned to the 325th Fighter Group's 317th Fighter Squadron.

In his only direct combat action while flying a P-47, Lowry was given probable credit for an Italian-made Macchi Mc.202 fighter that he engaged near Fiume, Yugoslavia, on

March 18, 1944. It was not until after the 325th Fighter Group had transitioned to P-51 Mustangs in the spring of 1944 that Wayne Lowry scored his first confirmed aerial victory. On June 6, 1944, during the 325th Fighter Group's shuttle mission to Russia, Lowry downed an Me-109 near Galati, Romania. Thereafter, in only two months, Lowry's score shot up precipitously to eleven confirmed German fighters and another probable. His last aerial victory, an Me-109, was scored near Ratibor, Poland, on August 7, 1944. Lowry continued to fly a full schedule of combat missions as a flight leader and sometime squadron leader, but he never again directly confronted a German airplane.

A mission that began with one song—"Into the Wild Blue Yonder"—was to end with another song, entirely—"I'll Be Seeing You."

From the time I had first picked up a book on World War I aces, I had always dreamed of becoming an ace. However, during the time in 1944 in which I was fulfilling my dream, I was haunted continuously by a song with words that I liked not at all: "We Had Wings Like an Angel." We all wanted fame and fortune. And we pilots wanted wings. (But I suspect that what many of us *really* wanted was Veronica Lake, who had starred in the show, *They Wanted Wings!*) Whatever it was we wanted, though, we learned that for glory the price comes high.

I paid for my glory as an eleven-victory American ace on October 4, 1944. That day, when I discovered myself over Munich, Germany, with a fuel shortage on my hands, I was overwhelmed with an overpowering desire to live.

My first response, of course, was to throttle back, lean out the mixture control, and reduce the RPMs to the point at which the airplane would barely stay aloft. I hoped that these elementary procedures would somehow get me to our own lines. But, in view of the amount of fuel I had aboard, and given the performance of the airplane, I knew the hope could not be fulfilled.

At first I pointed the plane on a course toward Switzerland, but I lost my nerve completely when I looked over the side and observed the Alps pointing directly up at me. I was afraid that I would spear myself if I bailed out over them, but chances were better, if I landed on top of one of the mountains, that I would have frozen to death before I could get to a lower elevation. I didn't have enough fuel aboard to fly all over Switzerland looking for a flat place to set my plane down, so I decided to head for the Adriatic Sea. I thought of bailing out over the water and getting picked up by Air-Sea Rescue, but then I remembered the details of a briefing we'd gotten from the Air-Sea Rescue people a short time back. They'd said they were saving twenty percent of the airmen who bailed out over the Adriatic. The thought of what happened to the other eighty percent had me bugged. Those people were probably hobnobbing with the mermaids. I was on the wrong end of those 80:20 odds, so I decided to take my chances over dry land.

I could have crash-landed—doing so would have given me a much better chance to escape—but I was afraid that I wouldn't be able to destroy the airplane before the Germans got it. To do so, the pilot had to crawl underneath the cowling, turn on a petcock, and set the plane on fire. I was afraid I couldn't find the petcock under those conditions, so I elected to bail out. It was okay with me; let the Germans have the airplane after it had crashed from two miles up.

Fear had me almost completely paralyzed. Having seen both friend and foe alike die because of fear on previous occasions, I was only too well aware of what I was up against. I could remember President Roosevelt's famous words, "The only thing we have to fear is fear itself," but I couldn't completely conquer the fear I was experiencing.

I did manage to lead my flight as far as far-northern Italy, but my fuel supply ran out long before we were able to get over friendly lines. I had only a few minutes left, and I needed every second of them to prepare for my exit.

By the time I finished going over the details of my exit in my mind, I was down to 10,000 feet. I knew it was time to leave. I had seen too many pilots die because they stayed with their airplanes too long; they tried to bail out when they were too low for their parachutes to deploy.

I immediately started my bail-out procedure. I first gave out several "Maydays" over the radio. However, I refused to engage in any heroic conversations with the other pilots in my flight. That would have been too much for me. I jettisoned the canopy and set the trim tabs full nose-down. I thus had to maintain considerable back pressure on the control column to maintain level flight. I got rid of my oxygen mask, throat mike, and the connection to my headset. Then I unfastened my safety belt and shoulder harness. In my panic, I unbuckled one leg strap on my parachute when I was getting out of my seatbelt and shoulder straps. I hastily put the leg strap back together again.

I was afraid of ripping my guts out on the tail group (the horizontal stabilizer and rudder) as I left the cockpit of the plane. We had been told that the way to avoid this was to kick the stick hard forward as you left the plane, and the reverse lift would throw you over the tail group. I didn't have complete faith in this procedure. I had previously rolled the trim tabs full forward, so now I rolled the plane on its back and simply dropped out. Just as I left the cockpit, I kicked the control stick hard forward to take advantage of the reverse lift. I came out of the plane beautifully, missing the entire tail group by a wide margin.

My airspeed when I left the plane was considerably over 200 miles per hour. I should have counted to "10" and waited for my personal airspeed to drop down to 120 miles per hour (the terminal velocity for a falling body) before I pulled the ripcord of the parachute. However, I was curious to learn whether the parachute was going to work or not, so I pulled the ripcord much sooner than that. The shock of the parachute opening stunned me. It sounded like a 75mm cannon going off in my ears. The leg and chest straps bit into me so hard that I became sick and vomited all the way to the ground. Also, my wallet and .45-caliber pistol were yanked from me. If I had been wearing low-cut shoes, they would have gone, too.

The trip to the ground probably took only ten minutes, but to me it seemed a lot longer than that. My comrades flew by me several times as I was descending in my parachute. Much later, they told me that they thought I had been seriously hurt because I was hanging limp in my parachute. Unfortunately, their presence and concern nearly did me in. As they flew close to look me over, the propeller wash from their planes caused my parachute to tip at a dangerous angle—to the extent that I thought it might collapse. I appreciated the concern my fellow pilots were showing for me, but at that time I wished they'd go away.

Landing in a parachute is like jumping off a ten- or twelve-foot wall. Both of my legs became paralyzed from the shock of hitting the ground so hard. However, I was to find out soon that I could walk—and even run—quite well if I had to.

As soon as I reached the ground, I was surrounded by several Italian civilians. When the girls threw their arms around me, I thought they might have mistaken me for a god who had descended from the heavens.

One of the men said that we were "blood brothers" and that he was going to get me out of there. I immediately hid my parachute under a shock of corn fodder, and we both took off at a dead run down a corn row. This Italian man really tried to help me escape, but there was very little he could do because we were surrounded by a whole division of German soldiers. As we ran through the corn, German soldiers whose rifles had fixed bayonets on them were already in the cornfield, coming toward us. We were only missing the Germans by five or six corn rows as we ran right through their lines. However, as I left the corn fodder behind, I saw that many other Germans were coming after me in staff cars, on bicycles, and on foot. I thought it was a little unfair of the enemy to throw a whole division against one poor American. I was determined to evade them, however, and I kept running all out.

My comrade and I actually made it three miles through the enemy horde. And then I got careless; I tried to cross a road without clearing myself. A German command car came careening around a corner and five German soldiers jumped out with their bayoneted rifles pointed at me. One of them spoke up in broken English: "For you, the *var* is *ofer.*"

The Italian man who had taken me in tow had shown a lot of guts. He was going to try to take me all the way through the whole German Army, and I believe we damned near made it. At first, I thought he was going to get killed for helping me, but I think he escaped. The last I saw of him, he had disappeared down a corn row at a dead run. The Germans didn't know who he was, so I hope and believe he made good his escape.

The Germans made me walk back with them the three miles I had run while trying to escape. They wanted to retrieve my parachute, but I couldn't find it. Either the other Italians had taken it, or I couldn't remember which fodder shock I had hidden it under.

It's hard to believe, but I was hard-pressed identifying myself to the Germans as an American pilot. My parachute was the last link I had with my career as a fighter pilot. I had no identification on me. I hadn't put on my dog tags that morning, and the violent opening shock of the parachute had taken my billfold and my pistol. They probably grabbed me simply because I had been running away from them and was foolish enough to get caught.

I had earlier read the Air Forces' brochure on what life was like as a prisoner of war. The pamphlet outlined expected behavior and what a pilot could expect in the way of treatment from the enemy. Basically, the brochure outlined a way of life that was a long way from pleasant. As I stood there in that cornfield, waiting to see what the Germans would do to me, I could clearly recall how I had recoiled in horror as I turned page after page of that booklet, as I became aware of just how bad things could get.

After my fruitless search for my parachute, the Germans put me in a command car. One soldier sat down beside me and pointed a pistol right at my throat—with the hammer cocked! I was afraid to move and even more afraid that the bumpy road over which we were traveling might cause the gun to go off accidentally.

Since the war, I've had quite a few Stateside heroes give

me advice as to what *they* would have done if they had been in the same fix. One of them wondered why I hadn't used my .45-caliber pistol to shoot my way out of that mess. I had to point out that I was surrounded by 20,000 Germans and that there are only seven rounds in a .45. And I didn't even have a pistol; it had been jolted off me when my parachute opened. Another one of those Stateside heroes said that if anyone ever pointed a gun at *his* throat, he'd take that damn gun away. Well, I was actually in that predicament, and I was afraid to move a muscle.

When we got to their camp, the Germans put me in a Bastille-type of prison located on the shores of the Adriatic Sea. This prison had solid masonry walls, almost three feet thick, with a sliding steel aperture that the Germans used to peer in at me once in a while. There were no windows and no other doors. I was left in total Stygian darkness for two days and three nights with no food and very little water. I could hear the waves of the Adriatic Sea lap-lapping against the walls. I could only imagine what horrors had preceded me in a prison such as this.

I could see my luminous wristwatch and could tell night and day. I had a little over a half pack of cigarettes on me, which I rationed four to a twenty-four-hour period of time. I ran out before the Germans let me out of the cell. Every now and then, I could hear the sliding steel aperture in the solid masonry door open, and I could make out a human eye peering in at me. So overpowering was my loneliness that I looked forward to a human eye looking in on me, even if it was the enemy.

The Germans finally moved me to a room in their camp and assigned a guard to watch over me. They gave me food then—dark German bread so sour I could barely eat it at first, even with the little pat of butter they provided. The German guards were rationed to four cigarettes a day, but my guards were so courteous that they never refused to give me a cigarette if I asked for one. I was enough of a con artist that I eventually got all the first guard's cigarettes, and then, when they changed guards, I got all of the next guard's cigarettes, too.

Several Italians took me in tow for several hours before I left the camp. They gave me much better food and even a little cognac, which was the last booze I was to see for seven months. Everyone was very friendly toward me—even the two German guards, who were supposed to be my enemies. We conversed in three languages—German, Italian, and English—but even at that we had a high old time for a few hours. I was then loaded into the back of a truck and taken partway across the Alps. The two German guards who accompanied me had a little English, and they managed to get across to me that they were very much impressed with the P-51 Mustang I had been flying. They seemed to agree that it was a much better plane than their best fighter planes, the Me-109 and the FW-190.

I was next loaded into a troop train along with two fresh German guards. These Germans were old men. It was very cold during our trip across the mountains. All the bridges in Germany had been bombed to smithereens by the Americans, but German ingenuity was so good that they had patched up the bombed-out bridges to the extent that a troop train could still get across.

On the second night, both of my guards went to sleep, and I almost escaped. I started to walk out the open door when the train was stopped, but both guards woke up and stopped me. It was just as well, as I probably would have frozen to death in my light coveralls before I could have found someone friendly enough to shelter me.

The rest of the trip was uneventful. After two or three days—maybe it was a little longer—I arrived at what was to be my new home for the next three weeks, the city of Frankfurt am Main, in far-western Germany. It was at the German interrogation center in Frankfurt that I picked up the severe nervous disorder that was to plague me the rest of my life. Today, nearly a half-century later, I sometimes still have to have tranquilizers to get any sleep at all at night.

The German interrogators were very intelligent men who could speak perfect English without any accent at all. Most of them had spent some time in the States. At first, I was put under pressure to answer a lot more questions than I was willing to answer. Because of my lack of identification, I was constantly threatened with being sent to a political prison, where, I was assured, I would be put in an oven. As an alternative, the interrogators offered to imprison me in a tiny cell, deep underground, with practically no food at all.

In the end, I suppose they got enough information out of me—name, rank, and serial number repeated over and over again—to positively identify me. In my desperation to identify myself, I also gave away information I was not supposed to reveal—the identifications of my group and squadron at the time I bailed out. I assumed that they already knew the unit identification from the checkerboard design on the tail of my airplane (the 325th Fighter Group had long been known as the Checkertail Clan, and the Germans had identified it as such many times on their propaganda broadcasts). Even when they had this information, I was made to do without more than a few scraps of food for ten days in a row while I had an endless barrage of questions fired at me, day and night.

From Frankfurt, I was put aboard another troop train. Accompanying me on this trip were people who had been taken prisoner in the unsuccessful American attempt to penetrate the German lines by parachute drop in September 1944. There were glider pilots, paratroopers, and even a Piper Cub pilot who had been forced down while spotting artillery fire. We all exchanged horror stories. A glider pilot told of being forced down in a clearing and then being shot at from all sides by the Germans. The paratroopers also had some interesting tales to tell, for this attempt to penetrate the German lines had been anything but successful.

We went all the way across Germany on bombed-out railroad lines that the Germans had successfully patched up, and we arrived at our new home around November 1, 1944. This was Stalag Luft 1, a prisoner-of-war camp for airmen that had been erected near Barth, a town on the Baltic deep in eastern Germany.

When we went through the main gate of the camp, we were greeted by all the people in that compound. One of them was a member of my own 317th Fighter Squadron. He threw his arms around me and said he was really glad to see me, but that he hated to see me *there*. And then he said, "And I suppose you ran out of gas." When I replied that I *really* had run out of gas, he wouldn't believe me and said, "Do you suppose that some Me-109 didn't puncture your gasoline tanks with bullets?" As it turned out, any fighter pilot who was worth his salt would never admit that he'd been shot down. They all claimed to have run out of gas.

There were many greetings from the people waiting in that compound to our new batch of prisoners of war. Many had served together in England or Italy. One of the questions asked was, "How's old Joe doing back in the squadron?" and the usual reply was "Oh, never mind old Joe; he'll be here in a couple of weeks." And, sure enough, the gates would open a couple of weeks later, and in would march old Joe. That's how high the losses were among American airmen at the time.

The main compound in which we were held prisoner at Stalag Luft 1 comprised five to six acres of ground entirely enclosed by two high barbed-wire fences spaced about ten feet apart. Between the fences was an impenetrable jumble of barbed wire. High guard towers were spaced about 100 feet apart around the periphery of the wired-in prisoner compound, with one or more guards in each tower. The guards were armed with automatic burp guns, and they had orders to shoot anyone who attempted to escape. About fifteen feet on our side of the inner compound fence was a lone strand of "warning" wire that we prisoners—*Kriegesgefangeners* in German—were told never to cross without permission from the German guards in the watch towers. If we did cross the warning wire, we would be shot.

Inside the compound were many barracks-type buildings, each housing approximately 400 men. Altogether, about 10,000 men were kept in Stalag Luft 1.

One of the most frequently used methods of attempting to escape was tunneling out. This involved a lot of arduous labor because the diggers had to hide dirt all around the compound in order to prevent the German guards from discovering what they were up to. In the early part of the war, some of these attempts to tunnel out were successful, but in the latter part of the war the Germans had installed seismograph equipment, and could detect any attempt to tunnel out. They let one tunnel get almost to the fence and then put up a big sign at the end of the tunnel: "Roses are red, violets are blue, your tunnel is finished, and so are you."

Stalag Luft 1 was located on the fifty-fourth parallel, where Alaska and northern Canada are, but it is warmed by the Gulf Stream, so the winters there are much less severe than in the mid-continental United States, which is at a much lower latitude. There were no severe snow storms as we experience in Nebraska and Wyoming.

The Germans' food ration was meager, to say the least; a week's ration for one man consisted of one loaf of bread, four ounces of butter, a few rutabagas or potatoes, and very little else. Someone in that compound figured out what it cost the Germans to feed us for one year at United States prices, and it came to fifty-four dollars and some cents. The Germans did, however, allow Red Cross parcels to come through, and we each received one parcel per week. The parcels were supplied by the U.S. government, but came through the International Red Cross. Those parcels were indeed a life saver for all of us; I don't see how we could have survived on the German ration alone.

Each Red Cross parcel contained one carton of cigarettes, a big chocolate candy bar, a can of Spam, and other goodies. We each kept our carton of cigarettes and chocolate candy bar and turned the rest of the parcel over to the *Kriegesgefangener* who had appointed himself head cook. This head cook portioned out the German ration and the Red Cross supplies so that everyone got something to eat at each meal, although it was never enough and we were hungry all the time. The lack of sex didn't bother us too much during our stay at Stalag Luft 1 because all any of us could think of was the nice big thick steak sandwiches we were going to eat when we got back to the States. Food was on our minds all the time.

Each German guard had a big German shepherd dog with him, and the dogs were so perfectly trained that they could tell an American from a German. The dogs were beautiful animals, but they were one-man dogs and had to be destroyed at the war's end. If you got out of line, a dog would knock you down and hold you by the throat until its handler arrived. This often happened to prisoners who left their barracks after dark. There were many *Kriegesgefangeners* who barely made it back to their barracks at dusk and slammed the door right in the face of a pursuing German shepherd.

One night around Christmas, we were all very hungry and the twenty men in my room got our heads together and decided we were going to eat one of those dogs. One *Kriegesgefangener* went outside the barracks just at dusk and got one of the dogs to chase him. This time, instead of slamming the door in the dog's face, the prisoner left the door wide open and allowed the dog to come into the barracks. The rest of us were in position on both sides of the doorway, and we all ganged up on the dog and tried to smother him with blankets. There were many screams from the men and snarls from the dog. I don't know to this day what went wrong, but we were unsuccessful—the dog got away through the still-open doorway. By then, several of us had been bitten and we had had enough of the whole thing. I'm not sure how we could have cooked a whole dog anyway because we had very few charcoal briquettes.

For outdoor exercise, we played touch football in the winter and softball in the spring. We had only one small playing field in that tiny compound, and, as there were 10,000 of us, only a very few actually got to play with the meager equipment that was available. You had to be really good to get to play, so fierce was the competition to get on one of the teams. However, I did succeed in making one of the softball teams in the spring.

We also went to a lot of classes. There were classes in almost everything—language, math, coaching . . . you name it. I had always wanted to learn a language besides English, but the Spanish and French classes were all filled up and I couldn't get in. The Germans offered to teach us German, but we refused because they were our enemies. That was foolish. We should have known that the Germans weren't going to be our enemies for the rest of our lives. I did manage to get into one of the coaching classes and enjoyed myself very much even though I was never the best athlete in the world. I learned a lot about keeping myself physically fit.

The war dragged on. We had a few radios in our compound, and some German-speaking *Kriegesgefangeners* kept track of the war. When they gave out the news, we would all chant "Come on, Joe [Josef Stalin]," and "Come on, Ike." The Germans were a little puzzled by who we meant when we said "Ike," but then it dawned on them. "Oh, you mean Eisenhower." When I first got there, the news was all bad. The Allies had failed to penetrate the German front in September and October of 1944, and later on, in December, was the Battle of the Bulge. We all thought that we were going to be cooped up for ten years. Later, in the spring of 1945, the news got better. The British and Americans broke through in Western Europe and, at the same time, the Russians were going great guns on the Eastern Front. We knew then that the war was going to end pretty soon, and there were innumerable bets made—for as much as several hundred dollars—as to when the war would end. Some of the bets were paid off, but most of them weren't because we quickly lost track of one another after the war ended.

During the last two or three weeks of the war, we had to do without Red Cross parcels because the Americans had bombed out all the German supply trains. Things got pretty grim at Stalag Luft 1. We were really hungry, but we were cheered by the fact that it was for a good cause. We would soon be liberated.

And then one day it happened. We woke up to find that there were no German guards in the high towers. They had all beat it to the west to surrender to the Americans. Lieutenant Colonel Frank Gabreski, the ranking officer in our compound, put his own men in those towers to prevent the rest of us from leaving. Gabreski didn't want us wandering about the countryside and getting hurt. However, Russian soldiers arrived a short time later. After the Russian commander ran over the front gate with a tank, he ordered Gabreski to let us go. And, with that, many of the *Kriegesgefangeners* poured through the gate and scattered all over the countryside in search of food.

The Communist soldiers we met were direct descendants of the Mongols who had overrun Europe during the Middle Ages. They wore grass in their boots for socks and rarely if ever took a bath. Each carried a huge pistol at his waist, which he fired at anything that irritated him.

The Germans in eastern Germany were anxious to give the Americans everything they had in order to keep the Russians from getting it. We all had small fortunes in the palms of our hands if we could have figured out some way of getting that loot out of eastern Germany.

After the first rush to leave the compound, Lieutenant Colonel Gabreski still wanted the remaining Americans to stay put and wait for the B-17s to come and get us, but some of the former prisoners elected to walk to freedom even though the Western Front was 300 miles away. I was one of them, and it was almost my undoing.

I walked for about twenty or thirty miles the first day, and stayed in a home when the Germans there invited me in for the night. I should have slept out on the ground, for I no sooner got in bed than four terrified German women piled in with me. A short time later, four Russians with drawn pistols came into my room. I thought that was the end of me, but one of them recognized my uniform and said in broken English, "Americanski pig; he has to have four women." I thus saved those German women from rape for one night at least, but I'm sure they all got raped the next night and other nights.

The next morning, the German family entreated me to take all their jewelry, but I demurred; I was afraid that the Russians would take it all away from me anyway. I walked for another twenty or thirty miles and then approached a Russian officer for food. This Russian was of Slavic appearance, more like the Russians I had met on the 325th Fighter Group's mission to Russia in June 1944. He gave me a loaf of bread and motioned me to a detention camp that was filled with displaced persons—Poles, Germans, and others. In only two days, I had hiked about fifty miles from one prisoner-of-war camp to another. Fortunately, the Russians had set up their defenses rather loosely, and I escaped up a gully that night.

I made my way across the rest of eastern Germany without being molested. It was just as well that I had made my escape because many Americans who bailed out over Russian lines during the final air battles over Berlin were held captive in Russia for a year or more after the war was over.

I made that loaf of bread the Russian officer had given me last a week, and I stayed away from the Russians and German homes after that. At long last, I made my way to the American lines. Just as I was coming in, a Negro sergeant spotted me. He ran out to meet me when I was still a long way off, and he threw his arms around me ecstatically. "Welcome home, Captain," he said to me. "Welcome home."

For me, at last, the war was over.

GLOSSARY & GUIDE TO ABBREVIATIONS

ack-ack antiaircraft gunfire
Airacobra U.S. Bell P-39 fighter
API Armor-Piercing Incendiary ammunition
Angels altitude in thousands of feet
Ar-234 German Arado twin-jet bomber
AT-6 U.S. North American Texan advanced trainer
A-20 U.S. Douglas Havoc twin-engine light attack bomber
A-26 U.S. Douglas Invader twin-engine attack bomber
Bandit enemy fighter
Beaufighter British Bristol 156 twin-engine strike fighter
Bogey unidentified airplane
B-17 U.S. Boeing Flying Fortress four-engine heavy
 bomber
B-24 U.S. Consolidated Liberator four-engine heavy
 bomber
B-25 U.S. North American Mitchell twin-engine medium
 bomber
B-26 U.S. Martin Marauder twin-engine medium bomber
CAVU Ceiling and Visibility Unlimited
Condor German Focke-Wulf FW-200 four-engine recon-
 naissance bomber
CPT Civilian Pilot Training (Program)
C-47 U.S. Douglas Skytrain twin-engine transport
Do-217 German Dornier twin-engine medium bomber
Element two fighters, flying as a unit
ETO European Theater of Operations
F4F U.S. Navy Grumman Wildcat fighter

Flak German antiaircraft (*Flieger Abwher Kannon*)

flight four fighters (two elements), flying as a unit

Flying Fortress U.S. Boeing B-17 four-engine heavy bomber

FW-190 German Focke-Wulf fighter

FW-200 German Condor four-engine reconnaissance bomber

G force of gravity (× 1)

GI Government Issue

Havoc U.S. Douglas A-20 twin-engine light attack bomber

Hawk U.S. Curtiss P-36 fighter

He-111 German Heinkel twin-engine medium bomber

IAR-80 Romanian fighter

IP Initial Point

Jagdgeschweder German fighter wing

Jug Nickname for P-47 Thunderbolt

Ju-52 German Junkers tri-motor transport

Ju-87 German Junkers Stuka single-engine dive-bomber

Ju-88 German Junkers twin-engine medium bomber

Kingcobra U.S. Bell P-63 fighter

Komet German Messerschmitt Me-163 rocket fighter

Kriegesgefangener Prisoner of war

Lancer U.S. Republic P-43 fighter

Liberator U.S. Consolidated B-24 four-engine heavy bomber

Lightning U.S. Lockheed P-38 twin-engine fighter

Marauder U.S. Martin B-26 twin-engine medium bomber

Mc.202 Italian Macchi Folgore (Thunderbolt) fighter

Me-109 German Messerschmitt fighter

Me-110 German Messerschmitt twin-engine heavy fighter

Me-163 German Messerschmitt Komet rocket fighter

Me-210 German Messerschmitt twin-engine bomber destroyer

Me-262 German Messerschmitt twin-jet fighter

Me-410 German Messerschmitt twin-engine heavy fighter

MiG-15 Soviet jet fighter

Mitchell U.S. North American B-25 twin-engine medium bomber

Mustang U.S. North American P-51 fighter
P-35 U.S. Seversky fighter
P-36 U.S. Curtiss Hawk fighter
P-38 U.S. Lockheed Lightning twin-engine fighter
P-39 U.S. Bell Airacobra fighter
P-40 U.S. Curtiss Warhawk fighter
P-43 U.S. Republic Lancer fighter
P-47 U.S. Republic Thunderbolt fighter
P-52 U.S. North American Mustang fighter
P-63 U.S. Bell Kingcobra fighter
RAF Royal Air Force
RCAF Royal Canadian Air Force
RP-63 U.S. Bell Kingcobra fighter target
SHAEF Supreme Headquarters, Allied Expeditionary Force
Spitfire British Supermarine fighter
Stuka German Junkers Ju-87 single-engine dive-bomber
Thunderbolt U.S. Republic P-47 fighter
USAAF U.S. Army Air Forces
USSAFE U.S. Strategic Air Forces in Europe
Warhawk U.S. Curtiss P-40 fighter
Wildcat U.S. Navy Grumman F4F fighter
YP-38 U.S. in-service test version of Lockheed P-38 Lightning twin-engine fighter

BIBLIOGRAPHY

Copp, DeWitt S. *A Few Great Captains: The Men and Events that Shaped the Development of U.S. Air Power*. Garden City, NY: Doubleday, 1980.

_____ *Forged in Fire: Strategy and Decisions in the Airwar Over Europe, 1940–1945*. Garden City, NY: Doubleday, 1982.

Maurer, Maurer (ed.). *Air Force Combat Units of World War II*. Washington, D.C.: Office of Air Force History, 1983.

McFarland, Stephen L., and Wesley Phillips Newton. *To Command the Sky: The Battle for Air Superiority Over Germany, 1942–1944*. Washington, D.C.: Smithsonian Institution Press, 1991.

Mets, David R. *Master of Airpower: General Carl A. Spaatz*. Novato, California: Presidio Press, 1988.

Mondey, David. *Concise Guide to American Aircraft of World War II*. London: Temple Press, 1982.

_____. *Concise Guide to Axis Aircraft of World War II*. London: Temple Press, 1984.

_____. *Concise Guide to British Aircraft of World War II*. London: Temple Press, 1982.

Morris, Danny. *Aces & Wingmen II, Volume I*. Usk, Washington: Aviation—USK, 1989.

Olmsted, Merle C. *The Yoxford Boys: The 357th Fighter Group on Escort Over Europe and Russia*. Fallbrook, California: Aero Publishers, Inc., 1971.

Olynyk, Frank J. *Victory List No. 5: USAAF (European Theater) Credits for the Destruction of Enemy Aircraft in Air-to-Air Combat, World War II*. Aurora, Ohio: Frank J. Olynyk, 1987.

_____. *Victory List No. 6: USAAF (Mediterranean Theater)*

Credits for the Destruction of Enemy Aircraft in Air-to-Air Combat, World War II. Aurora, Ohio: Frank J. Olynyk, 1987.

Schaffer, Ronald. *Wings of Judgment: American Bombing in World War II.* New York: Oxford University Press, 1985.

Shores, Chris. "America's Spitfires," *Air Enthusiast,* August–November 1981.

Stanaway, John. *Peter Three Eight: The Pilots' Story.* Missoula, Montana: Pictorial Histories Publishing Company, 1986.

Toliver, Raymond F., and Trevor J. Constable. *Fighter Aces of the U.S.A.* Fallbrook, California: Aero Publishers, Inc., 1979.

Truluck, John H., Jr. *And So It Was: Memories of a World War II Fighter Pilot.* Walterboro, South Carolina: The Press and Standard, 1989.

Williams, Mary H. *U.S. Army in World War II: Special Studies, Chronology: 1941–1945.* Washington, D.C., Center of Military History, 1984.

INDEX